COMPANY ACCOUNTS

AUSTRALIA AND NEW ZEALAND
The Law Book Company Ltd.
Sydney : Melbourne : Perth

CANADA AND U.S.A.
The Carswell Company Ltd.
Agincourt, Ontario

INDIA
N.M. Tripathi Private Ltd.
Bombay
and
Eastern Law House Private Ltd.
Calcutta and Delhi
M.P.P. House
Bangalore

ISRAEL
Steimatzky's Agency Ltd.
Jerusalem : Tel Aviv : Haifa

MALAYSIA : SINGAPORE : BRUNEI
Malayan Law Journal (Pte.) Ltd.
Singapore and Kuala Lumpur

PAKISTAN
Pakistan Law House
Karachi

COMPANY ACCOUNTS

JENNY BOUGH, LL.M. (London)

of Gray's Inn, Barrister, Tutor in law
at The University of Kent at Canterbury

LONDON   SWEET & MAXWELL   1987

Published in 1987 by
Sweet & Maxwell Limited
11 New Fetter Lane, London
Computerset by Promenade Graphics Ltd., Cheltenham
Printed in Great Britain by
Robert Hartnoll (1985) Limited, Bodmin, Cornwall

British Library Cataloguing in Publication Data
  Bough, Jenny
    Company accounts
    1. Corporations—Great Britain
    —Accounting
    I. Title
    657'.95'0941   HF5686.67

  ISBN 0–421–36020–8

PREFACE

Many entrepreneurs choose to incorporate their businesses. This business form has advantages but the law imposes various obligations on those involved as directors and managers of a company, not least among them being the requirements relating to the disclosure of information in the form of annual accounts. I have sought in this book to explain the statutory and non-statutory rules surrounding a company's annual accounts and, whilst not wishing to turn the reader into an accountant, I hope that an insight will be given as to the presentation and preparation of these accounts. In writing, I have concentrated on the needs of the legal practitioner who is, from time to time, confronted with problems connected with the annual accounts of a company. Hopefully, such lawyers will find in this book general guidance on what is a complex area of law. Although written as a handbook for legal practitioners, it may also prove helpful for those who are studying for professional examinations involving the law relating to company accounts.

I have endeavoured to summarise and explain the law as it was on March 31, 1987.

My thanks go to my family for their long suffering during the preparation of this book and also to my publishers for their great patience.

May 1987   Jenny Bough

CONTENTS

TABLE OF CASES

TABLE OF STATUTES

TABLE OF STATEMENTS OF STANDARD ACCOUNTING PRACTICE

1 INTRODUCTION

Business enterprises in the United Kingdom can be run in one of three ways, by a sole trader, a partnership or by a limited company. Whilst the formation and running of a company is the most regulated form of business enterprise, it is often used because its characteristic of limited liability is seen as an advantage. Whether or not the directors and officers of a company do in fact have the benefit of limited liability will depend to a large extent upon the willingness of financial institutions to accept a company's assets as security, rather than the assets of the entrepreneur.

Limited liability is not, however, the only reason for incorporating a business as a company. If an entrepreneur decides that, for whatever reason, this is the most advantageous form in which his business can operate, he will be required to comply with the legislation and case law which govern companies incorporated in Great Britain. Among those provisions are rules relating to the accounts which companies are expected to produce.

Annual accounts

All companies registered in Great Britain, whether public or private, have a duty to prepare annual accounts. These must be circulated to company members and delivered to the Registrar of Companies. This is, generally speaking, the rule whatever the size of company, from the family concern right up to the industrial giants such as ICI and Marks and Spencer. A few concessions are offered to the smaller company, for example, the ability to file modified accounts, but on the whole, the disclosure requirements are the same for all companies.

Disclosure of information, which goes to the heart of the company's business and its well being, can be seen as the price it pays for limited liability. The legislation demands that this information be supplied to the company's shareholders and also insists upon it being made public by requiring it to be filed with the Registrar of Companies. The reason for supplying information to shareholders is not hard to find. It is essential if they are to appraise sensibly their investment in the company. By registering the accounts with the Registrar of Companies, they become public documents and thus are available to would be investors, suppliers, customers and to competitors. The accounts may also be used to distribute to prospective financiers in the event of the company seeking outside funds. Those using the accounts are obviously interested in learning as much about the company as possible, whereas the company will be concerned not to disclose facts enabling competitors to glean anything of relevance which would help them to gain an advantage. There is therefore a conflict of interest when it comes to what information a company should disclose and how detailed that information should be. The present rules are complex and require a company to make public a substantial amount of detailed information.

Legislation

Until quite recently, legislation only provided a framework for accounts and the accountancy profession supplied some of the more detailed rules governing them. With the implementation of the EEC Fourth Directive on company accounts in 1981, the accounting requirements became more detailed and now represent a compromise between the German approach, which requires strict compliance with set rules, and the British approach which is to demand that accounts show what is termed a "true and fair view," rather than comply with detailed rules. The term "true and fair" is discussed further in Chapter 5.

As well as company legislation, there are occasionally further statutory requirements laid upon specific types of company, for example, estate agencies. On the whole, however, the accounting rules are to be found in the Companies Act 1985, which consolidates the previous legislation on the subject.

Professional standards

Accounts are generally believed to show a true and fair view if they comply with the standards set by the accountancy profession. These standards are known as "Statements of Standard Accounting Practice" or "SSAPs," and are discussed in Chapter 6 on the non-statutory accounting requirements. Certain accounting principles which were originally only contained in a standard are now incorporated into statute and these are discussed in Chapter 5. Further, in the context of distributable profits, legislation requires that generally accepted accounting principles should be followed.[1]

Stock Exchange

In addition to the accounting standards, if a company is listed on the Stock Exchange, it will be expected to provide the Stock Exchange with accounts which comply not only with the companies legislation and the accounting standards but also with the disclosure rules which are laid down by the Stock Exchange itself.

Classification of companies

The Stock Exchange requirements will of course only apply to public quoted companies. In comparison, the accounting rules set out in legislation and in the accounting standards will generally apply to all companies. There are, however, some exceptions so it is worth noting the distinction between public and private companies.

Public companies

A public company is "a company limited by share or limited by guarantee and having a share capital, being a company—

    (a) the memorandum of which states that it is to be public company, and

    (b) in relation to which the provisions of (the Companies Act 1985) or the former Companies Acts as to the registration or re-registration of a company as a public company have been complied with on or after December 22, 1980 . . ."[2]

The significance of December 22, 1980, is that the Companies Act 1980 introduced new definitions of private and public companies and required certain companies already in existence to re-register in by that date.

On registration the Registrar of Companies must be satisfied that the nominal value of the company's allotted share capital is not less than the authorised minimum[3] currently set at £50,000 but this amount may be altered by the Secretary of State, from time to time, by the means of a Statutory Instrument.[4]

[1] Companies Act 1985, Sched. 4, para. 91.
[2] *Ibid.* s.1(3).
[3] *Ibid.* s.11.
[4] *Ibid.* s.118.

Private companies

Special category companies

A public company must also have the words "public limited company" at the end of its name.[5] An acceptable alternative to "public limited company" is "p.l.c."[6]

A private company is simply defined as being "a company that is not a public company."[7] It must have as the last word in its name "limited," which can be abbreviated to "ltd."[8] There are certain exceptions to this rule[9] which concern a limited number of exceptional cases outside the scope of this book.

Apart from the categorisation of companies into public and private, the other division which is of importance when considering company accounts is the group of companies which are known as "special category companies." The special category classification comprises banking, shipping and insurance companies and for the purposes of the Companies Act 1985 these are defined as:

"(a) "banking company" means a company which is a recognised bank for the purposes of the Banking Act 1979 or is a licensed institution within that Act;

(b) "insurance company" means an insurance company to which Part II of the Insurance Companies Act 1982 applies; and

(c) "shipping company" means a company which, or a subsidiary of which, owns ships or includes among its activities the management or operation of ships and which satisfies the Secretary of State that it ought in the national interest to be treated under this Part of this Act as a shipping company."[10]

The importance of the special category companies is that they do not have to comply with the accounting provisions of the Act, which implement the Fourth Directive and are mainly contained in Schedule 4 to the Act. Instead they can follow the less burdensome rules which applied before the Companies Act 1981 and which are now contained in Schedule 9 to the Companies Act 1985. In due course they will be subject to their own EEC Directives. As each of the companies within this special category is so specialised, the pre–1981 accounting requirements are not examined here.

Statutory accounts

Companies subject to the Companies Act 1985 have to prepare annually a balance sheet and profit and loss account. Along with these documents and the notes to the accounts, a company's directors and its auditors must also prepare their own reports, which must be annexed to the accounts. These documents are sometimes referred to collectively as a company's statutory accounts. Another phrase which is used to describe these documents is "annual accounts" and this term is more fully explained in Chapter 3. The Statements of Standard Accounting Practice use yet another phrase—"financial statements." This phrase includes a company's balance sheet, profit and loss

---

[5] *Ibid.* s.25(1).
[6] *Ibid.* s.27(4).
[7] *Ibid.* s.1(3).
[8] *Ibid.* ss.25(2) and 27(4).
[9] *Ibid.* s.30.
[10] *Ibid.* s.257(1).

account, statement of source and application of funds,[11] notes and any other statements which are included with the accounts.

Management accounts

Generally, the law imposes no other burdens on what other accounts a company has to keep, although there are provisions governing what accounting records should be kept. These provisions are dealt with in Chapter 2. In practice, the keeping of internal or management accounts is common and can provide a very useful tool for directors or officers of a company enabling them to have access to up to date information invaluable in monitoring current performance and in charting the progress of the company in the future. These accounts are also discussed in Chapter 2.

True and fair

In examining the rules governing company accounts, two concepts underlie the subject. The first is "true and fair." This refers to the obligation that a company's accounts must present a true and fair view and it is a requirement which overrides all the other detailed rules and regulations. This subject, along with the most recent opinion as to the meaning of the term is discussed in Chapter 5 on Accounting Principles.

Materiality

The other concept is that of materiality. It is often a rule that only material amounts need be shown or disclosed, for example, paragraph 86 of Schedule 4 to the Companies Act 1985 specifically states that amounts which are not material in a particular context are to be disregarded. What is material will depend on the circumstances in each company, for there is no hard and fast formula for determining what is material in all cases. The basic test is that a matter will be regarded as material if knowledge of it would be likely to influence the users of the accounts.

With that test as a starting point, it will be a question of professional judgment as to what is material or not. The accountancy profession advises that in deciding that question, the following points should be considered:

"(a) The amount itself, in relation to
    (i)   the overall view of the accounts
    (ii) the total of which it forms or should form part
    (iii) associated items (whether or not in the profit and loss account or in the balance sheet)
    (iv) the corresponding amount in previous years;
(b) the description, including questions of emphasis;
(c) the presentation and context; and
(d) any statutory requirements for disclosure."[12]

What is material for one purpose may not be for another, even within the same set of accounts. An item may not be material in the context of the accounts as a whole but taken in the particular context it may well be.

It is therefore impossible to express materiality in quantitative terms and the concept would lose its usefulness if it were reduced to a formula which could be applied mechanically.

With the concepts of true and fair and of materiality as a base, the rules to be found in legislation and in other non-

---

[11] See pp. 46–67.
[12] The Interpretation of "Material," ICAEW Handbook, 2.206.

statutory sources then build a complex edifice which surrounds company accounts. The aim of this book is to set out those rules which are of general application, and thus provisions applying to particular types of company, such as the special category companies as defined in page 3 above are not included. All references are to the Companies Act 1985 unless otherwise stated.

2 ACCOUNTING RECORDS

The required records

One of the basic accounting requirements for all companies is that they must keep accounting records.[1] In general terms, these records must be sufficient to show and explain the company's transactions: more specifically:

> "The accounting records . . . shall be such as to—
> (a) disclose with reasonable accuracy, at any time, the financial position of the company at that time, and
> (b) enable the directors to ensure that any balance sheet and profit and loss account prepared . . . comply with the requirements of (the Companies Act 1985) as to the form and content of company accounts and otherwise."[2]

In particular, the balance sheet should give a true and fair view of the company's state of affairs and the profit and loss account, a true and fair view of the company's profit or loss.[3]

These wide requirements are further elaborated by statute:

> "The accounting records shall in particular contain—
> (a) entries from day to day of all sums of money received and expended by the company, and the matters in respect of which the receipt and expenditure takes place, and
> (b) a record of the assets and liabilities of the company."[4]

Where the company's business involves dealing in goods, its records must also contain:

> "(a) statements of stock held by the company at the end of each financial year of the company,
> (b) all statements of stocktakings from which any such statement of stock as is mentioned in paragraph (a) has been or is to be prepared, and
> (c) except in the case of goods sold by way of ordinary retail trade, statements of all goods sold and purchased, showing the goods and the buyers and sellers in sufficient detail to enable all these to be identified."[5]

Purpose   The primary purpose of these accounting records is that it should be possible to prepare statements from them which show the financial position of the company. This does not refer solely to the company's cash position but will also include other tangible assets, liabilities and profits or losses. The second arm of

[1] Companies Act 1985, s.221(1).
[2] *Ibid*. s.221(2).
[3] *Ibid*. s.228(2).
[4] *Ibid*. s.221(3).
[5] *Ibid*. s.221(4).

the statutory requirement is that the financial position of the company should be disclosed by its records, with reasonable accuracy "at any time." This implies that there should be some structure to the record keeping system and that the mere accumulation of documents will not satisfy the requirements. A company should establish a system which organises and labels the information, so that it can be retrieved as and when necessary. It is thought, however, that the requirement does not necessitate the installation of an instantaneous recording system, rather that the records are organised in such a way that the financial position can be ascertained at any selected date.[6] If a company does wish to computerise its records, any computerised or non legible records which meet the conditions set out above will be acceptable.[7]

Penalties When a company fails to keep proper accounting records, an officer of that company, who is in default, will be liable to imprisonment or a fine, or both. A defence is available to an officer who acted honestly and who can show that, in the circumstances, the default was excusable. The circumstances which have to be considered here are the way in which the company carried on its business.[8]

A company's failure to keep records, or proper records is also relevant when a company is being wound up as insolvent. In such a situation, the official in charge of the winding up must report a director of the insolvent company to the Secretary of State if he considers that the director's conduct makes him unfit to be a director. Once a director has been reported to the Secretary of State, the Secretary may apply to the court for a disqualification order. When hearing such an application, the failure to keep proper accounting records is one type of conduct to which the court must give consideration. Such failure may also be taken into account should the court have to consider ordering a director to contribute personally to an insolvent company's assets in the event of wrongful trading by that company.[9]

Special requirements Further legal requirements regarding its accounting records may be imposed upon a company because of the nature of the business in which it is engaged, for example, estate agents.[10] Consideration, therefore, must also be given to the legislation governing the particular business as well as to the general requirements of companies legislation.

Fraudulent trading Before leaving the content of accounting records, the Companies Act provisions relating to fraudulent trading are of interest. While not specifically dealing with records they do suggest another aim of the accounts. Under these provisions, it is an offence to trade with the intent of defrauding creditors. The offence is committed by a person who knowingly obtains credit when there is no reasonable prospect of the creditor being paid

---

[6] Financial and Accounting Responsibilities of Directors, ICAEW Handbook 1.401.
[7] S.I. 1985 No. 724.
[8] Companies Act 1985, s.223.
[9] Company Directors Disqualification Act 1986, s.9, Sched. 1.
[10] Estate Agents Act 1979, s.14 as amended Companies Consolidation (Consequential Provisions) Act 1985, Sched. 2.

Wrongful trading

once the debt falls due or shortly thereafter.[11] Further, a person who is a director of a company which goes into insolvent liquidation may also be held financially liable in the event of the company's wrongful trading. Liability will arise where, "at some time before the commencement of the winding up, that person knew or ought to have concluded that there was no reasonable prospect that the company would avoid going into insolvent liquidation." A winding up will be an insolvent liquidation if a company's assets are insufficient for the payment of its debts and other liabilities and the expenses of winding up.[12] The records, therefore, should be such that those carrying on the business of the company can assess whether or not there will be funds available to meet debts as they fall due.

Place where kept

Once a company has established its accounting records, the question of where they should be kept must be considered. Statute gives this decision to the directors and allows them considerable freedom of choice. The records must be kept either at the company's registered office or "such other place as the directors think fit." Wherever they are kept, the records must at all times be open to inspection by the officers of the company.[13] The same rule applies to records kept in a non legible form.[14] The term "officer" includes a director, manager or secretary[15] but as this is not a definitive list it may cover any person with authority over company affairs. The company's auditors may be regarded as officers of the company in some circumstances[16] but whether or not they are for these purposes is academic as they have a statutory right to inspect the company's books at all times.[17] If for some reason, a company keeps its accounting records outside Great Britain, it must send the accounts and returns which are derived from those records to Great Britain and keep them at a place there. These accounts and returns must also be open to inspection by the company's officers.[18]

Penalties

If a company fails to store its accounting records in accordance with statute or fails to make them available for inspection, any officer in default will be liable to the same penalties as for breach of the rules relating to the keeping and content of the records; the same defence is also available.[19]

Disposal of records

Company legislation

Company legislation specifies the length of time for which accounting records must be kept but as will be seen, there are other time limits to be observed. For company law purposes, a private company is required to keep its accounting records for

---

[11] Companies Act 1985, s.458; Insolvency Act 1986, s.213; *R.* v. *Grantham* [1984] 3 All E.R. 166.
[12] Insolvency Act 1986, s.214.
[13] s.222(1).
[14] S.I. 1985 No. 724.
[15] s.744.
[16] *Re London & General Bank* [1895] 2 Ch. 166; *Re Kingston Cotton Mill* [1896] 1 Ch. 6.
[17] s.237(3).
[18] s.222(2).
[19] s.223(1) and see also p. 7 above.

three years from the date on which they were made; whereas, for public companies, the period is six years. These provisions are subject to any rules made under section 411 of the Insolvency Act 1986, which apply in the event of a company being wound up.[20]

Penalties   An officer of a company will be guilty of an offence and liable to imprisonment or a fine, or both, if he fails to take all reasonable steps to ensure that the company preserves its records for the requisite time. An officer will also be guilty of an offence and liable to the same punishment if he intentionally caused the company's default.[21]

Limitation periods   Also to be considered when deciding the length of time that records should be retained, are the limitation periods set by contract and tax law. It may, therefore, be thought wise to retain information relating to simple contracts for six years from the date on which a cause of action could have arisen or 12 years in the case of specialty contracts.[22]

Tax legislation   The tax position is more complicated. Generally, the Inland Revenue has six years from the end of the chargeable period in which to raise an assessment.[23] In the case of the taxpayer's fraud or wilful default, an assessment may be made at any time.[24] Where there is negligence with regard to corporation tax returns, the Inland Revenue may go back a further six years from the date of the original assessment and the process may be repeated if necessary.[25] In addition to these powers of assessment, the Inland Revenue may require a taxpayer to produce any documents relating to his liability.[26]

A company employing staff will pay them under the Pay As You Earn (PAYE) system. Under these rules, all documents and records relating to the calculation or payment of employees' emoluments must be kept for at least three years.[27]

Customs and Excise   As well as the Inland Revenue's powers to call for records relating to tax, the Customs and Excise also has extremely wide powers. For the purposes of Value Added Tax, every taxable person is required to keep records and accounts, with all related documents, for up to six years.[28]

A taxpayer in breach of the various provisions relating to the keeping of records for tax purposes will be liable to prosecution. The particular statute should be consulted for details.

Original documents or copies?

Keeping original documents may cause problems for companies, especially when space is at a premium, so they may wish to consider storing the information in another way. While the

---

[20] s.222(4).
[21] s.223.
[22] Limitation Act 1980, ss.5 and 8(1).
[23] Taxes Management Act 1970, s.34.
[24] *Ibid.* s.36.
[25] *Ibid.* s.39.
[26] *Ibid.* s.20.
[27] Income and Corporation Taxes Act 1970, s.204; S.I. 1973 No. 334, para. 32(5) as amended by S.I. 1981 No. 44.
[28] Value Added Tax Act 1983, Sched. 7, para. 7, as amended by Finance Act 1985, Sched. 7.

original papers are of course the best evidence of the information contained therein, copies will be admissible in court. The court, however, must be able to rely on the trustworthiness of those copies and it is at the judge's discretion whether or not to allow copies and to specify any necessary method of authentication.[29] If a company does decide to copy or microfilm documents, care should be taken to ensure that all records are copied and that the copies are legible. Finally, a company storing its records in this way should ensure that a place of safe keeping is found for them.

Data Protection   A final consideration which those concerned with the keeping of company records should have in mind, is the need for registration under the Data Protection Act 1984. This need will arise when a company processes its records automatically and those records contain information about individual persons. The Act should be consulted for the precise requirements.

Management accounts

Purpose   Depending on a company's size, structure and the nature of its business, management or internal accounts may be kept. Generally, there is no statutory requirement to keep such accounts but companies should consider whether they are necessary for the proper running of their business. The management of any company needs to know how its business is progressing in order that it may adapt to changing circumstances. If a company seeks funding from outside sources, the lender will normally expect those managing the company to be receiving up to date information on how the company is developing. The nature of the information will depend upon many things but common to most businesses is the need to plan ahead and produce budgets and forecasts and having produced them to compare them with actual performance at regular intervals.

Another possible purpose of management accounts is to enable the directors to ascertain the company's distributable profits. While there is no statutory requirement that records should be kept for this end, the accountancy profession has advised that it is essential that a company's records should be such to enable them to distinguish between those reserves which are distributable and those which are not.[30] It is important that a company knows what profits are available to it for the purpose of distribution, and this includes the paying of dividends. The keeping of records which make this information readily assessable, will of course assist. Distributable profits are considered in detail in Chapter 11.

The above are some of the considerations which a company should bear in mind when designing and preparing its management accounts. Detailed consideration of the design of these accounts requires an examination of accounting principles and practice, which is thus outside the scope of this book.

---

[29] Civil Evidence Act 1968, s.6.
[30] The determination of realised profits and disclosure of distributable profits in the context of the Companies Acts; T.R. 481. See Appendix III.

3 ANNUAL ACCOUNTS

Introduction

The only accounts which the Companies Act requires to be produced regularly are a company's annual accounts. While the term "annual accounts" has no statutory definition, appearing only as a head note in the Act, it is a convenient description of the financial documents to which it refers. The documents which comprise the annual accounts are the balance sheet and profit and loss account, to which are added the directors' report, the auditors' report and the notes to the accounts. In certain circumstances, group accounts should also be included.[1] The provisions relating to group accounts are set out in Chapter 16.

Directors' duties The responsibility for preparing the balance sheet and profit and loss account is placed upon the directors of a company,[2] as is the duty to prepare group accounts when necessary.[3] No penalty is imposed upon directors for failing to prepare the requisite accounts, but as will be seen,[4] there are penalties for failure to lay the annual accounts before the general meeting and to deliver a copy of them to the Registrar of Companies. The absence of a penalty for failing to prepare the accounts is, therefore, of no practical importance. In the event of a company being wound up as insolvent, the extent of a director's responsibility for any failure to prepare annual accounts will be taken into consideration by a court in determining his fitness or otherwise to act as a director in the future.[5]

The financial year

The requirement that accounts be prepared annually is reached by a somewhat devious route. The Act actually requires the directors of a trading company to prepare, in respect of each accounting reference period, a profit and loss account. If the company is not a trading company an income and expenditure account should be prepared.[6] The balance sheet, which every company must prepare is required to show the state of the companies affairs as at the last day of the financial year.[7] The meaning given to the term "financial year" is somewhat circular as it refers back to the period in respect of which the profit and loss account is made up.[8] It does add, however, that that period need not necessarily be a year. Section 227 gives the means of calculating the beginning of the financial year once it is known what a company's accounting reference period is.

[1] Companies Act 1985, s.239.
[2] *Ibid.* s.227(1)(3).
[3] *Ibid.* s.229(1).
[4] See pp. 15–16 below.
[5] Company Directors Disqualification Act 1986, s.9, Sched. 1.
[6] Companies Act 1985, s.227(1).
[7] *Ibid.* s.227(3).
[8] *Ibid.* s.742(1).

Accounting reference period

**Accounting
reference date**

An explanation of "accounting reference period" is provided by section 224, which gives as the starting point the company's accounting reference date.[9] This date is central to a company's accounting life. As a company's accounting reference period ends on its accounting reference date, it is important that the date is chosen with care. The usual criteria are to choose a date when the company's stocks are at their lowest, and the company's activities are not at their peak, so that the necessary year end activities, for example, stocktaking, will not intrude upon what is the company's busiest time. A company is, therefore, well advised to choose an accounting reference date which best suits its purposes, and notify the Registrar of Companies of that choice within six months of the company being incorporated. If the Registrar of Companies does not receive notification of a company's choice of date within six months of the company's formation, the date is deemed to be March 31.[10] Should a company fail to make a choice within the time limit allowed and subsequently find that a year end of March 31 is not suitable, there are only limited grounds for making alterations.[11]

The importance of the accounting reference date in relation to a company's accounting reference period is that it sets the end of that time and thus determines the end of the company's financial year.[12]

**Length of
accounting
reference period**

The length of the accounting reference period may vary according to whether or not it is the company's first such period. If it is the first, the period will run from the date of the company's incorporation to its accounting reference date but that period must not be less than six months or more than 18 months.[13] So, for example, if a company is incorporated on January 1, 1986, and has its accounting reference date as March 31, its first accounting reference period will have to be January 1, 1986, to March 31, 1987, as if it ends on March 31, 1986, the period covered will only be three months. Alternatively, the first year cannot end on March 31, 1988, as this will span a period of more than 18 months. If on the other hand a company with an incorporation date of January 1, 1986, chooses August 31 as its accounting reference date, the first period must be January 1, 1986, to August 31, 1986, as to make it run until August 31, 1987, will mean that a period of more than 18 months is covered.

Subsequent accounting reference periods will be periods of 12 months ending with the accounting reference date.[13] In the first example, the second accounting period would be April 1, 1987, to March 31, 1988, and in the second example, September 1, 1986 to August 31, 1987. An accounting reference period will thus normally be one year, unless it is the first such period. There are, however, provisions which enable a company to change its accounting reference date thus shortening or extending an accounting period.

---

[9] *Ibid.* s.224(1).
[10] *Ibid.* s.224(2)(3).
[11] See pp. 13–14 below.
[12] Companies Act 1985, s.224(1)(2).
[13] *Ibid.* s.224(4).

Alteration of accounting reference date

The decision to alter a company's accounting reference period can only be taken at certain times and in limited circumstances. Alteration can be made either:

    (a) during a current accounting reference period, or
    (b) after the end of an accounting reference period.

Current period
At any time during a current accounting reference period, a company may notify the Registrar of Companies of a new accounting reference date.[14] The notice must specify whether alteration has the effect of either shortening or lengthening the accounting reference period.[15] If it is the former no formal restrictions apply, so that a company may alter its accounting reference date regularly. There are, however, practical restrictions, for not only will the formalities have to be observed (for example, notification of the change sent to the Registrar of Companies) but the accounts for each shortened period require to be audited with the resulting administrative work and additional fees.[16] This is, of course, the same for any alteration of accounting reference period.

A company wishing to alter its accounting reference date so that it extends the current accounting reference period faces certain restrictions. The alteration must not extend the current period to more than 18 months[17] and there must not have been an earlier extension of an accounting reference period within the previous five years. The five year period commences with the end of the first extended accounting reference period.[18] These rules can be illustrated as follows.

During accounting reference period January 1, 1986, to December 31, 1986, a company wishes to alter its accounting reference period to end on:

    (a) September 30, 1986—as this will shorten its current period, it may adopt this new period so long as the Registrar of Companies is notified before the date it wishes to adopt as the end of the accounting reference period, in this example, September 30;
    (b) March 31, 1987—this extends the current period to 15 months and it is therefore necessary to check that no other earlier accounting reference period has been extended within the last five years;
    (c) September 30, 1987—as this extends the current period to over 18 months, the alteration will be of no legal effect, regardless of whether or not there has been an extension within the preceding five years.

There are two exceptions to the above rules. First, even if there has been an earlier extension within the last five years, a member of a group of companies will be allowed to alter its accounting reference date in order to bring it into line with the

---

[14] *Ibid.* s.225(1).
[15] *Ibid.* s.225(4).
[16] See p. 117ff.
[17] Companies Act 1985, s.225(5).
[18] *Ibid.* s.225(6).

other companies within the group. Thus, a subsidiary may change its reference date to that of its holding company, or vice versa.[19] The second exception is whether the Secretary of State directs that a restriction shall not apply.[20]

After accounting reference date

The Registrar of Companies will accept notification of a change of accounting reference date at any time after the end of an accounting reference period only if its purpose is to bring that company's accounting reference period into line with that of its subsidiary or holding company. Even if that is the purpose, the notice will be of no effect if:

(a) it is given outside the period allowed for laying and delivering the accounts[21] relating to the previous accounting reference period[22]; or

(b) it specifies that the accounting reference period is to be extended and there has been an earlier extension of that period, within five years of the date on which the earlier extended period came to an end.[23]

The only exception to the last rule, is where the Secretary of State lifts the restrictions in a particular case.[24]

Laying and delivering accounts

Directors' duties

In addition to their duty to prepare the company's balance sheet and profit and loss account, together with the accompanying notes to the accounts, the directors must annex their report and the auditors' report to these documents.[25] The directors must then lay copies of these documents before the company in general meeting[26] and also deliver copies to the Registrar of Companies.[27] These tasks must be performed within a certain period. In the case of private companies, it is 10 months after the end of the relevant accounting reference period whereas public companies are permitted only seven months to lay and file their accounts.[28]

Exceptions

Two exceptions apply to the above rule. The first is where a company carries on business or has interests outside the United Kingdom, the Channel Islands and the Isle of Man. In this case, the directors may notify the Registrar of Companies of such interests and claim an extension of three months. It should be noted that if any documents comprised in the accounts are in a language other than English, an English translation must be annexed along with the necessary certification that they are a correct translation.[29]

---

[19] *Ibid.*
[20] *Ibid.* s.225(7).
[21] See below for applicable periods.
[22] Companies Act 1985, s.225(3).
[23] *Ibid.* s.225(6).
[24] *Ibid.* s.225(7).
[25] *Ibid.* s.239.
[26] *Ibid.* s.241(1).
[27] *Ibid.* s.241(3).
[28] *Ibid.* s.242(1)(2).
[29] *Ibid.* ss.241(3), 242(3).

The second exception applies to a company submitting accounts in respect of its first accounting reference period. Where that period begins on the date of the company's incorporation and is a period of more than 12 months, the period for laying and delivering accounts is reduced by the number of days by which the first accounting reference period exceeds 12 months. The period for laying and delivering accounts cannot be reduced to less than three months after the end of the first accounting reference period under this provision.[30]

Illustrations

To illustrate the working of the above rules, the following examples can be taken. Assuming that a private company's first accounting reference period covers January 1, 1986, to February 28, 1987, it will be 59 days over 12 months; the company will, therefore, have to deliver its accounts to the Registrar of Companies and lay them before a general meeting by October 31, 1987, rather than by December 28, 1987. In the case of a public company, the date would be July 31, 1986, rather than September 28, 1986.

Altering the facts slightly, if a company's first accounting period was January 1, 1986, to June 30, 1987, and the full brunt of the exception applied, that would leave a private company four months to lay and deliver its accounts. As a public company would have one month to comply with the statutory requirements were the normal formula to apply, the proviso to the exception comes into effect and a period of three months is allowed for filing accounts. Thus the period for laying and delivering a private company's accounts will end on October 31, 1987 (the straight exception applying), whereas for a public company it will end on September 30, 1987.

Change of accounting reference date

Where a company has shortened its accounting reference period, the time for laying and delivering its accounts will run from its new accounting reference date. If this results in a period of less than three months, a three month period will be substituted, which will commence with the date on which notice of the altered accounting reference date is given to the Registrar of Companies.[31]

Secretary of State's powers

The period for laying and delivering accounts may be extended in a particular case by the Secretary of State. He may give a company notice of his decisions where he thinks that special reasons exist which justify such an extension.[32]

Penalties

There are various penalties for breaches of the laying and delivering requirements. For failure to lay copies of a company's accounts before the company in general meeting, to deliver copies of the same to the Registrar of Companies or to annex a certified English translation of foreign documents, where necessary, within the required period, any person, who immediately before the end of that period, was a director of the company will be guilty of an offence and liable to a fine. A daily default fine will be imposed for continued contravention.[33] A director will have a defence to the charge if he can prove that he took all reasonable steps for ensuring that the rules regarding the

---

[30] *Ibid*. s.242(4).
[31] *Ibid*. s.242(5).
[32] *Ibid*. s.242(6).
[33] *Ibid*. s.243(1).

laying and delivering of accounts, and the provision of English translations of documents, where necessary, would be adhered to before the end of the time limit set for compliance.[34] It will be no defence to prove that a document was not prepared as required by statute.[35] The company may also be liable to a penalty, recoverable in civil proceedings by the Secretary of State when the requisite accounts have not been delivered to the Registrar of Companies on time.[36]

The penalties imposed are set on a sliding scale depending upon the length of the delay in laying or delivering the accounts:

> 0–1 month delay — £20
> 1–3 months' delay — £50
> 3–6 months' delay — £100
> 6–12 months' delay — £200
> a delay of 12 months and over — £450[37]

If the laying and delivering requirements have been broken and the default has not been remedied within 14 days after a notice requiring compliance has been served on the directors, a default order may be made against them ordering them to make good the default within a specified time.[38] Any member or creditor of the company or the Registrar of Companies may apply for the order and if an order is granted, the court may further provide that the directors shall bear all the costs of and incidental to the application.[39] Such an order may be made in addition to any criminal proceedings taken against directors.[40] In the case of a default order the Act does not provide the director with an "all reasonable steps" defence but the conduct of a particular director may be taken into account when the court exercises its discretion regarding who is to bear the costs of, and incidental to, the application.

Where accounts have been laid and delivered but do not comply with the requirements of the Act, any person who, at the time the accounts were so laid or delivered, was a director of the company, is guilty of an offence and liable to a fine.[41] As with the offence of failure to deliver and lay accounts, an "all reasonable steps" defence is available to any director who can prove that he took all reasonable steps for securing compliance with the requirements in question.[42]

Other recipients In addition to making the accounts available to the company in general meeting and delivering a copy of them to the Registrar of Companies, every member of the company, debenture holder and any other person who is entitled to receive notice of the company's general meetings must be sent a copy as of right. Amongst those in the last category would be a company's auditors who, by virtue of section 387, are entitled to receive any

---

[34] *Ibid.* s.243(2).
[35] *Ibid.* s.243(5).
[36] *Ibid.* s.243(3).
[37] *Ibid.* s.243(4).
[38] *Ibid.* s.244(1).
[39] *Ibid.* s.244(2).
[40] *Ibid.* s.244(3).
[41] *Ibid.* s.245(1)(2).
[42] *Ibid.* s.245(3).

documents sent to company members which relate to the company's general meetings. A copy of the accounts must by sent at least 21 days before the date of the general meeting.[43] The 21 days requirement may be waived by all members entitled to attend and vote at a general meeting.[44]

Those persons who are not entitled to receive copies of a company's annual accounts as of right, are:—

(a) in the case of a company not having a share capital, a member or debenture holder, who is not entitled to receive notices of the company's general meetings[45];
(b) a member of a company or a debenture holder who is not entitled to receive notices of general meetings of the company and of whose address the company is unaware[46];
(c) more than one of joint holders of any shares or debentures, where none of those joint holders is entitled to receive notices of general meetings[47]; or
(d) in the case of joint holders of shares or debentures, some of whom are entitled to receive notices of general meetings and some of whom are not, those not so entitled.[48]

Apart from the duty to send out copies of the accounts a company must also supply copies on request, free of charge, to any member or debenture holder of the company. This rule applies whether or not the member or debenture holder is entitled to receive copies as of right.[49]

Penalties The penalty for failure to supply copies of the accounts to those entitled as of right is a fine, which is imposed upon the company and every officer who is in default.[50] If a copy is not furnished within seven days of its being demanded, the company and every officer in default will be liable to a fine. A daily default fine will be imposed for continued contravention.[51] A company is only expected to supply copies of its annual accounts free of charge on one occasion and will have a defence, if charged with breach of the above provisions, if it is proved that the person has already demanded a copy of the document to which he is entitled and has been furnished with it.[52]

Publication of Accounts

A company will be deemed to have published its accounts if it publishes, issues or circulates them or otherwise makes them available for public inspection. Such action must be undertaken in a manner which is calculated to invite members of the public to read the accounts concerned.[53] This is normally achieved when

---

[43] *Ibid.* s.240(1).
[44] *Ibid.* s.240(4).
[45] *Ibid.* s.240(2).
[46] *Ibid.* s.240(3).
[47] *Ibid.*
[48] *Ibid.*
[49] *Ibid.* s.246(1).
[50] *Ibid.* s.240(5).
[51] *Ibid.* s.246(2).
[52] *Ibid.*
[53] *Ibid.* s.742(5).

a company files its accounts on public record at Companies House.

The publication of a company's accounts can be looked at under two headings—the publication of full accounts and for these purposes, this includes modified accounts[54] and the publication of abridged accounts.

Full accounts   Full accounts are those which a company is required to lay before the company in general meeting and deliver to the Registrar of Companies. The directors' report[55] and auditors' report[56] must be included with the full accounts.

If modified accounts are published the auditors' report which must accompany them will be the special report required by the modified accounts rules.[57]

A holding company, which is obliged to prepare group accounts, may only publish its individual accounts if it publishes its group accounts at the same time. The modified group accounts may only be published if the holding company's individual accounts are also modified.[58] The relevant auditors' report must be included with the group accounts, or with the group and individual accounts, as the case may be. As with an individual company, a holding company will have to publish the auditors' report which is laid before it in general meeting, or in the case of modified accounts, the special auditors' report which has to accompany those accounts.[59]

Abridged accounts   Abridged accounts are defined as:

> "any balance sheet or profit and loss account relating to a financial year . . . or purporting to deal with any such financial year, otherwise than as part of full accounts . . ."[60]

The definition also includes abridged group accounts.[61]

Interim statements, commonly published by public-quoted companies, will not normally be subject to the publication rules if the statement does not relate to a financial year. An interim statement which includes comparative figures relating to a full year period, may, however, be regarded as an abridged account if the comparative information can be said to take the form of a balance sheet or profit and loss account. A company listed on the Stock Exchange, is obliged to issue a preliminary profits statement.[62] This statement will probably have to comply with the statutory publication requirements for abridged accounts, as it will be in respect of a full financial year and the information which has to be disclosed closely follows the statutory provisions for a balance sheet and profit and loss account. Whether or not a preliminary profits statement falls within the abridged accounts

---

[54] See p. 30ff below.
[55] Companies Act 1985, s.254(1).
[56] *Ibid.* s.254(2).
[57] *Ibid.* s.254(5). For modified accounts audit report see p. 36 below.
[58] *Ibid.* s.254(3).
[59] *Ibid.* s.254(4). For modified accounts audit report see p. 36 below.
[60] *Ibid.* s.255(1).
[61] *Ibid.* s.255(2).
[62] See p. 53 below.

definition will depend upon the way in which the particular statement is drawn up.

Another form of financial information which many companies publish today is employee reports. If these cover a full financial year and equate to a balance sheet and profit and loss account then the publication rules will apply.

When a company publishes abridged accounts, it must publish a statement with those accounts which indicates:

(a) that the accounts are not full accounts;
(b) whether full individual or full group accounts (according to the type of abridged accounts published) have been delivered to the Registrar of Companies;
(c) whether the company's auditors have reported on the company's accounts for any financial year with which the abridged accounts purport to deal; and
(d) whether any report so made was unqualified.[63]

The auditors' report relating to the full accounts dealt with in the abridged accounts must not be published with the abridged accounts.[64]

Penalties   Should a company breach the publication rules, either in respect of the publication of full or abridged accounts, the company and any officer in default will be liable to a fine.[65]

Annual Return

In addition to the obligation to prepare and circulate its annual accounts a company is also obliged to supply the Registrar of Companies with certain information at least once in each calendar year, in the form of an annual return.[66] A return need not be made in the year of a company's incorporation nor necessarily in the following year, if an annual general meeting does not have to be held during that year.[67] The annual return is not connected with a company's annual accounts, although some of the information contained in it is of a financial nature.

AGM   The time limit for submitting an annual return depends upon when a company holds its annual general meeting. The general rule is that such meetings must be held at least once a year and that not more than 15 months may elapse between the date of one annual general meeting and the holding of the next. In the case of a newly incorporated company, so long as it holds its first annual general meeting within 18 months of its incorporation, it need not hold another in the year of its **Timing of** incorporation or in the following year.[68] An annual return must **annual return** be completed by a company and signed by a director and the company secretary within 42 days of an annual general meeting being held. It must then be forwarded forthwith to the Registrar

---

[63] Companies Act 1985, s.255(3). For "unqualified" see p. 118 below.
[64] *Ibid.* s.255(4).
[65] *Ibid.* ss.254(6), 255(5).
[66] *Ibid.* ss.363(1), 364(1).
[67] *Ibid.* ss.363(3), 364(2).
[68] *Ibid.* s.366(1)(2)(3).

Penalties of Companies.[69] Failure to comply with these requirements will result in the company and every officer in default being liable to a fine and, for continued contravention, a daily default fine. For these purposes, a shadow director is deemed to be a director of the company.[70] A shadow director is defined as "a person in accordance with whose directions or instructions the directors of the company are accustomed to act." Those who advise a company in a professional capacity will not be regarded as shadow directors.[71]

Information disclosed   A company having a share capital is obliged to make an annual return which includes the following information:

(a) the address of the company's registered office;

(b) the address of where the registers of members and of debenture holders are kept, if not the registered office;

(c) details of the company's share capital distinguishing between shares issued for cash and shares issued as fully or partly paid up otherwise than for cash; the particulars required to be shown include, *inter alia*, the amounts and categories of share capital, the amount called up on each share and any discounts allowed;

(d) particulars of the company's indebtedness as at the date of the return in respect of all registerable mortgages and charges, whenever created;

(e) details of past and present shareholders and their shareholdings; if a company has converted any of its shares into stock and the Registrar of Companies has been notified of the conversion, the amount of stock held by each member must be included in the annual return as well as the details relating to shares;

(f) all the details of the company's directors and secretary as appear in the company's register of directors and secretaries[72]; for these purposes, directors includes shadow directors.[73]

It will not be necessary to supply full details of past and present members and their shareholdings, if these details have been included in a return for either of the two immediately preceding years. In this event, all that need be supplied are particulars relating to:

(a) persons ceasing to be or becoming members since the date of the last return; and

(b) shares transferred since that date; or

(c) changes as compared with that date in the amount of stock held by a member.[74]

The information is necessarily less detailed for companies not having a share capital.[75]

---

[69] *Ibid.* s.365(1)(2).
[70] *Ibid.* s.365(3).
[71] *Ibid.* s.741(2).
[72] *Ibid.* Sched. 15.
[73] *Ibid.* s.363(8).
[74] *Ibid.* s.363(5).
[75] *Ibid.* s.364(1)(3).

Penalties   A fine and daily default fine in cases of continued contravention are imposed for failure to make an annual return in the prescribed form, liability resting upon the company and every officer of it who is in default. A shadow director is deemed to be an officer of the company for these purposes.[76]

---

[76] *Ibid.* ss.363(7)(8), 364(4)(5).

4 PRESENTATION OF ACCOUNTS

FORMATS

Introduction

In recent times, one of the most important influences upon company accounts has been that of the EEC. Before the passing of the Companies Act 1981, the form and content of company accounts was largely a matter of generally accepted accounting practice, governed by Schedule 8 to the Companies Act 1948. While Schedule 8 mapped out the content of the balance sheet and profit and loss account, it did not specify the form which those documents had to take and the provisions as to contents **Fourth Directive** were not exhaustive. The EEC Fourth Directive on company law was adopted in July 1978 and implemented by the Companies Act 1981. This statute introduced a new Schedule 8 to the 1948 Act which not only laid down formats which had to be followed when preparing a company's balance sheet and profit and loss accounts, but also provided detailed rules as to how certain items in the accounts were to be treated. The 1981 Act was subsequently consolidated with the other company statutes dating from 1948 and what was Schedule 8 to the Companies Act 1948 is now Schedule 4 to the Companies Act 1985.

The company law consolidation replaced the existing statutes with just four. The bulk of the statutory rules relating to company accounts is to be found in the Companies Act 1985. These rules generally apply to both public and private companies, although banking, shipping and insurance companies (known collectively as special category companies[1]) at present can choose whether or not to follow the formats or to adopt the form of accounts allowed by the Companies Act 1948 and now contained in Schedule 9 to the 1985 Act. In due course, special category companies will be the subject of EEC directives, which will in time be implemented in the United Kingdom.

Formats

Schedule 4 to the Companies Act 1985 gives a choice of formats for both balance sheet and profit and loss account. These formats are reproduced in Appendix I. In addition to the information shown in the formats, further disclosure must be made by way of notes to the accounts, which are then appended to the balance sheet and the profit or loss account.

Balance sheet For the balance sheet, there is a choice between two styles, one vertical (format 1), the other horizontal (format 2). As far as the information shown by these two formats is concerned, there is little to choose between them. The horizontal version presents

[1] See p. 3 above.

the data in two columns, headed "assets" and "liabilities," which gives the traditional look to the balance sheet, whereas format 1 presents the same facts in a slightly different order and in the vertical form. Format 1 shows figures for "net current assets (liabilities)" and "total assets less current liabilities" which are not specifically shown in format 2, although figures representing these amounts can be deduced from the information available therein.

Profit and loss account   The choice is wider for the profit and loss account. Not only is a vertical or a horizontal presentation offered, but also formats which lend themselves more to a particular type of business. Thus, either the profit and loss account format 1 or 3 would be appropriate for a company engaged in selling products as the headings cover such intems as "cost of sales" and "distribution costs." A manufacturing company might opt for either format 2 or 4 as these cater for amounts to be shown in respect of "raw material and consumables" and "staff costs." In practice, as no guidance is given in the Act as to the format which should be used by specific types of company, trading companies have tended to opt for formats 1 or 3 as these give away less detailed information about their operating results to their competitors. Formats 1 and 3 do not require the separate presentations of "raw materials and consumables" and "other external charges" as do the other two formats. The terms used in formats 1 and 3, "distribution costs" and "administrative expenses", are not defined, so a company, provided that the accounts show a true and fair view, may allocate what expenditure it thinks appropriate to these two headings. By virtue of the headings within formats 1 and 3, all remaining expenditure must be allocated to "cost of sales." For similar reasons, service companies have tended to select formats 2 or 4. Service companies seldom have substantial values attributable to "raw materials and consumables" or to "finished goods" and consequentially the bulk of their expenditure falls to be disclosed as "other operating charges" about which little additional information need be disclosed. Directors, whose responsibility it is to prepare the annual accounts,[2] may thus choose the format which reveals as little as possible about their company's operations, provided that the accounts show a true and fair view of the company's results for the particular financial period.

Form and content

General provisions   Section 228 is headed "Form and content of company individual and group accounts" and is central to understanding how the detailed rules work. The basic rule is that the form and content of the profit and loss account, the balance sheet and the notes to the accounts must comply with Schedule 4 to the 1985 Act. So, not only must the company provide specific information, it must also set it out in the way laid down by statute.

True and fair   The next central requirement is that the accounts shall show a true and fair view; that is, the balance sheet must give a true

[2] Companies Act 1985, s.227(1)(3).

and fair view[3] of the company's state of affairs as at the end of its financial year and the profit and loss account must show a true and fair view of the company's transactions and resulting profit or loss for the financial year.[4]

The primary presumption is that use of Schedule 4 formats will meet that true and fair standard. The statute, however, recognises that this will not always be the case and provides for deviation from strict compliance with Schedule 4 by giving the option of a true and fair override. Two situations only are envisaged as giving grounds for use of the override.

True and fair override
The first situation is where the Schedule 4 formats do not show a true and fair view because they do not give enough information.[5] In other words, whilst complying with the letter of the law, a misleading picture may be painted because all the information needed to judge either the state of the company's affairs or its profit or loss is not shown. In this situation, the Act authorises the addition of any other necessary information. The extra details should be given in the "incomplete" document, for example, if the balance sheet does not show a true and fair view, the additional information must be shown in that document. It will only be necessary to use the true and fair override where there is no suitable heading under which to show the necessary additional information. This is because Schedule 4 itself provides for any item in the formats to be shown in greater detail than required by the format adopted.[6] If the problem can be solved by expanding any item already in the format then the true and fair override need not be used and there will be no need to include a note to the accounts explaining the action taken. Such a note is necessary if the override is used.[7]

The second situation in which the true and fair override may be used is where a more radical departure from Schedule 4 is necessitated. Where the format used fails to give a true and fair view even if additional information were given, a company is allowed to ignore those provisions which result in the distorting view.[8]

There are three important points to note here.

(a) Special circumstances   It is clear from the wording of the provision that only in exceptional cases can the true and fair override be used. Use is limited to "special circumstances in the case of any company"; it is not available just because the company does not like the formats or that the preparation of accounts according to the Schedule 4 provisions involves extra costs. The test is, do circumstances which are peculiar to that company result in the Schedule 4 formats presenting a misleading picture?

(b) Limited departure   Departure from Schedule 4 is only to be made where necessary. The Act speaks of "departure from that requirement," that requirement being the one which distorts the

---

[3] See p. 38ff below.
[4] Companies Act 1985, s.228(2).
[5] *Ibid.* s.228(4).
[6] *Ibid.* Sched. 4, para. 3.
[7] See pp. 25–26 below.
[8] Companies Act 1985, s.228(5).

true and fair view. So, if for example, the balance sheet treatment of creditors was the distorting requirement, that would be the only item in the formats from which a departure could be made. The rest of the balance sheet would have to comply with the Schedule. It would be extremely unlikely that the whole format could be jettisoned under the true and fair override.

(c) Directors' responsibilities   While the provision does not state who is to decide that the "special circumstances" exception applies to a particular company, it is the directors who are authorised to depart from Schedule 4; the implication is, therefore, that the decision is theirs. This view, it is submitted, is supported by the fact that the obligation to prepare the accounts in the first instance is placed not on the company but on the directors. The "special circumstances" exception differs in this respect from the "additional information" exception, as in the latter, the Act does not impose the duty of disclosing the necessary additional information on anyone in particular. The reason for this could be that the "special circumstances" exception is a more radical departure from Schedule 4 and from the presumption that the statutory form and contents will normally give a true and fair view. Directors should, therefore, carefully review the facts which lead them to a decision that a radical departure should be made from Schedule 4 and it would be very unusual if the opinion of the company's auditors was not sought. While it is, in the final analysis, the decision of the directors whether a departure from the statutory form of accounts is to be made, the auditors may have to qualify their report as not complying with the Companies Act 1985[9] and the directors should consider whether this will adversely affect the company, for example, should the auditors' qualification relate to a material item, this may affect a company's ability to obtain financial support from banking and other institutions. A final point of note is that directors who misuse this exception will be guilty of an offence for failing to provide accounts which comply with the Companies Acts.[10]

If either example of the true and fair override is used, there must be a note to the accounts which gives the following information:—

(a) **Particulars**   the way in which the company has departed from the Schedule must be detailed. One way would be to state which headings or sub-headings have been omitted or changed and then briefly explain how that information has been shown. It is extremely unlikely in the case of a trading company that the total omission of headings to which a significant value was attributable, in particular in the profit and loss account, would give a true and fair view.

(b) **Reasons**   the Act does not expand on the way in which reasons for the departure should be shown, and thus, it is open to the directors to state that, in their opinion, the departure was necessary in order to present a true and fair view. It is suggested, however, that while within the letter

---

[9] See p. 118 below.
[10] See p. 16 above.

of the law, this is against its spirit and some idea of why the formats did not give a true and fair view should be given.

(c) **Effect** — again, if a very literal, narrow approach were taken, this requirement would be met by simply stating that the effect of the departure was to present a true and fair view of either the company's state of affairs or its profit or loss. It is hoped that directors using the true and fair override will attempt to be a little more forthcoming and show how a true and fair view is given by the changes made.

Interpretation   There are two points of general interpretation with which it is necessary to deal before turning to the details of the Schedule. The first is that any reference to a balance sheet or profit and loss account includes any notes thereto.[11] This emphasises that the Schedule 4 provisions which refer to notes to the accounts must be followed in the same way as rules regarding the balance sheet and profit and loss account themselves. Secondly, in the case of a company not trading for profit, for example, a charity, the term "profit and loss account" is to be taken as referring to its "income and expenditure account" and reference to profit or loss will then be read as reference to income or expenditure.

Schedule 4

The schedule is divided into seven parts as follows:

Part	Subject
I	Basic requirements with respect to the form and content of a company's accounts
II	Accounting rules and principles
III	Notes to the accounts
IV	Special provisions where the company is a holding or subsidiary company
V	Special provisions where the company is an investment company
VI	Special provisions relating to merger relief
VII	Interpretation of Schedule 4.

Part IV will be considered in Chapter 16 and Part VI in Chapter 17, whereas Part V falls outside the ambit of this book. The remaining parts will be discussed as follows, the general points immediately below, and those paragraphs dealing with specific issues will be covered under the subject heading.

Basic requirements   Part I offers a company a choice of format for its balance sheet and its profit and loss account, but certain "ground rules" apply whichever formats are chosen.

The basic rule is that the formats, whether for the balance sheet or the profit and loss account, must be followed exactly. The order of items shown in the formats and the headings and sub-headings used should be copied as they stand in the

[11] Companies Act 1985, s.742(2).

Schedule.[12] In the formats the headings and sub-headings are allocated letters and numbers for identification purposes only and these do not have to be shown on the face of a company's accounts.

Permissible alterations   As has been discussed in pages 24 to 26 above, the true and fair override permitting departure from the requirements of Schedule 4 is available in limited situations. In addition to which the Schedule itself sets out possible deviations from strict compliance with its terms. As will be seen there is a certain amount of overlap between the true and fair override and the deviations permitted by the Schedule. The latter permits the following departures from the formats.

(a) **Change of format used**   The general rule is that having chosen one of the two balance sheet formats and one of the four profit and loss account formats, a company must use those formats in subsequent years. The directors are, however, empowered to change to another of the specified formats if, in their opinion, there are special reasons for a change.[13] The points to note here are first that it is the directors' decision, and not, for example, that of the auditors; and secondly, that there must be special reasons for a change. It is presumed that the reasons for the change must have arisen since the original choice was made, otherwise the directors should have had them in mind when they first chose the formats the company was to use. An example of a change necessitating the choice of a new format could be a change in the type of business engaged in by a group of companies, which has been brought about by the acquisition of a new subsidiary. It is unlikely that a company would often be faced with circumstances which necessitated a change of this type and it would not be sufficient merely for the directors to decide that they did not really like the chosen format and that they want a change. There is no provision made for "cannibalising" formats, for example, by borrowing headings from each of the four profit and loss formats and piecing them together.

(b) **Greater detail**   If a company so wishes, any item in the formats may be shown in greater detail. This overlaps with the true and fair override, as does the next category. The result of this overlap is discussed below.[14]

(c) **Additional information**   New items may be introduced to the assets or liabilities, income or expenditure, which are not already shown in the formats. Certain items may not, however, be treated as assets in a balance sheet, namely:

— preliminary expenses;
— expenses of and commission on any issue of shares or debentures; and
— costs of research.[15]

---

[12] *Ibid.* Sched. 4, para. 1.
[13] *Ibid.* para. 2.
[14] *Ibid.* para. 3.
[15] *Ibid.*

(d) Adaptations   The directors have certain power to adapt the headings, sub-heading and arrangement of the formats.[16] There are two points to note. The first is that the special nature of the company's business must require such adaptation. Although, it is not spelt out by paragraph 3 of the Schedule, it is envisaged by the wording that the decision as to whether the company has such a special need is to be taken by the directors. The second point is that only those headings and sub-headings which have been allotted Arabic numerals may be adapted under this rule. This gives a very wide discretion to those compiling accounts, in particular, in relation to the profit and loss formats, but of course, it must be remembered that the true and fair requirement is paramount.

(e) Combination of items   As with "Adaptations" this only applies to items which have been allotted an Arabic numeral. These items may be combined if the items are not material to the true and fair view shown by either the balance sheet or the profit and loss account, or if the items are material but their combination facilitates assessing the state of affairs of the company, or its profit or loss for that year. In the latter case, the individual items must be disclosed in a note to the accounts.[17]

(f) Omissions   Any heading or sub-heading against which there is no amount to be shown can be omitted. This is, however, only possible where there was no amount shown against that item in the preceding year.[18]

Where a different format is adopted, a note to the accounts must be included giving particulars of the change and the reasons for it.[19] Such an explanatory note is not required for any of the alterations set out in (b) to (f) above. If the true and fair override is used a note to the accounts must also be given, but in this case, the note must give not only the particulars of the change and the reasons for it, but also its effect.[20]

The permissible changes to the formats can be summarised as follows:

— true and fair override additional information	—note required
— true and fair override radical change	—note required
— change from one format to another	—note required
— greater detail	—note not required
— additional information	—note not required
— adaptation of arrangement etc.	—note not required
— combination of headings	—note not required
— omissions	—note not required

[16] *Ibid.*
[17] *Ibid.*
[18] *Ibid.*
[19] *Ibid.* para. 2(2).
[20] *Ibid.* s.228(6).

If a company, therefore, wishes to alter the formats for any reason and does not wish to explain the alterations which it has made, it should avoid using the true and fair override. There is no reason, however, why a note of explanation should not be given even though it is not strictly required and this procedure is regarded by some as best practice.

Whilst the Schedule lays down what appears to be a firm rule that the formats shall be followed exactly as they are set out, it then proceeds to give wide powers to adapt those formats. It can be argued, however, that the spirit of the statute and of the Fourth Directive which the Act implements, require exact compliance with the formats, unless special circumstances dictate otherwise.

Corresponding amounts   The general rules, which relate to both balance sheet and profit and loss account, further require that each item shown in either of those two documents, must be accompanied by the corresponding amount for the financial year immediately preceding that to which the balance sheet or profit and loss account relates.[21] If the corresponding amount is not comparable with the previous year's amount, the statute requires that the earlier figure must be adjusted so that it can be compared with the later amount. Where such an adjustment is made, particulars of it and the reasons for it must be disclosed in a note to the accounts. It should be noted that companies are listed on the Stock Exchange usually give corresponding figures for the preceding five years.[22]

Set off   Finally, there is a general rule against set off:

> "Amounts in respect of items representing assets or income may not be set off against amounts in respect of items representing liabilities or expenditure (as the case may be) or vice versa."[23]

Set off is probably not used here in a way familiar to lawyers and thus is unlikely to include the legally enforceable right of set off. The argument to support this view is that the company's liability should reasonably be construed as being the amount it is liable to pay in legal proceedings which are commenced on the balance sheet date. This view is supported by the treatment of set offs by International Accounting Standard IAS 13. This standard prohibits the setting off of current assets against current liabilities, but gives two exceptions, namely in the case of a progress payment on contract work in progress or where "there is a legal right of set off and the off setting represents the likely manner of realisation of the asset or settlement of the liability." While this standard has not yet been brought into effect in England, its exemptions from the general prohibition against set off are sensible and would not be contrary to the spirit of the English legislation.

The type of set off which is prohibited by Schedule 4 would be where a debtor receivable from a third party is set against a creditor payable to the same third party and the resulting net balance only, being included in the relevant balance sheet

---

[21] *Ibid.* Sched. 4, para. 4.
[22] See p. 49 above.
[23] Companies Act 1985, Sched. 4, para. 5.

heading. The false impression given by such a procedure is obvious as the full extent of the amount owed to creditors or due from debtors would not be apparent.

MODIFIED ACCOUNTS

Introduction

The obligation placed upon companies to prepare annual accounts applies to all companies regardless of size. This is also true of the duty to lay such accounts before the company in general meeting. It is, however, possible for certain companies to deliver what are termed "modified" accounts to the Registrar of Companies. This does not mean that those companies which are eligible to deliver modified accounts are spared the rigours of preparing full annual accounts under Schedule 4, as these still have to be prepared, audited and laid before the company as normal. Delivery of modified accounts to the Registrar does mean that an additional set of accounts has to be prepared from the information included in the full accounts and a directors' statement and a special auditors' report added. The benefit of delivering modified accounts is that companies can restrict the information which is placed upon public record and is thus available to competitors. It is, therefore, for the individual company to decide whether the degree of confidentiality obtained by delivering modified accounts is worth the extra work and cost involved. This decision is for the directors of a company, if their company is eligible to deliver modified accounts.

Qualifications

In order to be regarded as eligible for these purposes, a company must qualify in particular financial years as either small or medium-sized.[24] Regardless of size, however, certain companies will never qualify, namely:

 (a) a public company;
 (b) a special category company[25]; and
 (c) subject to certain exceptions, a member of a group which is ineligible for this purpose.[26]

In this context, a group is defined as "a holding company and its subsidiaries together" and will be regarded as ineligible if any of its members are:

 (i) a public company or a special category company; or
 (ii) certain bodies corporate, other than companies.[27]

Even if a group is ineligible, a member of it may still take advantage of the modified accounts provisions if it is exempt from

[24] *Ibid.* s.247(1).
[25] See p. 3 above.
[26] Companies Act 1985, s.247(2).
[27] *Ibid.* s.247(3).

audit under the dormant companies rules[28] and was so exempt throughout the year for which it is sought to deliver modified accounts. Alternatively, the modified accounts provisions may be applied where the dormant company has resolved not to have an audit during that year.[29]

To qualify as either a small or medium-sized company, two or more of the following conditions must be satisfied:

	Small	*Medium-sized*
Amount of turnover for the year, not more than	£2m	£8m
Balance sheet total not more than	£975,000	£3.9m
Average number of employees in the year, not exceeding	50	250[30]

Turnover Whilst not defined in the context of modified accounts, Schedule 4 defines "turnover" as:

"the amount derived from the provision of goods and services falling within the company's ordinary activities, after deduction of:
(a) trade discounts;
(b) value added tax; and
(c) any other taxes based on amounts so derived."[31]

At the time of writing the only deductions for companies trading in England would be under the first two headings. The third category would cover taxes akin to sales tax, for example individual states sales taxes in the United States. Where a company's financial period is not a calendar year, the maximum figures for the qualifying conditions in relation to turnover must be proportionally adjusted.[32]

Balance sheet total The term "balance sheet total" is defined in terms of the formats set out in Schedule 4. For a company using the balance sheet format 1, it is the aggregate of the amounts shown under the headings "Called up share capital not paid," "Fixed assets," "Current assets" and "Prepayments and accrued income"; whereas for a company using format 2, it is the aggregate of the amounts shown under the general heading "Assets."[33]

Employees The average number of employees is calculated by ascertaining for each week in the financial year, the number of persons employed under contracts of service by the company in that week. The fact that a person was not employed for the whole week is irrelevant. The weekly number of employees is then added together and divided by the number of weeks in the financial year.[34]

In order to be eligible to deliver modified accounts for its

[28] See pp. 122–123 below.
[29] Companies Act 1985, s.247(4).
[30] *Ibid.* s.248(1)(2), as amended by S.I. 1986 No. 1865.
[31] *Ibid.* Sched. 4, para. 95.
[32] *Ibid.* s.248(5).
[33] *Ibid.* s.248(3).
[34] *Ibid.* s.248(4).

First financial year
Subsequent years

first financial year, a company must qualify as either a small or medium-sized company in respect of that year.[35] In subsequent years, it will have to meet the requirements for two consecutive years.[36] As an example of the way in which these provisions operate, assume that a company was, in 1987, in its fourth year and wished to deliver modified accounts; in order to do so it would have to meet the requirements as either a small or medium-sized company not only in its fourth year, but also in 1986, its third year.

If a company meets the relevant requirements in the first qualifying year and then fails to satisfy them in the second, it may still deliver modified accounts for that second year and also the following year if it succeeds in meeting the requirements in the third qualifying year.[37] Thus in the above example, if a company satisfied the criteria in 1985 and 1987 but not in 1986, it could deliver modified accounts in 1986 and 1987. If it only met the relevant conditions in 1985, it could take advantage of the modified accounts rules in 1986 but not in 1987. Thereafter, it would have to build up at least one qualifying year before it could again take advantage of the provisions and deliver modified accounts.

Holding
companies

A holding company may qualify to deliver modified accounts if it is required to prepare group accounts for itself and its subsidiaries under section 229 of the Act[38] and the holding company and its subsidiaries together satisfy the criteria for either a small or medium-sized company. In other words, the group is deemed to be a single company for these purposes, and as such must meet one of the set of qualifying conditions. The criteria must be met in the year for which modified accounts are to be delivered.[39] A holding company cannot, therefore, file modified accounts in respect of a year in which it does not qualify, whereas an individual company may do so in the

Group accounts

circumstances outlined in paragraph above. When the directors of the holding company are entitled to deliver modified accounts in respect of that company, they may also deliver modified accounts for the group.[40]

In deciding whether the criteria are met, the figures for turnover, balance sheet total and average number of employees must be taken from the group's consolidated accounts. If consolidated accounts have not been prepared, figures from the group accounts are to be used, with such adjustment as would have been made if the accounts had been prepared in consolidated form. If in the group accounts subsidiaries have been omitted from the calculations, they must be included when ascertaining the group's turnover, balance sheet total and average number of employees. The figures used in the calculations should be taken from the omitted subsidiary's accounts for the relevant year, with any adjustments as would have been made had those figures been used in the consolidated accounts.[41] Where the

---

[35] *Ibid.* s.249(2).
[36] *Ibid.* s.249(3)(4).
[37] *Ibid.* s.249(5)(6).
[38] *Ibid.* s.250(1).
[39] *Ibid.* s.250(2).
[40] *Ibid.* s.250(6).
[41] *Ibid.* s.250(3)(4).

financial year of an omitted subsidiary does not c[...]
of its holding company (and thus the figures for e[...]
the same period and are therefore not strictly com[...]
financial year to be used for the subsidiary's figure[...]
last before the end of the holding company's financial year.[42] For
example, if a holding company's financial year is April 6, 1986, to
April 5, 1987, and its subsidiary's financial year is June 1, 1986 to
April 30, 1987, the figures must be taken from the subsidiary's
accounts for the year ending April 30, 1986. A subsidiary may,
however, be omitted from the calculation of turnover, balance
sheet total and the average number of employees if it was not
included in the group accounts on the grounds of
impracticability.[43]

Having qualified as a small or medium-sized company, the
modifications permitted are to be found in Schedule 8 to the Act
and are set out below.

Small Companies

Individual accounts A modified balance sheet for a small company must show the
following items:

BALANCE SHEET[44]

Format 1	**Format 2**
	ASSETS
A Called up share capital not paid	A Called up share capital not paid

B Fixed assets
  I   Intangible assets
  II Tangible assets
  III Investments
	B Fixed assets
	  I Intangible assets
	  II Tangible assets
	  III Investments

C Current assets
  I   Stocks
  II Debtors
  III Investments
	C Current assets
	  I Stocks
	  II Debtors
	  III Investments
	  IV Cash at bank and in hand

D Prepayments and accrued income	D Prepayments and accrued income
E Creditors: amounts falling due within one year	LIABILITIES A Capital and reserves I Called up share capital

F Net current assets (liabilities)	II Share premium account
	  III Revaluation reserve
	  IV Other reserves
	  V Profit and loss account

[42] *Ibid.* s.250(5).
[43] *Ibid.* s.250(3).
[44] *Ibid.* Sched. 8, para. 2.

G Total assets less current liabilities	B Provisions for liabilities and charges
H Creditors: amounts falling due after more than one year	C Creditors
I Provisions for liabilities and charges	D Accruals and deferred income
J Accruals and deferred income	
K Capital and reserves	

K Capital and reserves
   I   Called up share capital
   II   Share premium account
   III Revaluation reserve
   IV Other reserves
   V   Profit and loss account

In the full accounts, each item under "Debtors" must be expanded to show amounts falling due after one year. This information has to be shown on the face of the full accounts or in notes to the full accounts. The same details must also appear on the face of the modified balance sheet or in the notes to the modified accounts. In the same way, the full accounts must show amounts falling due within one year and after one year, for each of the items shown under format 2 "Creditors." Separate disclosure of the aggregates for all of these items, must also appear either, on the face of the modified balance sheet, or in the notes to the modified accounts.[45]

The modified balance sheet should be accompanied by a limited form of notes to the accounts which should provide information on:

  (i)   accounting policies;
  (ii) share capital;
 (iii) particulars of allotments;
 (iv) particulars of debts;
  (v) basis of translation of foreign currency amounts into sterling; and
 (vi) corresponding amounts for preceding financial years.[46]

A small sized company need not deliver a profit and loss account or a directors' report. In addition to this, disclosure of its chairman's and directors' emoluments, pensions and compensation for loss of office is not required. Finally, details of a small company's higher paid employees may also be omitted.[47]

Group accounts   The modifications which apply to consolidated accounts are the same as for individual accounts. Thus, only a modified balance sheet and limited notes to the accounts need be delivered to the Registrar of Companies.[48] If the group accounts are not

[45] *Ibid.* para. 6.
[46] *Ibid.* para. 5.
[47] *Ibid.* paras. 3, 4.
[48] *Ibid.* paras. 13–17.

consolidated, the modified group accounts should give the same or equivalent information as would have been shown had modified consolidated accounts been produced.[49] The form of full group accounts is discussed in Chapter 16. It is, however, unlikely that a group of companies will be able to meet the necessary criteria enabling it to deliver modified group accounts under this heading because of the low thresholds which those criteria impose.

Medium-sized companies

Individual accounts The modifications granted to a medium-sized company are not as generous as those given to a small sized company. A full balance sheet and directors' report must still be filed, but certain items in the profit and loss account of a medium-sized company may be combined under the heading "Gross profit or loss." Those items are:

Format 1

Gross profit or loss
1. Turnover
2. Cost of sales
3. Gross profit or loss
6. Other operating income

Format 2

Gross profit or loss
1. Turnover
2. Change in stocks of finished goods and work in progress
3. Own work capitalised
4. Other operating costs
5.(a) Raw materials and consumables
   (b) Other external charges

Format 3

Gross profit or loss
A Charges
   1. Cost of sales
B Income
   1. Turnover
   2. Other operating income

Format 4

Gross profit or loss
A Charges
   1. Reduction in stocks of finished goods and in work in progress
   2.(a) Raw materials and consumables
      (b) Other external charges

[49] *Ibid.* s.250(6).

B Income
1. Turnover
2. Increase in stocks of finished goods and in work in progress
3. Own work capitalised
4. Other operating income.[50]

The only modification which is permitted to the notes of the accounts is that particulars of turnover, giving details of the different classes of business carried on by the company, need not be shown.[51]

Group accounts

The modifications granted to medium-sized companies are also given to groups of companies which qualify as medium-sized and for which consolidated accounts are prepared. Where consolidated accounts are not prepared, the modified group accounts should show the same or equivalent information that would have been shown had the modified accounts been consolidated.[52]

Directors' statement and auditors' report

Having prepared modified accounts, an individual company or the holding company of a group must comply with two further requirements before delivering such accounts to the Registrar of Companies. The first is that the balance sheet must contain a statement by the directors which should appear immediately above the directors' signatures. The statement must show that the directors have relied on sections 247 to 249 of the Companies Act 1985 as entitling them to deliver modified accounts and that their company is qualified to deliver such accounts because it is either a small or medium-sized company, as the case may be.[53] The directors' statement in respect of modified group accounts must also include reference to the fact that they are entitled to deliver modified group accounts by virtue of section 250 of the Act 1985.[54]

Directors' statement

Auditors' report

The second requirement is that modified accounts must be accompanied by a special auditors' report. The auditors are required to give their opinion, confirming the directors' statement, that the directors are entitled to deliver modified accounts in respect of the particular financial year. They must also include their opinion that any accounts comprised in the documents delivered as modified accounts are properly prepared as such, in accordance with the statutory requirements.[55] The auditors' report accompanying group modified accounts will differ in that reference will have to be made to the fact that those accounts are for a group rather than an individual company.[56]

Once the directors have decided to take advantage of the modified accounts rules, the auditors are under an obligation to

---

[50] *Ibid.* Sched. 8, para. 7.
[51] *Ibid.* para. 8.
[52] *Ibid.* paras. 18 and 19.
[53] *Ibid.* para. 9.
[54] *Ibid.* para. 21.
[55] *Ibid.* para. 10.
[56] *Ibid.* para. 22.

provide them with a report covering the points set out above.[57]

In the case of both individual and group accounts, the full auditors' report need not be delivered but if it is not, the full text of it must be reproduced in the special auditors' report.[58]

SSAPs　　　A final consideration with regard to modified accounts is whether the accountancy profession's Statements of Standard Accounting Practice should apply to them. As full accounts will have to be prepared for circulation to shareholders, it is difficult to envisage a situation in which modified accounts will not have been prepared from the full accounts. That being the case, the standards should have been applied where necessary to the full accounts. When modified accounts are delivered to the Registrar of Companies, however, the full disclosure required by any applicable standard will not apply, the reason being that the standards need only be applied to accounts giving a true and fair view and there is no requirement that modified accounts should give a true and fair view.

---

[57] *Ibid.* paras. 10(3), 22(3).
[58] *Ibid.* paras. 10(2), 22(2).

5 ACCOUNTING PRINCIPLES, CONCEPTS AND BASES

Introduction

The preparation of accounts is governed by certain accounting principles and rules, some of which are contained in statute but the majority of which are set out in statements of standard accounting practice (SSAPs) and statements of recommended practice (SORPs).[1] To a certain extent the statutory principles and rules overlap with those produced by the accountancy profession. In this chapter, the general principles, concepts and bases which underlie the preparation of accounts are discussed. Those relating to specific topics are to be found under the headings which deal with those subjects.

True and fair
Both the statutory requirements and the SSAPs issued by the accountancy profession seek to achieve some standardisation, not only in the presentation of accounts but also in the way in which they have been compiled. One idea is central to both sets of rules and that is that the accounts should show a true and fair view. In SSAP 2, "Disclosure of Accounting Policies", the need to show accounting policies adopted in the preparation of a company's financial statements is justified by reference to the necessity to give a true and fair view. The true and fair requirement is that a balance sheet must give a true and fair view of the state of affairs of the company at the end of its financial year, and a profit and loss account must show a true and fair view of the company's profit or loss for the financial year. This concept has been enshrined in company legislation since 1947, when it first appeared in section 13(1) of the Companies Act of that year, which was subsequently consolidated and became section 149(1)[2] of the Companies Act 1948.

Definition
The phrase "true and fair" has never been defined by statute, by the courts or by the accountancy profession itself. A definition or paraphrase would probably add little if anything to the understanding of "true and fair," for as Leonard Hoffman Q.C. and Mary Arden point out in their joint opinion on the concept of true and fair,[3] it is one of the many abstract or philosophical concepts known to the English legal system which are generally understood, but about which there is frequent controversy over their application to particular facts.

Guidelines
There are, however, several pointers which can be used as a guide to the meaning of true and fair, the first being that it is expected that in the majority of cases, the formats laid down in

---

[1] See p. 44ff below.
[2] Companies Act 1985, s.228(2).
[3] See Appendix II.

the Act for balance sheets and profit and loss accounts will present a true and fair view. That this will not always be the case is recognised by the exceptions to this rule which are permitted by the statute and discussed in Chapter 4.

Secondly, as Leonard Hoffman Q.C. and Mary Arden point out in their joint opinion, the true and fair concept involves judgment in questions of degree, for example, in relation to accuracy and comprehensiveness. It will also be a question of judgment how much disclosure will be necessary. It will always be possible that more than one presentation of a situation may reflect a true and fair view. In interpreting the concept, a judge will look for guidance from the practices of ordinary professional accountants. The use of accepted accounting principles relating to specific situations will be prima facie evidence that particular accounts are true and fair.

The Littlejohn Case
Since the joint opinion on true and fair was given, the status of Statements of Standard Accounting Practice has been considered in the case of *Lloyd Cheyham & Co. Ltd.* v. *Littlejohn & Co.*[4] In considering whether the accounting treatment of certain items had been negligent, Woolf J. considered the evidential role of SSAPs. He held that:

> "While they are not conclusive, so that a departure from their terms necessarily involves a breach of the duty of care, they are very strong evidence as to what is the proper standard which should be adopted and unless there is some justification, a departure from this will be regarded as constituting a breach of duty."

He went on to echo the point made in the joint opinion that users of accounts are entitled to assume that they have been drawn up in accordance with approved practice unless there is an indication in the accounts to the contrary.

Accounting principles

With the concept of true and fair as the aim when preparing and presenting accounts, the Companies Act 1985 sets out five accounting principles which must be applied to all items shown in a company's accounts[5]:

(a) a company is to be presumed to be carrying on business as a going concern;

(b) accounting policies are to be applied consistently from one financial year to the next;

(c) the amount of any item is to be determined on a prudent basis, and in particular:

    (i) only profits realised at the balance sheet date are to be included in the profit and loss account; and

    (ii) all liabilities and losses which have arisen or are likely to arise in respect of the financial year to which the accounts relate or a previous financial year are to be taken into account; this will include those which only

---

[4] [1986] PCC 389.
[5] Companies Act 1985, Sched. 4, para. 9.

become apparent between the balance sheet date and the date on which it is signed on behalf of the board of directors;

(d) all income and charges relating to the financial year to which the accounts relate are to be taken into account, without regard to the date of receipt or payment (the accruals principle); and

(e) in determining the aggregate amount of any item, the amount of each individual asset or liability that falls to be taken into account must be determined separately, this can be described briefly as the separate valuation principle.[6]

The statutory accounting principles are the same as the accounting concepts set out in SSAP 2, with the addition of the separate valuation principle.

Compliance   It is expected that all companies will follow these accounting principles but if the directors of a company believe that there are special reasons for departing from any of the principles in preparing the company's accounts, statute allows them so to do. If advantage is taken of this exception, then particulars of the departure, the reasons for it and its effect are to be given in a note to the accounts.[7] If the departure is material, it will also be commented on in the auditors' report as being both a departure from the requirements of the Companies Act 1985 and from SSAP 2.

Accounting concepts

SSAP 2, which seeks to encourage companies to give a clear explanation of the accounting policies in financial statements, defines the fundamental accounting concepts as the "broad basic assumptions which underlie the periodic financial accounts of business enterprises". These assumptions are several, but four are singled out, namely the going concern concept, the accruals concept, the consistency concept and the prudence concept. The following discussion considers both the statutory provisions and the requirements of the Standard.

Going concern   **The going concern concept**   The Act presumes that a company's accounts will be prepared on the basis that the company is carrying on business as a going concern.[8] In other words, it is presumed that the company will continue in operational existence for the foreseeable future. For these purposes, the accountancy profession has given the general advice that, while the foreseeable future can not be defined in precise terms, it should normally extend to a minimum of six months from the date of the audit report, or one year after the balance sheet date, whichever period is longer.[9] This presumption can of course be rebutted, for example, when a

---

[6] *Ibid.* paras. 10–14.
[7] *Ibid.* para. 15.
[8] *Ibid.* para. 10.
[9] Auditing Guidelines, "The auditors' consideration in respect of going concern," issued August 1985 by Auditing Practices Committee.

company can not meet its debts as they fall due or is under capitalised. This concept is crucial to the expression of a true and fair view when valuing assets to be shown in the balance sheet. The value of most assets to a company which is a going concern will be greater than their value if the company were to be broken up and sold (the break up basis). It may also be that once a company is no longer a going concern, new liabilities, such as redundancy payments will arise and need to be included in the accounts.

Consistency
The consistency concept Statute and SSAP 2 require that accounting policies be applied consistently from one financial year to another. In other words, like items should receive the same accounting treatment within each separate accounting period.[10] Where accounting policies are changed, the comparative figures in accounts are required to be restated to give a basis for comparison and the effect of material changes should be disclosed as extraordinary items under SSAP 6, "Extraordinary Items and Prior Year Adjustments."

Prudence
The prudence concept A company must use a prudent basis in determining the amount of any item included in its annual accounts. In particular, the Act concentrates upon two aspects of this rule:

(a) Only "realised" profits may be included in the profit and loss account. The term 'realised' is defined as "such profits of the company as fall to be treated as realised profits for the purposes of those accounts in accordance with the principles generally accepted with respect to the determination for accounting purposes of realised profits at the time when those accounts are prepared."[11] The question of what can be regarded as realised is considered in SSAP 2, which interprets it as meaning realised in the form of either cash or of other assets, for example, debtors, the ultimate cash realisation of which can be assessed with reasonable certainty. The concept of realised profits, which is important not only for the purpose of the profit and loss account but also in the context of a company's distributions, is discussed in more detail in Chapter 11.

(b) All liabilities and losses which have arisen or are likely to arise in respect of either the financial year in question or a previous financial year must be taken into account. This is so even if they only become apparent between the balance sheet date and the date on which the balance sheet is signed on behalf of the directors. Thus, if after the balance sheet date but before the balance sheet has been signed, a manufacturing company makes a material loss on a contract because it is prevented from delivering stocks included in the balance sheet by the contracted delivery date, an appropriate proportion of the loss must be reflected in the annual accounts.[12]

Accruals
The accruals concept The financial statements must take into account all income and charges relating to the financial year in

[10] Companies Act 1985, Sched. 4, para. 11.
[11] *Ibid.* para. 91.
[12] *Ibid.* para. 12.

question, regardless of when they are received or paid.[13] It is possible that there may be a clash between this concept and the prudence concept. No guidance is given in the Act as to the course of action to be followed in such circumstances, but SSAP 2 requires that in this situation, the prudence concept must prevail.

Separate valuation

The separate valuation principle   The total value of any particular group of assets must be arrived at by adding together the individual values of the items within the group, rather than by applying an average price to all.[14] This will not always be practical, for example, in the case of small items which are constantly being replaced. Provision is therefore made for certain assets to be included in the balance sheet at a fixed quantity and value.[15] There is a further exception where there is a legal right of set off, in which case assets and liabilities can be set off against each other, an action otherwise prohibited by the Act.[16]

Accounting bases

Having discussed the four fundamental concepts, SSAP 2 goes on to examine accounting bases. It defines accounting bases as the methods by which the concepts have been expressed or applied to financial transactions and items; in other words they are the flesh on the bones of the accounting concepts. One of the reasons that the development of bases had been necessary is that many business transactions have financial effects which are not contained in one accounting period, for example, the acquisition of new equipment which will reduce the unit cost of production and thus increase profit for at least five years. No hard and fast rule can be laid down in such situations, as gauging the future financial effects of a particular transaction is not an exact science. The Standard lists matters which are particularly problematical, for example, the future benefits to be derived from stocks and all types of work in progress at the end of the year and the future benefits to be derived from fixed assets. In answer to these problems, certain accounting rules have been formulated, in the case of the two examples given, there are bases for calculating the amounts at which stocks and work in progress are to be derived[17] and rules for determining the depreciation of fixed assets.[18] Once a particular base is adopted by a company, it will become that company's accounting policy on that matter.

The fact that there may be a number of accounting bases which could justifiably be used for one particular item means that a company's financial position and the view presented in its accounts can only be properly appreciated if its accounting policies are disclosed. Hence the Standard requires disclosure of accounting policies for dealing with items which are material or

[13] *Ibid*. para. 13.
[14] *Ibid*. para. 14.
[15] *Ibid*. para. 25.
[16] *Ibid*. para. 5.
[17] See pp. 69, 70–71 below.
[18] See p. 56ff below.

critical in determining the profit or loss for the year. Disclosure should be made in the notes to the accounts and the explanations of the policies given in as clear, fair and as brief a manner as possible.

As the proliferation of numerous accounting bases for one item can be both confusing and misleading, the accountancy profession has sought to eliminate the element of discretion in certain cases where some degree of agreement as to the proper accounting treatment can be attained. This is done by means of the issue of Statements of Standard Accounting Practice on specific topics.[19]

It will be seen that, although the Companies Act 1985 does not go into the subject of accounting bases and accounting policies, the provisions which it terms "historical accounting rules" and "alternative accounting rules" are to some extent concerned with the same issues as SSAPs. In some cases, the Standards are more detailed than the Act and occasionally there is a clash between the two. The various accounting bases or rules are discussed in the context of the disclosure requirements of the particular financial statement in which they occur.

---

[19] See p. 44ff below.

6 NON-STATUTORY ACCOUNTING REQUIREMENTS

Introduction

Apart from the statutory obligations which are imposed upon directors regarding the way in which a company presents its financial information, there are also non–statutory requirements relating to the preparation of accounts and their contents. Some of these rules apply to all companies, whereas others govern only companies listed on the Stock Exchange. The major accountancy bodies, in an attempt to harmonise the way in which accounts are prepared and presented, have issued and continue to issue Statements of Standard Accounting Practice (SSAPs) which govern all accounts which are required to show a true and fair view. In order for an auditor, being a member of a major accountancy body, to express agreement with the true and fair view disclosed in a set of accounts, he must be satisfied that relevant SSAPs have been correctly applied or reasons for deviation therefrom have been fully disclosed and the resulting difference quantified. In addition, Statements of Recommended Practice or SORPs, have recently been introduced, compliance with which is advised but not compulsory. Both SSAPs and SORPs are discussed in more detail below.

Public companies which are listed on the Stock Exchange will also have to comply with that body's disclosure requirements, in addition to both the statutory rules and the Standards issued by the accountancy profession. The financial information which the Stock Exchange obliges quoted companies to disclose is examined below, while the financial data which a company will have to submit to the Stock Exchange when applying for a listing is discussed in Chapter 18.

Statements of Standard Accounting Practice

Preparation Statements of Standard Accounting Practice are prepared by the ASC and approved by that body before being voted on by the members of the Consultative Committee of Accountancy Bodies (CCAB). Having been approved, the Standards are then issued.

Before a Standard is issued, it will have been published as an exposure draft (ED), in order that comments on its details can be received before the final version is approved. Compliance with an exposure draft is not of course compulsory as there is no guarantee that its provisions will not be altered, but an exposure draft should not be completely ignored when it comes to the preparation of accounts and, unless the draft is particularly controversial, it should be regarded as good practice until such time as it is finally approved by members of the CCAB.

The legal status of SSAPs is discussed in the context of generally accepted accounting principles in Chapter 5.

Application

Not all Standards are of general application, for example, SSAP 3, "Earnings per share," will only apply to listed companies and SSAP 12, "Foreign currency translation," will only be relevant to those with a foreign element in their assets, liabilities or business transactions.

Compliance

Compliance with SSAPs is compulsory for all professional accountants who assume responsibilities in respect of financial statements intended to show a true and fair view. It must be said, however, that as the Standards are not intended to be a comprehensive code of rigid rules, compliance will not always be practicable or, in certain cases, appropriate. In these situations, it is permissible to modify the provisions or to follow an alternative method of accounting treatment, provided that any departure from a Standard is noted and explained. Whether or not the accounting treatment of a particular item should depart from a relevant Standard is left to the professional judgment of the accountant concerned, who should have regard for both the spirit and the precise terms of the Standard, as well as the overriding requirement that a company's annual accounts must present a true and fair view. SSAPs need not, however, be applied to items whose effect is judged to be immaterial to an understanding of a particular set of financial statements.

In addition to ensuring that the Standards are complied with and any significant departure noted, auditors are also obliged to consider whether they agree with any departure. In the event of their agreement with any departure, they must justify their concurrence, whether it is stated or implied, in their report. If they do not agree with any departure and cannot persuade the company concerned that it should comply with a Standard, the auditors will qualify their audit report. The seriousness of any qualification will depend upon the nature of the departure, for example, if a company does not disclose its accounting policies as it required to do by SSAP 2, and it has prepared accounts on a basis other than the going concern basis, an auditors' qualification in this respect will have serious consequences as it may have to question the solvency of the company and thus may lead to the withdrawal of financial facilities by banks and other such organisations.

In the case of accountants other than auditors, they are expected to use their best endeavours to ensure that the Standards are observed and to explain the existence and the purpose of them to non accountant directors and officers. If a standard is not complied with, the accountant is expected to disclose any significant departures and give an explanation of the reasons for it in the accounts. If the effect of such departure is material, this should also be quantified, unless to do so would be impracticable or misleading.

As accounting methods and practices are continually changing and evolving, existing SSAPs are subject to review as and when necessary and new Standards introduced when needed. The Standards should be considered as the basis for all accounts intended to give a true and fair view of financial position and profit or loss, but as the scope of this book is restricted to companies incorporated under the Companies Act, the Standards will be discussed in terms of these companies only.

Individual Standards are discussed in the context of the particular item to which they relate. There is, however, one Standard which does not relate to information shown in statutory accounts, SSAP 10, "Statements of Source and Application of Funds," an explanation of which follows.

Funds flow statements

Statements showing the source and application of a company's funds are generally speaking not required by law but SSAP 10, "Statements of Source and Application of Funds", requires that such statements be included with a company's audited accounts, if its turnover or gross income is £25,000 or more per annum. This statement which is also known as a funds flow statement is, however, potentially one of the most useful parts of a company's annual accounts for the management of a company, as it will show a company's principal sources of working capital and the way in which those funds have been applied. While SSAP 10 sets out the minimum requirements for funds flow statements, a company can develop its statement to its own needs, thus sharpening its usefulness as a management tool. Companies with a turnover or gross income below this limit should, therefore, consider producing a statement of the source and application of funds for internal use wherever it is thought desirable so to do.

Contents

A funds flow statement provides information which supplements a company's balance sheet and profit and loss account. From the statutory accounts, it will be possible to assess the amount of profit or loss which a company has made during its financial year and the disposition of the company's resources at the beginning and end of that year. A funds flow statement will demonstrate the movements in assets, liabilities and capital which have taken place during the year and the effect of such movements on the company's net liquid funds, thereby providing the user of the company's accounts with a fuller understanding of its affairs. "Net liquid funds" are defined as cash at bank and in hand and cash equivalents (for example, investments held as current assets) less bank overdrafts and other borrowings repayable within one year of the accounting date. SSAP 10, however, makes it clear that a funds flow statement does not aim to provide an indication of a business' capital requirements or the extent of seasonal peaks of stocks, debtors, etc.

As has been seen, the funds flow statement should show the funds which have been made available to a company during the period under review and the way in which they have been used. This will be achieved by showing the profit or loss for the period and any adjustments made to that figure in respect of items which do not represent a flow of funds, for example, depreciation. In addition to this information, the following other sources and applications of funds should be shown, but only where they are material:

"(a) dividends paid;
(b) acquisitions and disposals of fixed and other non–current assets;
(c) funds raised by increasing, or expended in repaying or

redeeming, medium or long–term loans or the issued capital of the company;

(d) increase or decrease in working capital sub–divided into its components, and movements in net liquid funds."

SSAP 10 further requires that the figures used in a funds flow statement should generally be identifiable in the profit and loss account, balance sheet and the notes to the accounts. In the event of those published figures having to be adjusted, details of the adjustments should be given to enable the related figures to be rapidly located.

In preparing the statement, "setting off" should be kept to a minimum in order that the full significance of the movements reported can be appreciated. Thus, if one building is purchased during the year and another sold, rather than deducting one from the other and showing the net result, the purchase cost and sale proceeds should generally be kept separate in a funds flow statement.

Groups The statement of the source and application of funds for a group of companies should reflect the operations of the group. If during the financial year, subsidiary companies have been acquired or disposed of, these purchases or disposals should appear either as separate items, or by showing the effects on the separate assets and liabilities dealt with in the statement. In addition, the effects of the acquisition or disposal should be shown by way of footnote. Group accounts are discussed in greater depth in Chapter 14.

Corresponding previous year All companies preparing a funds flow statement for the period under review, whether for an individual company or for a group of companies, should include a statement for the corresponding previous year.

Audit Once a funds flow statement has been prepared, it should be audited as part of the annual accounts. If a statement of the source and application of funds is not prepared in accordance with SSAP 10, a company's auditors should report its omission, although its absence will not affect the truth or fairness of the company's annual accounts. As the statement is not part of the annual accounts as defined by statute, it does not have to be laid before the company in general meeting or registered with the Registrar of Companies, although most companies preparing such a statement will include it.

Listed companies A company seeking a listing on the Stock Exchange will have to supply a source and application of funds statement for the company or the group, along with the other financial information that is required. Once a listing has been granted, the Stock Exchange expects a member to comply with the current accounting standards, and thus a listed company should include a funds flow statement with its annual accounts.

Statements of Recommended Practice

In addition to the Statements of Standard Accounting Practice, the ASC also publish Statements of Recommended Practice
Types (SORPs). There are two types of SORP; the first is developed and issued by the ASC itself and the second type, while it is

developed and issued by an "industry" group which is representative of the industry concerned, has to be approved and franked by the ASC prior to its issue. The term "industry" in this context, refers to specific industries or sectors, including parts of the public sector. An industry group will be recognised by the ASC and its purpose will be to develop SORPs relating to that industry. Before any SORP is franked, the ASC will have reviewed the proposed statement and the procedures involved with its development.

Purpose   A particular subject will be dealt with by a SORP, rather than by a SSAP, when the ASC believes that it would not be appropriate to issue a Standard at that time. The primary aim of SORPs is to introduce a more uniform accounting treatment of the matters with which they deal.

Compliance   As their title suggests, SORPs are recommended practice and, unlike Standards, members of the CCAB are not obliged to comply with their provisions. Should a company decide not to follow a Statement of Recommended Practice, this departure will not need to be noted in a company's accounts. Companies are, however, encouraged to comply with any relevant Statement, and to disclose any departure from its provisions in the notes to their accounts, along with the reasons for the departure. SORPs will be designed so as to take account of the provisions of Standards, but may not be used to alter or extend SSAPs.

At the time of writing, the only SORP to have been issued deals with Pension Scheme Accounts.

Stock Exchange requirements

Introduction   While all listed companies will be public, not all public companies are necessarily listed. Companies that wish to be listed, will have to satisfy the Stock Exchange that they are suitable applicants and once a listing has been obtained, companies are subject to Continuing Obligations, under which the Stock Exchange places certain information requirements upon them.

Until recently the basis of the requirement to supply information was contractual, all listed companies entered into what was known as the listing agreement. As a result of three EEC Directives known as the Admission Directive, the Listing Particulars Directive and the Interim Reports Directive, the Stock Exchange decided that a formal listing agreement was no longer necessary. The Directives were implemented by The Stock Exchange (Listing) Regulations 1984.[1] The information requirements imposed by the Directives, and now by Statutory Instrument can not be waived, but those imposed by the Stock Exchange itself may be waived by the Council of Stock Exchange.

The aim of the obligation to supply continuing information is set out in the Stock Exchange's own manual "Admission of Securities to Listing" (the "Yellow Book") and is

---

[1] S.I. 1984 No. 716.

"to secure immediate release of information which might reasonably be expected to have a material effect on market activity in, and prices of, listed securities . . . The guiding principle is that information which is expected to be price-sensitive should be released immediately it is the subject of a decision. Until that point is reached, it is imperative that the strictest security within the user is observed."

The "user" in this context is the listed company. The ultimate sanction imposed by the Stock Exchange for breach of these rules is the suspension of the listing of the securities of the company at fault.

All listed companies are required to notify the Stock Exchange of any information which would enable investors in the company and the public to judge the position of the company and which would avoid the establishment of a false market in the company's listed securities. Provision is made for companies to be able to pass on any such information in strict confidence to persons with whom they are negotiating, with a view to the making of a contract or the raising of finance. Information should be released in a particular matter when it has reached the stage that it must go beyond the directors and the small group of employees and advisers necessarily concerned.

The Stock Exchange has recommended that listed companies should include a ten year historical summary in their financial statements. In practice, many companies have adopted a five year period for such summaries. In addition, listed companies are obliged to comply with the following requirements relating to their accounts.

Annual accounts   The Stock Exchange requires listed companies to issue their annual report and accounts within six months of the end of the accounting reference period to which they relate. An extension of this time limit may be granted where a company has significant interests outside the country of incorporation. This is in addition to the statutory requirements as to the laying and delivering accounts. Where a listed company is a member of a group, the group accounts should take the form of consolidated accounts. The company's own individual accounts must be published along with group accounts, where they contain significant additional information. The Stock Exchange requires that the following information is given in a company's annual report and accounts:

(a) **Departures from standard accounting practice**   The standard accounting practices referred to here are the Statements of Standard Accounting Practice, which are issued by the accountancy profession.[2] Any significant departure from an applicable Standard should be noted. In addition, the Stock Exchange normally requires companies to have regard to Statements of Recommended Practice issued by the principal accountancy bodies.[3]

(b) **Trading forecasts and results**   When there is a material difference between a trading forecast and the actual results shown

[2] See pp. 44–47 above.
[3] See pp. 47–48 above.

in the accounts, this must be accompanied by an explanation of the difference.

(c) **Geographical analysis**   A geographical analysis is required of net turnover and contribution to trading results of those trading operations, which the company or group carries on outside the United Kingdom and the Republic of Ireland. Transactions within a group, however, should be excluded. The detail needed to be shown is that which would enable a proper appraisal of the overall business. The Companies Act contains a similar requirement, to show the amount of turnover attributable to markets which are substantially different from each other. The term "market" is used to mean a market delimited by geographical bounds.[4] The statutory obligation is, therefore, wider. For example, if a company exports to two substantially different markets within one geographical area, disclosure would be necessary under the statutory requirement but not for Stock Exchange purposes.

(d) **Name of the principal country in which each subsidiary operates**   This requirement is in addition to the Companies Act provision that the country of incorporation of each company must be disclosed.[5] In the case of both the statutory and the Stock Exchange obligations, there are exceptions to the disclosure rules where, in the opinion of the directors, disclosure would be harmful to the business of the disclosing company or to any of its subsidiaries. In such a situation, the Secretary of State must agree that the information need not be disclosed. Where disclosure would result in particulars of excessive length being given the information need not be disclosed so long as the amounts involved are not material.[6] The approval of the Secretary of State is not required in this case.

(e) **Holdings of 20 per cent. or more**   Where a group has an interest of 20 per cent. or more in the equity capital of a company which is not a subsidiary, the following details must be given:

    (i)   the principal country of operation;
   (ii)   particulars of its issued capital and debt securities; and
  (iii)   the percentage of each class of debt securities attributable to the company's interest; disclosure will have to be made both where the company has a direct interest in the securities and where its interest is indirect.

This is similar to the Companies Act provision, but the statute requires that interests of 10 per cent. or more must be disclosed.[7] In both cases, disclosure will be excused if the amounts involved are not material and compliance with the requirement would lead to particulars of excessive length being given.

(f) **Bank loans etc**   A company's borrowings should be analysed into two categories, showing bank loans and overdrafts separately

---

[4] Companies Act 1985, Sched. 4, para. 55.
[5] *Ibid.* Sched. 5, para. 1.
[6] *Ibid.* paras. 3,4.
[7] *Ibid.* paras. 7–13.

from other borrowings of the company or group. The aggregate amounts repayable as at the end of the financial year should then be disclosed for each category, showing those due:

(i) in one year or less, or on demand;
(ii) between one and two years;
(iii) between two and five years; and
(iv) in five or more years.

It will be noted that the information is more detailed than that required under the Companies Act, which only requires an analysis of creditors falling due within one year, after one year and after five years.[8]

(g) Capitalised interest   The requirement here is to show the amount of interest capitalised in respect of the financial year, by the company or group during the year. An indication of the amount and treatment of any related tax relief should also be included.

(h) Directors' interests in the capital of any member of the group   To a certain extent this mirrors Companies Act requirements to be found in sections 323 to 329 of the Act but the Stock Exchange goes further and obliges companies to disclose any changes in directors' interests since the end of the financial year. The purpose behind this requirement is to disclose those holdings through which directors may influence voting, so that investors will be aware of such influence.

(i) Other interests in shares   Details of any interest of 5 per cent. or more in shares of the company held by a person other than any director must be given if the interests appear on the register kept by the company for the purposes of section 211 of the Companies Act.

(j) Close company   A statement must be given showing whether, so far as the directors are aware, the company is a close company for taxation purposes. The statement should also indicate whether or not there has been any change in that respect since the end of the financial year. Where the directors are in any doubt as to the company's standing for these purposes, this fact should be made known in the statement. Once the situation has been clarified, the Stock Exchange should be informed accordingly.

(k) Contracts of significance   The Stock Exchange requires disclosure of contracts of significance in which a director is, or was, materially interested. Particulars of such contracts will have to be given where they subsist during, or at the end of, the financial year. This requirement is similar to the provisions of the Companies Act which require disclosure of contracts in which a director has a material interest, whether that interest is direct or indirect.[9] There are two differences between the statutory provisions and the Stock Exchange obligations:

[8] See p. 72 below.
[9] Companies Act 1985, Sched. 6, paras. 1,2,3, and 9.

(a) statute requires the reporting of contracts in which a director is materially interested, and the decision as to whether an interest is material or not, is left to the board of directors without any further guidance being given. This contrasts with the approach of the Stock Exchange provision which requires that disclosure should be made of "a contract of significance." This phrase is then defined as "one which represents in amount or value a sum equal to 1 per cent. or more of:
  (i) in the case of a capital transaction or transaction of which the principal purpose is the granting of credit, the net assets of the company; or
  (ii) in other cases the total purchases, sales, payments or receipts, as the case may be, of the company."
(b) the Stock Exchange further requires that the negative must be reported if there are, or were, no such contracts which subsisted during or at the end of the financial year.

(l) Contracts of significance with a corporate substantial shareholder   Particulars of any such contract, made between a company or one of its subsidiaries and a corporate shareholder should be disclosed. The phrase "contracts of significance" has the same meaning as for (k) above. "Corporate shareholder" is defined as "any corporate shareholder entitled to exercise or control the exercise of 30 per cent. or more of the voting power at general meetings of the company, or one which is in a position to control the composition of the company."

(m) Provision of services by a corporate substantial shareholder   Particulars of any contract for the provision of services by such a person to the company or any subsidiary must be disclosed. There is, however, an exception in the case of the shareholder whose principal business it is to provide such services, and the contract is not a contract of significance. "Corporate substantial shareholder" and "contract of significance" bear the same meanings as above.

(n) Waiving of director's emoluments   When any director has waived, or agrees to waive, his emoluments, particulars of the arrangement must be disclosed, along with details of the emoluments which have accrued during the past financial year. Emoluments include those from the company or any of its subsidiaries. This goes beyond the statutory requirement which only requires details of emoluments which have been waived to be given.[10]

(o) Waiving of dividends   Waivers of dividends by any shareholders must be reported together with details of the dividends which were payable during the past financial year. Provision is made for the waiver of dividends of minor amounts to be excluded, provided that there has been some payment made on each share during the relevant calendar year.

---

[10] *Ibid.* Sched. 5, para. 27.

(p) Purchase of own shares   When a company purchases its own shares, its shareholders have to sanction the purchase. The Stock Exchange requires that the details of this authority should be given. If the purchase is not made through the market or by tender or partial offer to all shareholders, further particulars of the transaction must be disclosed. When a company purchases its own shares after the end of the particular financial year and the date of the report, the company is required to furnish the same details as are required by the Companies Act.[11] This means that a company listed on the Stock Exchange has to disclose the particulars of its purchase earlier than it would have to if it were not listed.

In addition, in respect of any director proposed for re-election at a forthcoming annual general meeting, a company's directors' report should contain a statement showing the unexpired period of any service contract which that director has with the company. This only applies where the director concerned has a service contract of more than one year's duration. If the director does not have such a contract, the directors' report must contain an appropriate negative statement.[12]

Half-yearly reports   The Stock Exchange further requires a listed company to report on its activities and profit or loss earned during the first six months of its financial year. A company has four months, from the end of the six month period, in which to send the half-yearly report to the holders of listed securities. Alternatively, it may insert the report as a paid advertisement in two national daily newspapers. In both cases, a copy of the report must be sent to the Stock Exchange.

The half-yearly report, not being a creature of statute, does not necessarily have to be audited, but directors are expected to ensure that the same accounting policies that are followed in the annual accounts are followed with regard to this report also. Should the accounting information not have been audited, this must be stated.

If a company changes its accounting reference period, it must consult the Stock Exchange as to the period to be covered by the half yearly report.

Preliminary profits statement   A preliminary profits statement, covering a company's full financial year is also required to be issued in advance of a company's annual report and accounts. The basis for this statement will be the draft annual accounts, and as it covers a full year and will closely resemble a profit and loss account, it will probably be classified as a form of abridged accounts. This being the case, the statutory provisions as to publication of accounts will apply.[13]

Contents   The information required to be disclosed in the half yearly report and preliminary profits statement will relate to a company's or group's activities and profit or loss during the relevant period.

---

[11] *Ibid.* Sched. 7, paras. 7 and 8.
[12] See also p. 152ff below.
[13] See pp. 17–19 above.

A half yearly report or the preliminary profits statement must contain, in tabular form, figures relating to the following items:

(i) net turnover;

(ii) profit or loss before taxation and extraordinary items;

(iii) taxation on profits (United Kingdom taxation and, if material, overseas taxation and the share of associated companies taxation is to be shown separately);

(iv) minority interests;

(v) profit or loss attributable to shareholders, before extraordinary items;

(vi) extraordinary items (net of taxation);

(vii) profit or loss attributable to shareholders;

(viii) rates of dividend(s) paid and proposed and amount absorbed thereby;

(ix) earning per share expressed as pence per share; and

(x) comparative figures in respect of the above items for the corresponding previous period.

The half yearly report should also contain an explanatory statement relating to the group's activities and profit or loss during the relevant period. The purpose of the report is to enable investors to make an informed assessment of the trend of the group's activities and trading results. Thus any significant information aiding this assessment must be given, along with an indication of any special factor which has influenced the activities and results for the particular six month period. It should also be possible to compare this information with that for the corresponding period of the preceding financial year. The report should further aim to refer to the company's or group's anticipated results for the full current financial year.

7 ASSETS AND LIABILITIES

Assets

Classification Assets are shown in both the balance sheet formats under the two main headings of "Fixed assets" and "Current assets." Fixed assets are defined as those intended for use on a continuing basis in the company's activities, whilst current assets are all those assets which are not classified as fixed.[1] It will, therefore, depend upon the nature of the particular company as to whether certain types of assets are included as either fixed or current assets. For example, a word processor to a company selling such equipment will be part of its stock in trade. As it will not be used on a continuing basis, it will be classified as a current asset. On the other hand, to a pharmaceutical company, a word processor used in the administration of the company on a continuing basis, will be classified as a fixed asset. The difference is not always clear cut and the way in which assets which fall between the two categories are classified will depend upon the circumstances of and the company's intentions in a particular case.

Certain items, however, cannot be treated as assets for the purpose of a company's balance sheet and they are:

(a) preliminary expenses;
(b) expenses of and commission on any issue of shares or debentures; and
(c) costs of research.[2]

As these items cannot be shown as fixed assets, they must be written off to the profit and loss account. In the case of the first two types of expenditure, an alternative would be to charge them against the share premium account, if any.

Research costs Those expenses which fall within the first two items above are well established. The question of what will constitute research costs, however, is a little more difficult. The statute does not provide a definition of research, although SSAP 13, "Accounting for Research and Development," states that pure or basic research is "original investigation undertaken in order to gain new scientific or technical knowledge and understanding. Basic research is not primarily directed towards any specific practical aim or application . . . ." Applied research is defined as "original investigation undertaken in order to gain new scientific or technical knowledge and directed towards a specific practical aim or objective."

The purpose of expenditure on pure and applied research is usually to maintain a company's business and its competitive position and thus the benefit of such expenditure will be experienced in one particular accounting period. These costs should, therefore, be written off as they are incurred. The

[1] Companies Act 1985, Sched. 4, para. 77.
[2] *Ibid.* para. 3.

development of new and improved products does not however merit the same accounting treatment where the expected benefit will probably be received over more than one period. In this case, the appropriate accounting treatment would be to match such expenditure against future revenue. The requirements which SSAP 13 sets with regard to this type of expenditure are discussed more fully on pages 59 and 60 below.

Fixed assets

Under the historical cost accounting rules, a fixed asset should be shown in the balance sheet at either its purchase price or production cost.[3] A company may, however, choose to use the alternative accounting rules and include a fixed asset at its current cost or market value. The valuation of assets under these rules is discussed more fully in Chapter 8.

Valuation   When calculating the purchase price of an asset, any expenses incidental to its acquisition may be added to the actual price paid for it. The production cost of an asset is arrived at by adding together:

(a) the purchase price of the raw materials and consumables used;

(b) the costs directly incurred by the company in the production of the asset;

(c) a reasonable proportion of indirect costs which relate to the period of production, for example, where the manufacture of a product takes up half of a company's factory, 50 per cent. of the rent or rates for the period of manufacture could be included in the production cost; and

(d) any interest on capital borrowed to finance the production of the asset, but only to the extent that it accrues in respect of the period of production.

When an amount of interest is included in the production cost of an asset, the fact of its inclusion and the amount of interest so included should be disclosed in a note to the accounts.[4]

Depreciation   If the historical accounting rules are applied and an asset is shown at either its purchase price or production cost, a provision for depreciation must be made if that asset has a limited useful economic life.[5] According to SSAP 12, "Accounting for Depreciation," depreciation is "a measure of the wearing out, consumption or other loss of value of a fixed asset, whether arising from use, effluxion of time or obsolescence through technology and market changes." Some assets, such as leaseholds, may have a predetermined useful life, whereas in other cases, an asset's useful life may be diminished by extraction or consumption (such as land used for mining purposes), dependent upon the amount of use it receives (for example, office furniture) or reduced by obsolescence (in the case of a company which depended upon the latest technology, computer software

---

[3] *Ibid.* para. 17.
[4] *Ibid.* para. 26.
[5] *Ibid.* para. 18.

could be such an asset) or physical deterioration (such as company cars).

Where a fixed asset does have a limited useful economic life, its purchase price or production cost must be reduced by an amount calculated to write off its cost systematically over the period of the asset's useful life. If it is estimated that the asset will have a residual value at the end of that time, then the amount to be written off is its purchase price or production cost less that estimated residual value.[6] The aim of systematically writing off the value of an asset over its useful economic life is to allocate a fair proportion of the cost to each accounting period during the asset's useful life. How this allocation is achieved will be for the management of a company to decide taking into account all relevant considerations, such as technical developments, commercial and accounting practices.

It will be necessary to review depreciation policy annually and should it be decided that the term of an asset's useful life has altered, SSAP 12 requires that the amount which has not been depreciated should be charged over the revised remaining useful life. If, however, it is decided that the commercial value of the asset is less than that included in the accounts, it should be written down immediately and this amount should be depreciated over the remaining useful life. Should a company change its depreciation policy during the life of an asset, then the new method should be applied to the written down value of the asset, from the date of the change. Where the effect of the change is material, it should be disclosed in a note to the accounts and, where the change in policy is material, it may be necessary to restate the previous year's figures to provide reasonable comparatives.

Diminution in value If a fixed asset diminishes in value, regardless of whether or not it has a limited useful life, then provision for diminution in value must be made if the reduction in value is expected to be permanent. The provision may be shown either in the profit and loss account or in a note to the accounts. Should the reduction prove not to be permanent, the provision may be written back by the amount of the increase in value and this amount shown in the profit and loss account or in a note to the accounts.[7]

When a fixed asset shown under the heading "Investments" in the balance sheet diminishes in value, provision for the diminution should also be made. The provision may be shown in either the profit and loss account or in a note to the accounts. If at a later date, the value of the investment rises, then the provision may be written back by the amount of the increase and the necessary disclosure made.[8]

Notes to the accounts Each item under the general heading "Fixed assets," whether it appears in the balance sheet or in the notes to the accounts, must be accompanied by notes to the accounts containing the following additional information:

(a) the aggregate amounts in respect of each item as at the date of the beginning of the financial year and as at the

---

[6] *Ibid.*
[7] *Ibid.* para. 19.
[8] *Ibid.*

balance sheet date (*i.e.* the financial year end) respectively; and

(b) the effect on any amount shown in the balance sheet in respect of any item of:

    (i) any revision made during that year relating to any asset included at a value determined under the alternative accounting rules (these rules are set out in Chapter 8);

    (ii) any acquisitions and disposals during the year of any assets; and

    (iii) any transfer to and from that item during the year.[9]

The aggregate amounts mentioned above are based on the purchase price or production cost of each item, or on the valuation determined under the alternative accounting rules if that basis has been used. In either case, any provisions for depreciation or diminution in value must be stated separately, giving the following details:

(a) the cumulative amount of such provisions;

(b) the amount of any such provision made in respect of the financial year;

(c) the amount of any adjustments made in respect of any such provisions during that year in consequence of the disposal of any asset; and

(d) the amount of any other adjustments made in respect of any such provisions during that year.[10]

In addition to the statutory requirements, SSAP 12 requires the disclosure of further details in respect of each major class of depreciable asset. These details are the depreciation methods used and the useful lives or the depreciation rates used.

Government grants   When a company has received a government grant in respect of any capital expenditure, the grant will have to be entered in the company's accounts. Whilst there are no specific statutory provisions on the way in which government grants should be treated, the accountancy profession has published SSAP 4, "The Accounting Treatment of Government Grants," which seeks to standardise the way in which such grants are dealt with in company accounts.

In order to show the progressive effect of the grant over the life of the asset to which it relates, the Standard requires that grants relating to fixed assets should be credited to the profit and loss account over the expected useful life of the asset, thus matching the grant to the depreciation charge. A company may do this by one of two methods:

(a) by deducting the amount of the grant from the acquisition cost of the fixed asset; or

(b) by treating the amount of the grant as a deferred credit, a portion of the grant will then be transferred annually.

If the first method is adopted, it will result in a conflict with the statutory rule that fixed assets must be shown at purchase

[9] *Ibid.* para. 42.
[10] *Ibid.* para. 32.

price or production cost.[11] As in effect the company has not paid for the full cost of the asset, if the asset were shown according to the statutory rule and the government grant ignored, a true and fair view might not be presented. Thus, if the first method of accounting for government grants is chosen, the true and fair override should be invoked and particulars of the departure from the statutory requirements would have to be disclosed along with the reasons for the departure and its effect.[12]

It is arguable that the first method is also in breach of the rule against set off.[13] This, however, would only be the case if government grants could be classified as liabilities, which is doubted.

If the second method of accounting for grants, as set out in SSAP 4, is adopted and the grant treated as a deferred credit, the Standard requires that in the event of the deferred credit being a material amount, it should be shown separately in the balance sheet. It should not be shown as part of the shareholders' funds.

Both the balance sheet formats divide "Fixed assets" into three categories, intangible and tangible assets and investments, and those categories are further subdivided into specific items. The Act then contains requirements relating to certain of those specific types of asset.

Intangible assets

This heading includes the following items:

Development costs
As has been seen on page 55 above, research costs may not be treated as an asset. Development costs, however, may be shown as a fixed asset if there are special circumstances warranting their inclusion as such.[14]

The Act itself gives no further guidance and does not define the phrase "special circumstances." Assistance is, however, provided by SSAP 13, "Accounting for Research and Development," which requires that development costs should be written off to the profit and loss account in the period in which they are incurred, unless it is anticipated that the expenditure will secure potential future benefits. If this is the case, it will be more appropriate to match the development costs against the future revenue. Before development costs can be capitalised, the following conditions must be satisfied:

(a) there must be a clearly defined project;
(b) the expenditure on the project must be separately identifiable;
(c) the technical feasibility and ultimate commercial viability of the project must be reasonably certain;
(d) future related revenues must be reasonably expected to cover all costs of the project, including future costs; and
(e) adequate resources exist, or must be reasonably expected to be available, to enable the project to be completed.

---

[11] See p. 56 above.
[12] See p. 24ff above.
[13] Companies Act 1985, Sched. 4, para. 5.
[14] *Ibid*. para. 20.

It will be a question of judgment in each particular case whether or not these conditions can be met, especially as regard should also be had to the accounting concept of prudence.[15]

Where development costs are capitalised and shown as a fixed asset, the Act requires that the following information should be given in a note to the accounts:

(a) the period over which the amount of those costs originally capitalised is being or is to be written off; and
(b) the reasons for capitalising the development costs in question.[16]

SSAP 13 requires that this information be given as an explanation of the accounting policy used in the capitalisation of development costs in the notes to the accounts.

According to the Standard, capitalisation of development costs should only be continued until commercial production begins. Thereafter, such costs should be amortised or depreciated. The period chosen for amortisation should be calculated with reference to either the sales revenue or the use of the product or process, or the period over which the product or process is expected to be sold or used. It will be necessary to review the policy applied at the end of each accounting period. Should circumstances change so that the deferral of development expenditure can no longer be justified, any costs which are judged to be irrecoverable should be written off. Once written off, the Standard prohibits any reinstatement.

While SSAP 13 is not incorporated into the Companies Act, it does serve as an authoritative guide as to what can be deemed to be "special circumstances" in this context and what is to be considered as the proper accounting treatment for development costs. There are, however, two areas of conflict between the Act and SSAP 13, in relation to writing off expenditure which can no longer be considered to have its original life.

The Act requires that provision should be made where a diminution in value is permanent,[17] as does SSAP 13, but the Standard goes on to rule that a provision should also be made when the diminution is expected to be temporary, which is not provided for by the statute. The second conflict is that the Act requires that a provision must be written back if the diminution proves to be temporary, which the Standard does not. The conflicts can be approached in one of two ways. A company can follow the Act and risk their auditors qualifying their audit report, unless the directors can persuade them that the company's circumstances are such that the Standard should not be followed, or it can apply the Standard, using the true and fair override[18] to justify departure from the requirements of the Act.

Concessions, patents etc. Amounts may only be shown under "concessions," patents etc. if the assets were acquired for valuable consideration and are not required to be shown under goodwill. Also the assets in question must have been created by the company itself.[19]

---

[15] See p. 41 above.
[16] Companies Act 1985, Sched. 4, para. 20.
[17] See p. 57 above.
[18] See p. 24ff above.
[19] Companies Act 1985, Sched. 4, para. 8, note 2 to the balance sheet formats.

Goodwill   Goodwill is considered in Chapter 17 on Acquisitions and
Mergers.

Tangible assets

Valuation   The principle categories of tangible asset are set out below but
before examining these categories, the methods of valuing such
assests must be considered. As has been seen on page 56, assets
are usually valued at production cost. Tangible assets may,
however, be shown at a fixed quantity and value, if they are of a
kind which are being constantly replaced and their overall value
is not material to assessing the company's state of affairs. This
method of valuation only applies where the quantity, value and
composition of the assets are not subject to material variation.[20]
This is known as the use of a "base stock" value and it is
generally restricted to the subheadings "Plant and machinery"
and "Fixtures, fittings, tools and equipment." Whether the
assets which come under either of these subheadings will qualify
to be shown at a base stock figure will depend upon the nature of
the particular company's business. A common use for this
method of valuation will be in respect of a company's tools. For
example, if, in order to operate its business, a company requires
three power drills, which are frequently replaced, instead of
including them at production cost or purchase price, depreciating
them over their useful economic life and disclosing all additions
and disposals during a particular period, they can be shown at a
base stock figure and any additions or disposal proceeds charged
or credited to the profit and loss account. No provision for
depreciation will be needed.

Land and   Where a company has deviated from strict compliance with
buildings   the layout of its chosen balance sheet format and in order to
facilitate assessment, has combined items under the heading of
"Land and buildings," a breakdown of the amounts relating to
freehold and to leasehold properties must be given in a note to
the accounts. Amounts in respect of leasehold properties must be
broken down further to show how much is attributable to land
held on long lease and how much to land held on short lease.[21]
For these purposes, a lease includes an agreement for a lease. A
long lease is one which, at the end of the financial year, has at
least 50 years to run. A lease not falling within this definition is
deemed to be a short lease.[22]

A provision for depreciation will not normally need to be
made in respect of freehold land as its value remains relatively
stable. Land may, however, be subject to reductions in value, for
example, land held by a mining company, the value of which
would decrease as the minerals were extracted from it. The value
of land might diminish for other reasons, such as social change or
the closure of a company which provided substantial employment
in an area. Where freehold land does decrease in value for
whatever reason, it should be written down using the same
principles which SSAP 12 applies to other fixed assets with a
limited useful economic life.

[20] *Ibid*. para. 25.
[21] *Ibid*. para. 44.
[22] *Ibid*. para. 83.

Where the market value of any interest in "Land and buildings" is materially different from the value at which it is included in the accounts, paragraph 1 of Schedule 7 to the Act requires directors to quantify the difference or state the market value. This information should be shown in the directors' report, further details of which are given in Chapter 12.

In the case of buildings, a provision for depreciation will generally be made as in most cases these will have a limited life.

SSAP 12 does not apply to investment properties. Due to their special nature, these are subject to different accounting treatment which is examined on pages 66 and 67 below.

Investments

Investments appearing under the "Fixed asset" heading must be accompanied by the notes required for all fixed assets which are set out on pages 57 and 58 above. Investments held as "Current assets" require much less detail to be given. On the other hand, regardless of whether investments appear under "Fixed assets" or "Current assets," the notes to the accounts

Listed

must record how much of that amount represents listed investments, distinguishing between investments listed on a recognised stock exchange and other listed investments.[23] Listed investments are those investments which have been granted a listing on a recognised stock exchange or on any stock exchange of repute (other than a recognised stock exchange) outside Great Britain.[24] The only recognised stock exchange in Great Britain at present is the Stock Exchange in London. As the definition applies to listed investments only, these particular disclosure requirements will not apply to investments traded on the Unlisted Securities Market.

In respect of listed investments, there must also be shown the aggregate market value of those investments where that amount differs from the book values of those investments. The market value and the stock exchange value will both have to be shown where the market value is taken to be higher for the purposes of the accounts.[25]

Investment in companies

Where one company has invested in another company, further details are required to be given. Those relating to investments in companies other than subsidiaries depend upon the extent of the interest acquired. The principle categories of investment are:

— shareholdings exceeding 10 per cent.;
— shareholdings exceeding 20 per cent.;
— investments in related companies; and
— investments in associated companies.

The disclosure requirements relating to subsidiaries are dealt with in Chapter 16 on Group Accounts.

Shareholdings over 10 per cent.

The equity share capital of a company is deemed to be its issued share capital, excluding any class of those shares which, neither as respects dividends nor as respects entitlement to return of capital, carries any right to participate beyond the specified amount in a distribution.[26] Generally speaking, this means that

[23] *Ibid.* para. 45.
[24] *Ibid.* para. 84.
[25] *Ibid.* para. 45.
[26] *Ibid.* s.744.

ordinary shares will be regarded as a company's equity capital, whereas, preference shares will not. It is, however, impossible to lay down hard and fast rules as each case must be judged on the rights attaching to the particular shares.

The three categories which govern the level of disclosure for company's holding investments, other than in subsidiaries, are:

(a) where the investment exceeds 10 per cent. of the nominal value of one class of the allotted equity share capital[27];

(b) where the investment exceeds 10 per cent. of the nominal value of the total allotted share capital[28]; and

(c) where the value of the investment included in the investing company's accounts exceeds 10 per cent. of the investing company's assets.[29]

Where the criteria detailed in (a) above is met and the company owns shares of another class or classes in the same company, the investing company must comply with the information requirements set out below, in respect of those other class or classes of share.[30]

Where an investment falls within any of the above categories, the information to be disclosed is as follows:

(a) the name of the company in which the investment has been made;

(b) in the case of a company incorporated in Great Britain, the part of Great Britain in which it is registered, but only if that company is registered in England and Wales and the investing company is registered in Scotland, or vice versa;

(c) if that company is incorporated outside Great Britain, the country in which it is incorporated;

(d) the identity of the class or classes of share held; and

(e) the proportion of the nominal value of the allotted shares of a particular class which a shareholding in that class of shares represents; this information must be given for each class of share held.[31]

Exemptions   There are two exemptions to the above rules. The first concerns shares held in a company which is incorporated outside the United Kingdom or, being incorporated in the United Kingdom, carries on business outside it. In either case, if the investing company's directors are of the opinion that disclosure would be harmful to the business of the company or to the company in which the shares are held, they may seek the approval of the Secretary of State to release them from the duty to give the requisite information.[32]

The second exemption allows the investing company to avoid disclosure where it has investments in more than one company and compliance with the above rules would result in the giving of particulars of excessive length. It is for the directors to decide whether or not that is the case. Where they are of the

---

[27] *Ibid.* Sched. 5, para. 7.
[28] *Ibid.* para. 8.
[29] *Ibid.* para. 9.
[30] *Ibid.* para. 7.
[31] *Ibid.* paras. 7,8,9.
[32] *Ibid.* para. 10.

opinion, however, that a shareholding principally affects either their company's profit or loss or the amount of its assets, then disclosure must be made in respect of that holding and a statement must be included showing that disclosure has only been made of investments which principally affect either the company's profit or loss or its assets. Where the exemption is used, the omitted particulars, together with the information which has been included, must be annexed to the company's next annual return. This exemption does not apply to an investment in a company, which is 10 per cent. of the investing company's assets.[33]

Shareholdings over 20 per cent.

Shareholdings exceeding 20 per cent.   The disclosure required under this heading applies where a company (Company A) holds shares in another company (Company B) which exceed 20 per cent. of the nominal value of Company B's allotted share capital. The same information as is required for holdings exceeding 10 per cent. must be given by the investing company, Company A, together with details showing the aggregate amount of the capital and reserves and the profit or loss of the company in which the investment has been made. These figures must be calculated as at the end of Company B's financial year. Where two companies share the same year end, that financial year will be the one for which the disclosure is to be made by Company A. Where the year ends differ, the information should be obtained from Company B's accounts last before the end of the financial year of the investing company.[34]

Exemptions

There are various exemptions from this disclosure requirement. First, where the investment is shown in Company A's financial statements by way of the equity method of valuation disclosure need not be made. Paragraph 17(2) of Schedule 5 to the Act, which sets out this exemption, does not give any indication as to what is meant by this method of valuation. A definition of the equity method of valuation or accounting can, however, be found in SSAP 14, "Group accounts," and involves showing the investment at

(a) its cost; and
(b) the investing company's share of the post acquisition retained profits and reserves of the company; less
(c) any amounts written off in respect of (a) or (b).

Secondly, an exemption is given to a company which is not obliged by statute to deliver a copy of a relevant balance sheet and does not in fact publish such a balance sheet in Great Britain or elsewhere. A relevant balance sheet is one in which it would have been necessary to show the required information had not the exemption applied.[35] Company A, the investing company, may only take advantage of this exemption if the shares held by it do not amount to at least one half, in nominal value, of Company B's allotted share capital. Thirdly, the information is not required if it is not material.[36] Finally, the requirements do not apply where disclosure would be harmful to either of the companies involved

[33] *Ibid.* paras. 11, 12.
[34] *Ibid.* paras. 15, 16.
[35] *Ibid.* para. 17.
[36] *Ibid.*

or where it would result in particulars of excessive length being given.[37]

Stock Exchange rules Companies which are listed on the Stock Exchange are obliged by that institution to make further disclosure in respect of their shareholdings which exceed 20 per cent.[38]

Related companies **Investments in related companies** For the purposes of the Act, a related company is "any body corporate (other than one which is a group company in relation to that company) in which that company holds on a long term basis a qualifying capital interest for the purpose of securing a contribution to that company's own activities by the exercise of any control or influence arising from that interest." A "qualifying capital interest" means "an interest in shares comprised in the equity share capital of that body corporate of a class carrying rights to vote in all circumstances at general meeting of that body corporate." Where Company A owns a qualifying capital interest of between 20 per cent. and 50 per cent., it is presumed that Company B is related to Company A.[39] Company A is, however, not related to Company B as Company B holds no interest in Company A's capital. A group company is a company which is a holding company or a subsidiary of another company.[40]

Provision is made in the accounts formats for related company details to be given in both the balance sheet and the profit and loss account. In the balance sheet, shares in, loans to, and amounts owed by related companies must be given. In the profit and loss account, income from shares in related companies must be disclosed.

Associated Companies **Investments in associated companies** The disclosure requirements in relation to associated companies are to be found in SSAP 1, "Accounting for Associated Companies." The definition of an associated company is very similar to that of a related company. An associated company is defined by SSAP 1 as

"A company not being a subsidiary of the investing group or company in which:
(a) the interest of the investing group or company is effectively that of a partner in a joint venture or consortium and the investing group or company is in a position to exercise a significant influence over the company in which the investment is made; or
(b) the interest of the investing group or company is for the long term and is substantial and, having regard to the disposition of the other shareholdings, the investing group or company is in a position to exercise a significant influence over the company in which the investment is made."

There is no hard and fast test to determine whether an investing group or company has a "significant influence" over another. Among the indications which would suggest that such an influence might be present are the holding of 20 per cent. or

[37] *Ibid.* para. 18.
[38] See p. 50 above.
[39] Companies Act 1985, Sched. 4, para. 92.
[40] *Ibid.* para. 81.

more of a company's equity voting rights and participation in a company's financial and operating policy decisions.

Whilst there is much overlap between the definitions of related and associated companies, there are differences and of the two, related companies is the wider category. It may be that disclosure of a holding in another company will have to comply with both the Act and SSAP 1 but it is possible for a company to be related to but not an associate of the investing company. In such a case, the Act and not the Standard should be followed. An associated company will almost invariably be a related company, in which case the provisions of both statute and SSAP 1 should be met.

The Standard requires that details of the investment made in an associated company should be disclosed, either at valuation or at cost, less any amounts written off. Particulars of any loans to or from the associated company, and of its assets and liabilities should be disclosed where the individual balances are material in the context of the investing company's balance sheet.

Investment properties   **Investment properties**   Statute provides no special rules for accounting for investment properties. There is however an accounting standard on the subject: SSAP 19, "Accounting for Investment Properties." The Standard defines an investment property as

> "an interest in land and/or buildings:
> (a) in respect of which construction work and development have been completed; and
> (b) which is held for its investment potential, any rental income being negotiated at arm's length."

Properties which are owned and occupied by a company for its own purposes are not included in the definition. For example, an office block which is used solely by the company's staff and for the running of its own operations and a property let to and occupied by another group company will not be investment properties for the purpose of SSAP 19.

Property held as an investment, could be shown under the "Other investments and loans" sub-heading of "Investments." Where the value of such properties is material, a separate heading should be used in order that a true and fair view is shown.

Valuation   Those properties which properly fall within the investment property category require different accounting treatment from other fixed assets. The value of other fixed assets, with the possible exception of freehold land, the value of those assets diminishes and in order for the accounts to reflect a true and fair view, provision for depreciation must be made. Investment properties, however, are not consumed in the business operation and it is the current value of these assets and any changes in that value which are important. As a consequence, SSAP 12, "Accounting for Depreciation," does not apply to investment properties, which must be included in a company's accounts at their open market value.

Whilst the Standard does not require that a valuer should be qualified or independent, it does recommend that in the case of a major enterprise, for example a listed company, having investment properties which represent a substantial proportion of its total assets:

(a) the properties should be valued annually and that the valuer should hold a recognised professional qualification and have recent post-qualification experience in the location and category of the properties concerned; and

(b) an independent valuer should value the properties at least every five years.

Where the value of an investment property changes, the Standard requires that the change is reflected as a movement on an investment revaluation reserve, and should not be taken to the profit and loss account. A provision for diminution in value need only be passed through the profit and loss account when the valuation of an individual property falls below its original cost. This does not apply to pension fund accounts nor to the long term business of insurance companies. Changes in value in these cases should be attributed to the relevant fund account.

Disclosure   The Standard then requires that the following information should also be disclosed:

(a) the names of the persons making the valuation of the property;

(b) particulars of the valuers' qualifications; it should be noted that the Standard does not require a company to use qualified or independent valuers;

(c) the bases of valuation used by the valuers; and

(d) if the valuer is an employee or an officer of the company or group which owns the property, a note of this fact.

Finally where an investment property has changed in value, SSAP 19 requires that the carrying value of investment property and the investment revaluation reserve should be displayed prominently in the company's financial statements.

If the provisions of SSAP 19 are complied with and no charge for depreciation is made in respect of investment properties, this will be contrary to statute which demands that all fixed assets be depreciated.[41] Statute does, however, demand that the accounts present a true and fair view, so a company with investment properties can comply with SSAP 19, and satisfy statutory requirements by using the true and fair override. If this course of action is taken, the particulars of the departure, the reasons for it and its effect must be noted in the accounts.[42] In order to disclose the effect of not depreciating investment properties, it will be necessary to calculate the amount of depreciation which would have been charged had the company not decided to include it in its accounts at its open market value.

Leased assets   There are no provisions relating specifically to leased assets in the Act, but the accountancy profession has attempted to provide a set of rules to ensure that companies who have a significant amount of leased assets disclose the effect of these leases in their financial statements. SSAP 21, "Accounting for Leases and Hire Purchase Contracts," applies to the annual accounts of both lessors and lessees. It requires, *inter alia*, that

[41] See p. 56 above.
[42] See p. 24ff above.

where leased assets effectively take the place of fixed assets, although ownership of an asset vests in the lessor, the asset should be capitalised as a fixed asset and provided for as a liability in order that the balance sheet shows a true and fair view of the company's assets and commitments. While this Standard was issued in August 1984 it was brought into full effect on July 1, 1987.[43] The Standard should be consulted not only for the detailed accounting treatment of leased assets, but also for the definition of the type of leases which it covers.

Own shares   This item is included under the "Investments" sub-heading for both fixed and current assets. This does not apply to a company's own shares which it obtains by purchase, as these shares must be treated as cancelled upon purchase. Rather it covers other circumstances in which a company might hold its own shares, for example on forfeiture or by gift. Where there is such a shareholding, the company must show the nominal value of the shares separately from the market value.[44]

Current assets

Valuation   It is a basic requirement that "Current assets" must be shown at either their purchase price or production cost.[45] In assessing the purchase price of an asset, any expenses incidental to its acquisition may be added to the actual price paid. In calculating the production cost of any item, the starting point is the purchase price of the raw materials and consumables used. To this may be added the direct costs incurred by the company in bringing the asset to its current location and stage of production. A reasonable proportion of the indirect costs of production may also be added, in so far as they relate to the relevant period of production. Any interest on capital borrowed to finance the production, to the extent also that it relates to the relevant period of production may also be included. If any interest is included, the amount of interest so added must be disclosed in a note to the accounts.[46] Transportation costs, however, may only be taken into account to the extent that they relate to moving the asset to its current location. The cost of transportation to the eventual customer must not be included in this figure.[47]

It may be that no records exist from which the purchase price or the production cost of an asset can be obtained or that the information is only available with unreasonable expense or delay. If this is the case, the asset may be valued at the sum ascribed to it in the earliest available record of its value made on or after its acquisition or production by the company. When this is done, the fact that this method of valuation has been used must be given in the accounting policy notes to the accounts.[48]

Where the net realisable value of any current asset is lower than either its purchase price or production cost, that asset

---

[43] As a general rule, SSAP 19 came into effect on July 1, 1984, as regards the financial statements of lessors and finance companies and w.e.f. July 1, 1987, for those of lessees and hirers.

[44] Companies Act 1985, Sched. 4, para. 8, note 4 to balance sheet formats.

[45] *Ibid.* para. 22.

[46] *Ibid.* para. 26.

[47] *Ibid.*

[48] *Ibid.* paras. 28, 51.

should be included in the balance sheet at its net realisable value.[49] SSAP 9, "Stocks and Work in Progress," defines net realisable value as:

> "the amount at which it is expected that the items of stocks and work in progress can be disposed of without creating either profit or loss in the year of sale, *i.e.* the estimated proceeds of sale less all further costs to completion and less all costs to be incurred in marketing, selling and distributing directly related to the items in question."

Where the net realisable value at the end of a particular year is lower than its purchase price or production cost, the value included in the balance sheet will be the net realisable value. Should the net realisable value increase for any reason, in a subsequent period, then the valuation at the subsequent year end should be included at the latest net realisable value.[50]

Valuing current assets by using purchase price, production cost or net realisable value will not always be practicable. For this reason other methods of valuing stocks and fungible assets are permitted by statute. These are discussed below.

Stocks and fungible assets
For the purposes of the balance sheet formats, stocks are required to be analysed under the headings of "Raw materials and consumables," "Work in progress," "Finished goods and goods for resale" and "Payments on account." The Act also talks

Fungible assets
in terms of "fungible" assets. An asset will be regarded as fungible if assets of that description are substantially indistinguishable one from the other. Investments may be included in this category.[51]

Valuation
In arriving at the purchase price or production cost of stocks or fungible assets, the Act permits the use of several methods of valuation and it is for the directors of a company to decide which method is most appropriate. The methods which may be used are:

(a) first in, first out (FIFO);
(b) last in, first out (LIFO);
(c) a weighted average price; or
(d) any other methods similar to any of the above methods.[52]

Having chosen a particular method of valuation, if the amount included in the balance sheet for an individual class of asset differs materially from what the Act calls "the relevant alternative amount," then the amount of that difference must be disclosed in a note to the accounts. The "relevant alternative amount" is the replacement cost of the particular assets at the balance sheet date. The directors may instead use, if they think it would provide a more appropriate standard of comparison, the most recent actual purchase price or production cost before the balance sheet date.[53]

In deciding which valuation method to use, directors should consider the guidance given by SSAP 9, "Stocks and Work in

---

[49] *Ibid.* para. 23.
[50] *Ibid.*
[51] *Ibid.* para. 27.
[52] *Ibid.*
[53] *Ibid.*

Progress." This Standard advises against the use of the LIFO method as it does not consider that it will normally bear a reasonable relationship to actual cost. SSAP 9 requires that stocks and work in progress be shown at the total of the lower of cost and net realisable value of the separate items. Disclosure of the accounting policies used in calculating cost and net realisable value must be made.

Raw materials and consumables
Work in progress

Provision is made for a company to show assets of this type at a fixed quantity and value.[54]

Work in progress should normally be shown at its purchase price or production cost, as is required for other current assets. Long-term contract work in progress, however, causes problems owing to the fact that it will straddle more than one financial year. A long-term contract is defined in SSAP 9, as

> "a contract entered into for manufacture or building of a single substantial entity or the provision of a service where the time taken to manufacture, build or provide is such that a substantial proportion of all such contract work will extend for a period exceeding one year."

An amendment to this definition, is proposed by Exposure Draft (ED) 40, "Stocks and Long Term Contracts" which seeks, *inter alia*, to clarify the one year period by stressing that this need not be the sole distinguishing feature of a long term contract. Because of the nature of long term contract work in progress, SSAP 9 seeks to take into account an element of the profit to be made on such a contract in the period in which it is made, although the contract at that time will not have been completed. Due to the uncertain nature of things, this should only be done in limited circumstances, when it is possible to gauge the expected profit with some degree of certainty.

There are conflicts between the way the Act treats this type of profit and the provisions of SSAP 9 on the subject. One minor conflict is that the balance sheet formats and the notes thereto require that payments received on account, or progress payments, shall be shown separately in the balance sheet, either under "Creditors," or as a deduction from stock. SSAP 9, on the other hand, states that they should be shown separately as a deduction in arriving at the balance sheet amount of long-term work in progress. Under the Standard, it is possible that any such amount be included in the notes to the accounts. The primary consideration must be that these items are clearly disclosed so as to be comprehensible to users of the accounts. That being the case, it is difficult to see that breach of either the statute or the standard will be anything other than technical. ED 40 also offers guidance on this and should be consulted for further details.

There is another area of difference which is more significant. It has been seen that like other current assets, work in progress should be shown at its purchase price or production cost, making no allowances for the inclusion of unrealised profits. SSAP 9, however, requires that

> "the amount at which long-term work in progress is stated in periodic financial statements should be cost plus any

---

[54] *Ibid.* para. 25.

attributable profit, less any foreseeable loss and progress payments received and receivable."

The reasoning behind this requirement is that if the profit arising from a long term contract were accounted for on the completion of the work, it would not reflect a true and fair view of the results of the activity of the company during the year. It would instead show the results of the contracts which have been completed during the period.

The Standard is thus in conflict with the Act in relation to the inclusion of attributable profit and the set off of assets and liabilities.[55] Each case should be looked at on its facts. If it is deemed necessary to include an amount for attributable profit in order that the accounts show a true and fair view, this may be done, so long as the departure from the Act and the reasons for it are noted in the accounts.[56] A solution to this problem is offered by ED 40. Where it is possible to gauge accurately the expected profit on a section of a contract, it is suggested that that profit may be included. That section may then be accounted for as a sale and debtor rather than as work in progress. It is recommended that the Exposure Draft be consulted where problems of this nature arise as detailed guidance for a range of possible situations is given.

There is a further point to note, which concerns the inclusion of realised profit in the profit and loss account. This is considered on pages 87–88 below.

Debtors   It is necessary to analyse debtors according to when the debts fall due. Debts falling due after more than one year must be shown separately for each item included under "Debtors."[57] It is the due date of the debt which is of importance, rather than the date on which the company expects to receive payment. The Act requires only a division between debts of under a year and those of over a year. There is no provision for debtors falling due after more than one year to appear under 'Fixed assets' as they do not fall within the definition of this category and therefore must be shown as "Current assets." It may be, however, that where a company has a long term debt that is material, in order for the accounts to show a true and fair view, a new heading should be created between the fixed and current assets headings, so that the significance of the long term debt can be appreciated.[58]

Where a company has investments in associated companies,[59] any unsettled trading balances in favour of the investing company should be included under "Current assets" in the investing company's balance sheet, in accordance with SSAP 1, "Accounting for Associated Companies." If the amount is material in relation to the accounts of the investing company, it should be disclosed separately.

Prepayments and accrued income   It will be seen from the formats that prepayments and accrued income may be shown either under "Debtors" or as a separate heading. If it is decided to show this item under "Debtors," it should be remembered that it will then have to be

---

[55] *Ibid.* para. 5.
[56] See also p. 24ff above.
[57] Companies Act 1985, Sched. 4, para. 8, note 5 to balance sheet formats.
[58] *Ibid.* para. 3.
[59] See pp. 65–66 above.

analysed according to age, as with any other item appearing under that heading. This requirement does not apply if a separate heading is used.

Cash at bank and in hand   One of the areas when the rule against set off must be borne in mind is in the consideration of what is to be shown under the heading "Cash at bank and in hand" in the balance sheet. The rule against set off states that "Amounts in respect of items representing assets or income may not be set off against amounts in respect of items representing liabilities or expenditure (as the case may be), or vice versa."[60]

It is not thought that this rule affects the legal right of set off.[61] In the present context of cash at bank, this means that a company can show the net amount it owes to its bank at the balance sheet date, providing that there is an arrangement with the bank that set off should apply. When set off is applied, however, like should be set off against like, for example, the amount which the company has deposited with the bank against the amount which it owes, where both are due on demand.

Liabilities

Creditors   **Creditors**   The Act makes specific provision as to what detail must be disclosed in respect of creditors. On the face of the balance sheet creditors must be analysed according to age, with amounts falling due within one year and after one year being shown separately for each of the items required under this heading. The aggregate amount for each age category must be shown separately for these items.[62]

Further details must be disclosed in the notes to the accounts in respect of each item under "Creditors" namely:

(a) the aggregate amount of any liability included, which falls due for payment or repayment after the end of five years beginning with the day next following the end of the financial year; this does not include debts which are payable or repayable by instalment;

(b) where any liability is payable or repayable by instalments any of which fall due for payment after the end of the five year period, the aggregate amount of the liability at the balance sheet date and of any instalments falling due after the end of that period must be disclosed separately;

(c) in relation to each debt within (a) and (b) above, the terms of payment or repayment and the rates of any interest payable on the debt should be disclosed; if this disclosure would, in the opinion of the directors, lead to a statement of excessive length, a general indication of these matters may be given;

(d) where security has been given by a company in respect of any item under "Creditors," the aggregate amount of the liability to which that security relates and an indication of the nature of the securities so given must be disclosed.[63]

---

[60] Companies Act 1985, Sched. 4, para. 5.
[61] See pp. 29–30 above.
[62] Companies Act 1985, Sched. 4, para. 8, note 13 to balance sheet formats.
[63] *Ibid*. para. 48.

It should be noted that the requirement to disclose the nature of any security given does not include contracts under which goods have been supplied subject to a Romalpa or "reservation of title" clause, the reason being that title does not pass immediately under such a contract so the unpaid supplier cannot be said to hold any security for the debt owed to him. The member's handbooks of both the Institute of Chartered Accountants in England and Wales and the Chartered Association of Certified Accountants contain guidance statements which recommend disclosure of the accounting policies applied to Romalpa clauses where the amount involved is material. If practicable, the amount of creditors covered by such clauses should also be shown.

Companies listed on the Stock Exchange are required to give a more detailed analysis of their creditors.[64]

Other creditors

Other creditors including taxation and social security The Act requires that liabilities in respect of taxation and social security payments are separately shown in the balance sheet and notes thereto. This is important in that these liabilities are preferential creditors.[65] Having these details clearly disclosed in the balance sheet enables the reader to assess the company's situation more clearly. Liabilities which are likely to appear under "Taxation and social security" are, for example, corporation tax, VAT, ACT on dividends, PAYE and national insurance deductions. Under "Other creditor," items such as dividends and creditors not specifically provided for elsewhere in the formats should appear. Deferred taxation should not be shown here as the formats provide for it to be shown under "Provisions for liabilities and charges."

As with the other headings involving creditors, amounts should be analysed according to age, showing amounts due within a year separately from amounts falling due after a year.[66]

Dividends

An item which is not specifically provided for, but which should appear under "Creditors" is dividends. These should be shown once they have been declared; until then, there is no liability on the company to pay them. The aggregate amount of dividends which have been recommended are required to be shown in the notes to the accounts.[67] This information is in addition to the need to disclose the aggregate amount of any dividends paid or proposed separately as additional items in the profit and loss account.[68] SSAP 8, "The Treatment of Taxation under the Imputation System in the Accounts of Companies," further requires proposed dividends to be shown under "Creditors", exclusive of the related ACT, which should appear under "Taxation and social security." Should a company have any arrears of fixed cumulative dividends on its shares, then it is required by the Act to show the amount of the arrears and the period for which the dividends for each class of share is in arrear.[69]

---

[64] See pp. 50–51 above.
[65] Insolvency Act 1986, ss.175, 386, Sched. 6.
[66] Companies Act 1985, Sched. 4, para. 8, note 13 to balance sheet formats.
[67] *Ibid.* para. 51.
[68] *Ibid.* para. 3.
[69] *Ibid.* para. 49.

Accruals and deferred income

Accruals and deferred income Provision is made for "Accruals and deferred income" to be shown either under "Creditors: amounts falling due within one year" and "Creditors: amounts falling due after more than one year," or under a separate heading of its own. If it appears separately, it will not be necessary to analyse the items included according to age, but in relation to balance sheet format 1 directors will need to ensure that a true and fair view is given by the heading "Total assets less current liabilities."

Debentures

Debenture loans Debentures are deemed to include debenture stock, bonds and any other securities of a company, whether constituting a charge on the assets of the company or not.[70] The question of what constitutes a debenture in any particular case will depend upon the interpretation of the document creating it.

"Debenture loans" appear as a sub-heading on the face of the balance sheet. Amounts shown here must distinguish between convertible loans and non convertible debenture loans.[71]

Where a company has issued debentures during the financial year, it must show the following details in the notes to the accounts:

(a) the reason for making the issue;
(b) the classes of debentures issued; and
(c) as respects each class of debenture, the amount issued and the consideration received by the company for the issue.

Where a company has any redeemed debentures which it has the power to reissue, particulars of these must also be given. Should a nominee or trustee for the company hold any of the company's debentures, the nominal amount of the debentures and the amount at which they are stated in the accounting records must be given.[72] Finally, the detailed information specified above is required to be shown for debentures.

Liabilities and charges

Provisions for liabilities and charges The heading "Provisions for liabilities and charges" is deemed by the Act to refer to "any amount retained as reasonably necessary for the purpose of providing for any liability or loss which is either likely to be incurred, or certain to be incurred but uncertain as to amount or as to the date on which it will arise."[73] Amounts which a third party can require a company to pay at the balance sheet date will appear under "Creditors," whereas, "Accruals" covers those amounts which a company is legally obliged to pay but which have not fallen due at that date. It might be thought that a provision for doubtful debts would be a suitable item for inclusion under the heading "Provision for liabilities and charges" but the correct procedure is to deduct it from the asset to which it relates. The reason for this is that where the net realisable value is lower than the value at which the debtor is included in the company's records, then the Act requires that the

---

[70] *Ibid.* s.744.
[71] *Ibid.* Sched. 4, para. 8, note 7 to balance sheet formats.
[72] *Ibid.* para. 41.
[73] *Ibid.* para. 89.

asset must be shown in the balance sheet at the lower value.[74] Items which should be shown under this heading are amounts provided to meet pension liabilities and similar charges, provisions for taxation (predominantly deferred taxation) and other similar provisions. Where the liability to tax may be calculated with reasonable accuracy and the date of the payment is determinable, as, for example, for corporation tax liabilities, the provision is generally included in "Creditors."

The following information must be shown, either on the face of the balance sheet or in the notes to the accounts, in respect of each item under this heading and of each material provision included in the item "Other provisions":

(a) the amount of the provisions as at the date of the beginning of the financial year and as at the balance sheet date respectively;

(b) any amounts transferred to or from the provisions during that year; and

(c) the source and application respectively of any amounts so transferred.

The amount of any provision for taxation, other than for deferred taxation must be shown separately.[75]

Pension costs   There are no further statutory requirements regarding the accounting treatment of pension costs or as to the disclosure of additional information relating to them. Pension costs are, however, the subject of a proposed Statement of Standard Accounting Practice, Exposure Draft (ED) 39, "Accounting for Pensions Costs." Until it is approved by the major accountancy bodies, compliance with the exposure draft is not mandatory, but it should be regarded as the best practice on the subject until approval has been given. The exposure draft only applies to the disclosure of material items in relation to contractual pensions schemes and arrangements where, as a result of established custom or practice there is a probability that benefits will be paid.

While from the point of view of the employee, pension contributions might be regarded as deferred remuneration, from the employer's view point, the cost of a pension scheme is part of the cost of the employee's services. The cost of providing a pension should therefore be recognised over the period during which the employer obtains benefit from those services. In **Defined** schemes which ED 39 calls "defined contribution" schemes, the **contribution** cost to the employer is known, as the rules of the scheme will **schemes** specify the contribution to be made to the scheme by the **Defined benefit** employer. The alternative is a "defined benefit" scheme, where **schemes** the benefit to be obtained by the employee is specified or the method of its calculation defined and the company finances the scheme accordingly. In this type of scheme the benefits paid may depend upon either the revalued career average or the final pay of the employee, and actuarial advice will be needed in order to determine the cost of financing such a scheme.

Disclosure   ED 39 examines how an employer should account for the costs of both types of schemes and also provides for the disclosure of certain information regarding the scheme chosen in a

[74] *Ibid.* para. 23.
[75] *Ibid.* paras. 46, 47.

company's financial statements. Sufficient information should be disclosed to enable the user of the financial statements to have a broad understanding of the significance of the pension arrangements. In the case of a defined contribution scheme this will usually be satisfied by indicating the nature of the scheme and the amounts included in the profit and loss account and balance sheet. As defined benefit schemes impose greater obligations upon the employer, the following additional information should also be given;

    (a)   the accounting policy applied in relation to the scheme;
    (b)   the actuarial valuation method used;
    (c)   the cost charged, explanations of the charge; and
    (d)   certain actuarial information.

Disclosure in relation to defined benefit schemes should relate not only to the current year but also given an indication of significant changes in relative future costs that are expected under the actuarial assumptions and method used. Where a company or group has more than one scheme it will be permissible to provide the disclosure on a combined basis so long as the overall significance can still be appreciated.

Taxation   **Taxation including deferred taxation**   As mentioned on page 73 above, provisions made in the accounts for taxation liabilities whose amount and payment date are not readily assessable should be included under this heading.

Deferred taxation   Details relating to deferred taxation are required to be disclosed in this section of the balance sheet and the notes thereto. Provisions for deferred tax arise from the different bases on which profits are arrived at for the purpose of corporation tax computations and at which profits are stated for financial accounts purposes and from the inclusion of certain assets at a valuation greater than cost.

    The difference arises mainly from certain expenses included in the accounts not being allowable deductions for tax purposes and certain allowances for tax purposes having no equivalent in the financial accounts. A company's future accounting and investment policies may reveal that benefits taken in the computation of the corporation tax liability for the current year will reverse in future periods. This liability is quantifiable and should be provided for as deferred tax.

    Where alternative accounting rules[76] have been adopted and an asset, for example, freehold property, has been revalued, it will be necessary to evaluate the potential liability to Capital Gains Tax were the asset to be disposed of at the valuation. The directors' intentions towards the asset will need to be re-examined each year to determine whether the potential liability need be included as a provision in the accounts.

    Deferred taxation need only be provided to the extent to which a company's directors consider it will eventually become payable. SSAP 15, "Accounting for Deferred Tax," requires, *inter alia*, that details of both the provisions included in the

---

[76] See Chap. 8.

accounts for deferred tax, and the total potential liability need to be disclosed.

Contingent liabilities, guarantees and other financial

Financial commitments

commitments   The notes to the accounts must give details of the company's liabilities contingent upon the occurrence of a particular event. This class of liability together with the disclosure requirements for each is divided into the headings outlined below.

Charges

(a) Where company assets are charged to secure the liabilities of any other person, particulars must be given of the charge and, where practicable, the amount secured[77]

Other contingent liabilities

(b) In the case of a contingent liability not provided for in the accounts, the amount or estimated amount of that liability must be disclosed, together with its legal nature and whether any valuable security has been given by the company in connection with that liability and if so, details of that security.[78] Contingent liabilities are also the subject of an accounting standard. SSAP 18, "Accounting for Contingencies," requires that all material contingent losses must be provided for in a company's accounts, if it is probable that a future event will confirm a loss that can be estimated with reasonable accuracy at the date on which the board of directors approves the annual accounts the aggregate amount of that liability must be given. If the event is not probable, then it is only necessary to disclose approximate details of contingent losses, where material, in the notes to the accounts. The note must state the nature of the contingency, the uncertainties that are expected to affect the ultimate outcome, and a prudent estimate of the financial effect, or a statement that an estimate is not practicable. Where the possibility of loss is regarded as too remote, no disclosure need be made.

Capital expenditure

(c) The aggregate value of contracts for capital expenditure, or an estimate of that value is required to be stated, so far as not provided for as a liability in the accounts. Also the aggregate or estimated value of capital expenditure authorised by the directors which has not been contracted for should be disclosed.[79]

Pension commitments

(d) The term "pension commitments" is not defined by the Act and it is thought that it includes not only pensions payable by a company but also a company's commitment to maintain a pension fund such that it is able to meet current and future pensions. The Act requires that a company must disclose any pension commitments which are included under any provision shown in the balance sheet and any such commitment for which no provision has been made. With regard to pensions payable to past directors, separate particulars must be given of that commitment.[80]

Other financial commitments

(e) Particulars must be given of any other financial commitments, for which a company has not provided and which are relevant to assessing the company's state of affairs.[81] While the scope of this requirement could be far reaching, it is thought

[77] Companies Act 1985, Sched. 4, para. 50.
[78] *Ibid.*
[79] *Ibid.*
[80] *Ibid.*
[81] *Ibid.*

that it does not necessitate the disclosure of a company's normal trading operations. A financial commitment within this category would need to be an agreement in principle which took a company into a new area of business or materially expanded an existing enterprise so that its size made it an operation which the company did not normally undertake.

8 ALTERNATIVE ACCOUNTING RULES

Introduction

In addition to the historical cost accounting rules which are the subject of Section B of Schedule 4, Section C of the Schedule contains what are described as "alternative accounting rules." These rules seek to take into account inflation when arriving at the value of certain items in a company's accounts. There is no obligation placed upon companies demanding that these rules must be used, as the Section C is couched in permissive terms.

Further, it is possible for a company to use a mix of historical cost accounting rules and alternative accounting rules. If this is done, there must be a valid reason for so doing, for a senseless use of the two sets of rules may result in the accounts presenting a view which is other than true and fair.

Scope of the rules

The alternative accounting rules permitted by the Act relate to five types of asset.[1]

Intangible fixed assets

(a) **Intangible fixed assets, other than goodwill** Such assets may be included at their current cost. As goodwill is not included in this category, it must be shown at the value of the consideration for which it was acquired, less any amounts by which it has been written down. Goodwill is discussed further in Chapter 17.

Tangible fixed assets

(b) **Tangible fixed assets** Under the alternative accounting rules, it is permissible to include these assets at a market value. Market value will be determined either as at the date of the assets last valuation or at their current cost. Exposure Draft 37, "Accounting for Depreciation," specifies that where this rule is used, companies should keep the valuations of any assets to which it is applied up to date. It should be noted that compliance with the Exposure Draft is not mandatory, but it should be regarded as best practice, until such time as it is approved by the major accountancy bodies and becomes a Standard.

Investments

(c) **Fixed asset investments** Investments shown under "Fixed assets" may be included either:

  (i) at a market value determined as at the date of their last valuation; or
  (ii) at a value determined on any basis which appears to the directors to be appropriate in the circumstances of the company.

[1] Companies Act 1985, Sched. 4, para. 31.

If the second alternative is adopted, particulars of the method of valuation used and the reasons for adopting it must be disclosed in a note to the accounts.

(d) Current asset investments These investments may be included at their current cost.

Stocks

(e) Stocks It is permissible to show stocks at their current cost.

The Act does not define the term "current cost." SSAP 16, "Current Cost Accounting," however, attempted to deal with issues of inflation or current cost accounting, and the principles contained in that Standard should be applied when calculating the current cost of any asset, unless reasons exist for choosing another method of valuation. SSAP 16 has had a chequered history and its mandatory status was suspended on June 6, 1985. It deals with an area in which there are no hard and fast rules. A company would therefore be wise to seek professional advice in cases of difficulty.

Revaluation reserve

When the alternative accounting rules are used, it will usually be the case that the value at which assets are included in the accounts will differ from the amounts at which they would have appeared had the historical cost accounting rules been used. In this situation the Act requires that the difference be debited or credited (as the case may be) to a revaluation reserve. Any provisions for depreciation or diminution in value calculated on a valuation other than one arrived at under the alternative accounting rules should be taken into account by the company when calculating the amount to be taken to the revaluation reserve. Any adjustments to such provisions should also be taken into consideration.[2]

The revaluation reserve must be reduced by any amount which the directors believe is no longer necessary for the purpose of the accounting policies adopted by the company. An amount, however, may only be transferred from the reserve to the profit and loss account in limited circumstances. Those circumstances are:

(a) the amount in question was previously charged to that account; or
(b) it represents realised profits.

A note to the accounts must set out the taxation treatment of any amounts credited or debited to the revaluation reserve.[3]

Both the balance sheet formats include a heading entitled "Revaluation reserve" but the Act allows companies to adopt another name for this reserve if they so wish. Whatever it is called, it should appear in the place allocated to the revaluation reserve in the formats.[4]

Application of the rules

The alternative accounting rules must be applied in conjunction with other rules laid down by the Schedule. Thus in valuing its

[2] *Ibid.* para. 34.
[3] *Ibid.*
[4] *Ibid.*

assets under these or the historical cost accounting rules, a company must follow the accounting principle that assets should be valued separately.[5]

It has been seen that any surplus arising on the revaluation of assets must be transferred to the revaluation reserve. A subsequent permanent reduction in the valuation of an asset must reduce the revaluation reserve but only to the extent to which the revaluation of the particular asset created the reserve. Any excess must be charged to the profit and loss account. The amount of the diminution below original cost must be provided for by writing it off against a revenue reserve, in other words, the company's realised profits are reduced because there has been a reduction in the worth of the company. To provide for it through a capital reserve, ie the revaluation reserve, would not result in the balance sheet showing a true and fair view of the state of the company's affairs. When the reduction in value of an asset is split between capital reserve and the profit and loss account, the total reduction in value is required to be disclosed in the notes to the accounts.[6]

Depreciation   When calculating the depreciation of an asset which has been valued under the alternative accounting rules, the calculations must be based upon the value ascribed to that asset under one of the valuation methods set out on pages 79–80 above.[7] Thus when applying the depreciation rules to an asset valued in this way, the asset's current valuation must be substituted for references to its purchase price or production cost.

As the depreciation charge in relation to a fixed asset valued according to the alternative accounting rules is based on that valuation of the asset and not on its historical cost, there may be a difference between the charge calculated on this basis and the charge had it been calculated on the historical cost of the asset. Where this difference is significant, the difference between the charges must be shown separately, either in the profit and loss account or in a note to the accounts.[8] The accounting Standard on depreciation, SSAP 12, contains rules similar to the statutory rules for calculating depreciation when the alternative accounting rules have been used. SSAP 12 requires a charge for depreciation of assets, which are shown at the revaluation figure in a company's financial statements, to be based on the revalued amount. In the event of this resulting in a material increase in depreciation compared to previous years' depreciation charges, then a note to the accounts must show the charge split between the depreciation applicable to original cost and that applicable to the change in value or revaluation. Although it is not a requirement of SSAP 12, it was normal practice before the alternative accounting rules, were enacted in 1981, to charge depreciation to the profit and loss account. The statutory provisions, which are now contained in Schedule 4 to the Companies Act 1985, may give a company a choice in this matter.

Split depreciation   It would seem that a company could either debit all of the depreciation charge to the profit and loss account, or split the

---

[5] See p. 42 above.
[6] Companies Act 1985, Sched. 4, para. 34.
[7] *Ibid*. para. 32.
[8] *Ibid*.

element of the charge which is based on the historical cost and that based on the revaluation amount. The depreciation based on the historical cost would then be charged to the profit and loss account, with the balance being charged to the revaluation reserve.

This method of dealing with depreciation is known as "split depreciation" and has the advantage that the depreciation charged to the profit and loss account is based upon a constant figure and is therefore known in advance, with the result that the reported earnings per share figures will be comparable. This will not be the case if depreciation is based upon the revaluation, as the depreciation charge will change with each new valuation, and it will be noted that companies using the alternative accounting rules for any assets are expected to revalue those assets regularly.

At present, split depreciation appears to be permissible both under the Act and SSAP 12. There is, however, doubt as to the acceptability of this method, as it is argued that it leads to the balance sheet being drawn up on a mix of historical cost and alternative accounting rules, and the profit and loss account only on the historical cost accounting rules. The Accounting Standards Committee (ASC) considers that the balance sheet and profit and loss account should be treated similarly in accounting terms and proposes to amend SSAP 12 to prohibit the use of the split depreciation method. Companies may, therefore, still use split depreciation until the ASC formally prohibits it.

There is, however, one situation in which, at present, split depreciation may not be used and this where full current cost accounts are prepared in accordance with SSAP 16. In this case, the excess depreciation charged on revalued assets should be charged to the current cost profit and loss account.

Disclosure   When advantage has been taken of the alternative accounting rules, the Act requires the disclosure of certain information, namely:

(a) the items affected by the choice and the basis of valuation adopted for each such item; this information is to be disclosed in a note to the accounts; and

(b) in the case of each balance sheet item affected (except stocks), the following details must be shown separately in the balance sheet or in a note to the accounts:
    (i) the comparable amounts determined according to the historical cost accounting rules; or
    (ii) the differences between those amounts and the corresponding amounts actually shown in the balance sheet in respect of that item.

In this context, "comparable amounts" means the aggregate amount which would have been shown in respect of that item if the historical cost accounting rules had been applied, and the aggregate amount of the cumulative provisions for depreciation or diminution in value which would have been permitted or required by those rules.[9]

---

[9] *Ibid.* para. 33.

9 RESERVES

Introduction

There are three main headings in the balance sheet under which reserves may be shown, namely "Revaluation reserve," "Other reserves" and "Profit and loss account."

Where reserves would have been shown as separate items on the face of the balance sheet, but have in fact been combined in order to facilitate assessment, and any amount has been transferred to or from any such reserve, then additional information must be given in respect of the aggregate of reserves shown in the same item. The information must be shown either in the notes to the accounts or on the face of the balance sheet itself and must include the following particulars:

(a) the amount of the reserve as at the date of the beginning of the financial year and as at the balance sheet date;
(b) any amounts transferred to or from the reserves during that year; and
(c) the source and application respectively of any amounts so transferred.[1]

The revised Standard, SSAP 6, "Extraordinary Items and Prior Year Adjustments," requires that a company's financial statements should include a statement of movements on reserves. This statement should follow on immediately after the profit and loss account. Where it does not, reference must be made on the face of the profit and loss account indicating where the statement may be found.

Revaluation reserve

This reserve must appear on the face of the balance sheet but may be shown under a different title.[2] It will consist of the aggregate of the excess of valuations of fixed assets over the original cost.

Other reserves

The heading "Other reserves" is broken down into four categories: "Capital redemption reserve," "Reserves for own shares," "Reserves provided for by the articles of association" and "Other reserves." Each of these sub-headings is examined in the following paragraphs.

Capital redemption reserve
Where a company either redeems or purchases its own shares wholly out of its profits, an amount equal to the nominal value of the shares acquired must be transferred to a reserve

[1] Companies Act 1985, Sched. 4, para. 46.
[2] *Ibid.* para. 34.

called the "Capital redemption reserve."[3] If the shares are acquired wholly or partly out of proceeds of a fresh issue of shares and the aggregate amount of those proceeds is less than the aggregate nominal value of the shares acquired, the amount of the difference should also be transferred to the capital redemption reserve.[4] This rule does not, however, apply if a private company uses the proceeds of a fresh issue of shares together with a payment made out of the company's capital for the acquisition of its own shares.[5]

The statutory rules relating to the reduction of share capital also apply to the capital redemption reserve, except that this reserve may be used by a company to pay up its unissued shares to be allotted to company members as fully paid bonus shares.[6]

Reserve for own shares

This reserve is for funds which a company wishes to set aside for the purchase of its own shares. Any amounts transferred to this reserve will have to be taken from realised profits in order that the requirements governing the funds available to a company for the acquisition of its own shares are met. These requirements are discussed in detail in Chapter 14.

Specified reserves

Reserves provided for by the articles of association   It will depend upon the individual company's articles of association as to the reserves which appear under this sub-heading.

Other reserves

The residual category "Other reserves" will include all reserves which do not have a specific place in the formats, both realised and unrealised. It is advisable, however, to place any reserve which is material under a separate heading or disclose its nature and the amount to which it relates in the notes to the accounts, in order to preserve a true and fair view.

Profit and loss account

Profit and loss account

The term "Profit and loss account" is not always used, as some companies prefer the heading "Revenue reserves." While this is strictly against the provisions of the Companies Act (for the rules governing adaptations to the formats see page 28 above), this classification is generally accepted and understood in the United Kingdom, and thus is unlikely to confuse a person who refers to the balance sheet. It must, however, appear as a separate item on the face of the balance sheet and be accompanied by the additional information set out on page 83 above.

On the face of every profit and loss account there must be shown as additional items any amount set aside, or proposed to be set aside to, withdrawn from or proposed to be withdrawn from, reserves.[7] These disclosure rules are separate from the rules which apply to the reserve entitled "Profit and loss account".

[3] *Ibid*. s.170(1).
[4] *Ibid*. s.170(2).
[5] *Ibid*. s.170(3).
[6] *Ibid*. s.170(4).
[7] *Ibid*. Sched. 4, para. 3.

Realised and distributable reserves   No distinction is made in the Act regarding the disclosure of realised or unrealised reserves. Neither is a company required to separate its distributable reserves from its undistributable ones. As it is important, especially to shareholders, to know if reserves are available for distribution, a company may find it necessary to disclose the amount of any undistributable reserves, where that amount is material, in order that the accounts present a true and fair view. The subject of realised and distributable reserves is covered in more detail in Chapter 11 on distributable profits.

Directors' report   In their report, the directors should disclose the amount, if any, which they propose should be carried to reserves.[8]

Prior year adjustments   SSAP 6, "Extraordinary Items and Prior Year Adjustments," defines prior year adjustments as those material adjustments applicable to prior years that arise either from changes in accounting policies or from the correction of fundamental errors. Normal recurring corrections and adjustments of accounting estimates made in previous years do not fall within this definition.

Under SSAP 2, "Disclosure of Accounting Policies," companies are expected to apply accounting policies consistently. In the event that a change in accounting policy is justified, for example, in the case of a newly acquired subsidiary coming into line with the accounting policies used by other members of the group, SSAP 6 states that those cumulative adjustments applicable to previous year, which have no bearing on the current year's results, should be accounted for by restating those previous years. This will result in the opening balance of retained profits being adjusted. The effect of the change should be disclosed by showing the amount involved separately in the restatement of the previous year, unless it is not practicable so to do.

In exceptional circumstances, an adjustment to the previous year's results will also have to be made in the event of a company's financial statements containing a fundamental error. SSAP 6 defines a fundamental error as one which is significant enough to destroy the truth and fairness of the accounts and which would have led to the withdrawal of the financial statements had the error been recognised at the time. The error should be corrected by adjusting the previous year's results.

---

[8] See also Chap. 12.

10 PROFIT AND LOSS ACCOUNT

Introduction

The choice of formats available for the profit and loss account allow a company to adopt the format which best suits its purposes, even if those purposes are to hide as much information as it can from the eyes of their competitors. One of the factors common to all the formats is that only realised profit or loss may be included in the account.[1] The term "realised" is examined under "Distributable profits" in Chapter 11, page 100. Another requirement applicable to all profit and loss accounts formats is that all profit and loss accounts must show the amount of the company's profit or loss on ordinary activities before taxation.[2] As the information required to be shown differs from formats 1 and 3 to formats 2 and 4, not all the items considered below will apply to each format.

Turnover

Definition The statutory definition of "turnover" is:

> "the amounts derived from the provision of goods and services falling within the company's ordinary activities, after deduction of:
> (a) trade discounts,
> (b) value added tax, and
> (c) any other taxes based on the amounts so derived."[3]

This definition is mirrored in all but one respect by the requirements contained in SSAP 5, "Accounting for Value Added Tax." The one difference is that the Standard also deals with gross turnover and requires companies wishing to show this total to show the VAT relevant to that turnover as a deduction in arriving at the turnover exclusive of VAT.

Disclosure Certain particulars of turnover must be shown in the notes to the accounts.

(a) **Classes of business** Where a company has carried on two or more classes of business during the course of a financial year, it must disclose in respect of each class, the amount of the turnover attributable to that class and the amount of the profit or loss of the company before taxation which is, in the opinion of the directors, attributable to that class. Disclosure is only required where the directors are of the opinion that their company carries on two or more classes of business which are substantially different from each other. If, in the directors' opinion, classes of

---

[1] Companies Act 1985, Sched. 4, para. 12.
[2] *Ibid.*, para. 3.
[3] *Ibid.*, para. 95. See also p. 31 above.

business are not substantially different from each other, they are to be treated as one class.

(b) Substantially different markets   The expression "markets" is defined in terms of markets delimited by geographical bounds. Disclosure of the amount of turnover attributable to each market is required where, in the course of the financial year, the company has supplied markets that, in the opinion of the directors, differ substantially from each other. Where markets are not regarded as substantially different from each other, they are to be treated as one market.[4]

In analysing the source of turnover for the purposes of (a) and (b) above, or (as the case may be) of profit or loss, the directors must consider the manner in which their company's activities are organised. Disclosure of amounts relating to a particular class of business or market is not necessary if the particular amount is immaterial, in which case it may be included in another class or market. Finally, if the directors believe that the disclosure of any of the particulars of turnover would be seriously prejudicial to the interests of the company, that particular need not be shown, but the fact that the information has not been disclosed must be stated.[5]

Companies which are listed on the Stock Exchange are also required to give details of the net turnover and the contribution to trading results on a geograpical basis.[6]

Cost of sales, distribution costs and administration expenses

These terms are not defined by the Act so much depends on the individual company as to what items they allocate to each heading. The primary guideline is that the profit and loss account must show a true and fair view of the company's profit and loss[7] but it is possible to do this and still allocate expenditure to these items so as to reveal as little information as possible to competitors about the company's operations. Where a company is in doubt as to the correct accounting treatment of any expense, the directors should consult an accountant, either in house or perhaps their auditors, who will be familiar with the company and its method of operation.

Gross Profit

Long term contracts   The valuation of stock and work in progress affects the calculation of gross profit in format 1. The valuation rules are discussed in Chapter 7[8] but there is one apparent anomaly affecting the profit and loss account. SSAP 9, "Stocks and Work

[4] *Ibid*. para. 55.
[5] *Ibid*.
[6] See p. 50 above.
[7] Companies Act 1985, s.228(2).
[8] See p. 69ff above.

in Progress," requires the recognition of attributable profit and foreseeable losses connected to long term contracts. The question has arisen as to whether profit thus recognised could be regarded as "realised." In September, 1982, the Consultative Committee of Accountancy Bodies, issued the technical release, TR 481, "The determination of realised profits and disclosure of distributable profits in the context of the Companies Acts 1948 to 1981," as a guidance statement for accountants belonging to its member bodies. The text of this technical release appears in Appendix III. The release advises that a conflict between the Act and SSAP 9 would not arise if attributable profits were treated as realised, the reason being that the relevant principles of recognising profits in SSAP 9 are based upon the concept of "reasonable certainty" as to the eventual outcome and are not in conflict with the statutory accounting principles. Exposure Draft 40 has subsequently provided additional guidance on this matter by recognising certain work as complete and taking it to turnover instead of to work in progress. This overcomes the apparent conflict between the Act and the Standard.

Difference between formats   Format 1 requires that a figure defined as "Gross profit or loss" be shown as a separate item, and the same number can be accordingly deduced from the information set out in format 3. This particular amount is not obtainable from formats 2 and 4, although a more accurate calculation of a manufacturing company's direct production costs may be obtained from the detailed disclosure relating to materials and labour costs required by formats 2 and 4. This will be an important factor for directors to consider when they decide upon the format to be adopted for the profit and loss account.

Costs attributable to employees and directors

Staff costs   Formats 2 and 4 require disclosure of "Staff costs" under the subheadings "wages and salaries," "social security cost" and "other pension costs," and the same information is required to be disclosed in notes to the profit and loss account where formats 1 and 3 are used.[9] The information to be shown under "social security costs" will be any contributions by a company to any state social security or pensions scheme, fund or arrangement. This includes the employer's contribution to the National Insurance Scheme. The amounts shown under "pension costs" will include any other contributions by a company for the purposes of any pension scheme established to provide pensions for employees, any sums set aside to pay pensions and any amounts paid by a company in respect of pensions without first being so set aside.

The personnel to be taken into account when calculating the amounts required to be disclosed under "Staff costs" are those employed by a company. A person will be employed when he or she has a contract *of* service with the company.[10] A person who

---

[9] Companies Act 1985, Sched. 4, para. 56.
[10] *Ibid.*

has a contract *for* service is regarded as self employed and the fees paid by a company to such worker can be included in the heading "Other operating charges" in formats 2 and 4. The dividing line between the two categories is very thin and categorisation is not always easy. An analysis of the difference between the two is outside the scope of this text and a work on employment law should be consulted.

Another category of personnel which will normally be excluded from "Staff costs" is that of casual labour. These people are regarded as not having a contract of employment. Their exact tax status is dependent upon employment law and the PAYE regulations. The salaries of casual labour will, however, have to be included if it is necessary to do so in order to show a true and fair view of a company's profit or loss. This is usually the case where a company is dependent upon casual labour, for example in the hotel industry.

Staff numbers   In addition to the financial information relating to staff, further particulars of the number and categories of employees are required to be given in the notes to the accounts. The details which are required to be disclosed are:

(a) the average number of persons employed by the company in the financial year; and

(b) the average number of employees within each category of persons employed by the company in the financial year.[11]

The average number of employees and the average number of employees within a particular category are to be calculated by dividing the relevant annual number by the number of weeks in the financial year. The relevant annual number is found by ascertaining for each week in the financial year the number of persons employed under contracts of service in that week, and the number of employees in the category in question. In both cases, the weekly totals are then added together and divided by the number of weeks in the financial year.[12] Where the accounts are for a period other than a calendar year, this calculation should be adjusted so that a simple mathematical average for the period is obtained.

It is for the directors to select the categories they wish to use, having regard to the manner in which the company's activities are organised.[13] Possible categorisation might be into full time and part time employees, or into production, sales and administration workers.

For the purposes of "Staff costs" and the additional particulars of employees which must be disclosed, any director who has a contract of service with a company must be included as an employee. The details set out in the following paragraphs must be disclosed whether or not a director can be classified as an employee.

Directors' remuneration   The following information relating to directors must be shown in the notes to the accounts.

Aggregate emoluments   For these purposes, the term "emoluments" includes fees and percentages, any sums paid by

[11] *Ibid.*
[12] *Ibid.*
[13] *Ibid.*

way of expenses allowances (insofar as those sums are charged to United Kingdom income tax), any contributions paid in respect of him under any pension scheme and the estimated money value of any other benefits received by him otherwise than in cash.[14]

The aggregate amount of emoluments paid to directors must be shown. This sum will include any emoluments paid to or receivable by a person in respect of his services:

(a) as director of the company (Company A);
(b) as director of any of Company A's subsidiaries, whilst he is also director of Company A; and
(c) in connection with the management of Company A or any of its subsidiaries.

The notes must show the division between emoluments in respect of services as director, whether of the company or its subsidiary and other emoluments.[15]

It should be noted that a director's remuneration may not be paid free of income tax, whether it is paid to him as a director or in any other capacity. It is also unlawful to calculate a director's remuneration by reference to or varying with either the amount of his income tax or any rate of income tax.[16]

The requirement to show directors' emoluments has to be complied with by all companies. The following rules, however, do not apply to companies which are not part of a group and whose directors, in aggregate, do not receive more than £60,000.[17]

Banded emoluments The disclosure required under this heading is that the number of directors whose emoluments fall within specific bands must be shown The bands are at present:

£0   — £ 5,000
£5,001 — £10,000 and continuing up in bands of £5,000 as far as necessary.

The emoluments of the chairman and the highest paid director must be shown separately, unless they are the same person, in which case the amount will be disclosed under "Chairman's emoluments."[18] For the purpose of banding, emoluments include the same amounts as for "Aggregate emoluments" above, except that contributions paid in respect of him under a pension scheme must be excluded.[19] Information relating to the aggregate amount of pensions paid to directors is shown separately.[20]

The emoluments of directors who discharged their duties as such wholly or mainly outside the United Kingdom are to be disregarded for disclosure under this heading.[21]

---

[14] *Ibid.* Sched. 5, para. 22.
[15] *Ibid.*
[16] *Ibid.* s.311.
[17] *Ibid.* Sched. 5, para. 23.
[18] *Ibid.* para. 25.
[19] *Ibid.* para. 26.
[20] See p. 91 below.
[21] Companies Act 1985, Sched. 5, para. 25.

Emoluments waived The number of directors whose emoluments would have been included under "Aggregate emoluments" above, had they not waived the rights to those emoluments,directors must be disclosed, along with the aggregate amounts of the emoluments waived.[22] Companies governed by the Stock Exchange also have to disclose particulars of any agreement under which current or future emoluments are waived.[23] Agreements concerning the waiver of emoluments paid by a subsidiary are included as well as the emoluments due from the company of which a person is a director.

Chairman's emoluments In addition to the information on directors' remuneration separate disclosure must be made with regard to a company chairman. A chairman is defined as:

> "the person elected by the directors to be chairman of their meetings and includes a person who, though not so elected, holds any office (however designated) which in accordance with the company's constitution carries with it functions substantially similar to those discharged by a person so elected."[24]

The emoluments of any person who acted as chairman during the financial year must be disclosed, so far as attributable to his period of office, unless his duties as chairman were wholly or mainly discharged outside the United Kingdom.[25] Emoluments in this context has the same meaning as for "Aggregate emoluments" above.

Pensions, etc. Where a payment is to be made in consideration for or in connection with a director's retirement from office, particulars of it, including the amount which it is proposed to pay, must be shown. The payment should also be approved by the company.[26]

The aggregate amount of pensions paid to or receivable by past or present directors must be disclosed. Pensions to be included in this amount are those paid to such directors in respect of:

(a) their directorship of the company (Company A);
(b) their directorship of any of Company A's subsidiaries held at a time when they were also director of Company A; and
(c) their services in connection with the management of Company A. A or any of its subsidiaries.[27]

The aggregate amount must be broken down to show pensions in respect of services as director, whether of the company or its subsidiary, and other pensions.[28] If a pension is paid to or receivable by a nominee of a director and disclosure would have been required had it been paid direct to the director,

---

[22] *Ibid.* para. 27.
[23] See p. 52 above.
[24] Companies Act 1985, Sched. 5, para. 24.
[25] *Ibid.*
[26] *Ibid.* s.312.
[27] *Ibid.* Sched. 5, para. 28.
[28] *Ibid.*

then that pension should also be included in the information shown.[29] Pensions are deemed to include any superannuation allowance, superannuation gratuity or similar payment. Where a director is in receipt of a pension from a scheme funded by the company and past contributions paid by the company are sufficient to finance the payment of the pension, then the receipt of the pension need not be disclosed.[30]

The Act defines a pension scheme as "a scheme for the provision of pensions in respect of services as director or otherwise which is maintained in whole or in part by means of contributions". Contributions in this context means:

> "any payment (including an insurance premium) paid for the purposes of the scheme by or in respect of persons rendering services in respect of which pensions will or may become payable under the scheme, except that it does not include any payment in respect of two or more persons if the amount paid in respect of each of them is not ascertainable."[31]

Directors' compensation

Before a company can lawfully make any payment to a director as compensation for loss of office, the particulars of the proposed payment must be disclosed to the members of the company and approved by the company. The particulars must include the amount which it is proposed to be paid. This procedure must also be followed where it is proposed to make a payment in consideration or in connection with a director's retirement from office.[32]

The aggregate amount of any compensation to directors or past directors in respect of loss of office must be disclosed in a note to the accounts. This amount will include not only compensation for loss of the office of director, but also for the loss of any other office held in connection with management of the company's or a subsidiary's affairs while the person was a director. Sums paid as consideration for or in connection with a person's retirement are also to be regarded as compensation for loss of office. The notes must distinguish between compensation paid in respect of the loss of office as director, whether of the company or its subsidiary, and compensation paid in respect of other offices.[33]

Supplementary information

In respect of directors' emoluments, pensions of past and present directors and compensation for loss of office, the following points must be taken into consideration.

The amounts shown under each of the above headings must include all sums paid by or receivable from the company, its subsidiaries and any other person in respect of services connected with the management of the company and its subsidiaries. Sums to be accounted for to the company or any of its subsidiaries, and certain other amounts should be excluded.[34] If any sum is

---

[29] *Ibid.*
[30] *Ibid.*
[31] *Ibid.* para. 33.
[32] *Ibid.* s.312.
[33] *Ibid.* para. 29.
[34] *Ibid.* para. 30.

excluded on the ground that the recipient is liable to account for it as above but the liability is thereafter wholly or partly released or it is not enforced within a period of two years, then the sums must be shown in the notes to the accounts. Where the amount is partly released or not enforced only that amount need be shown. Disclosure should be made in the first accounts in which it is practicable to do so and the amounts should be clearly identified.[35]

In the case of compensation paid to a director for loss of office, the notes to the accounts must distinguish between the sums respectively paid by or receivable from the company, the company's subsidiaries and persons other than the company and its subsidiaries.[36]

The amounts shown under each heading are the sums receivable in respect of the financial year covered by the annual accounts, regardless of when those amounts are paid. In the case of sums not receivable in respect of a period, the amounts paid during that year should be disclosed.[37]

If any sums paid by way of expenses allowance are charged to United Kingdom income tax after the end of the relevant financial year, the amount charged must be shown in a note to the first accounts in which it is practicable to show them and it must be clear to what the amount relates.[38]

Where the disclosure requirements relating to directors and chairmen require an analysis of the amount disclosed, the directors may use their discretion as to how to apportion such payments.[39] An example which would require the exercise of such discretion would be in connection with directors' emoluments, where it is necessary to distinguish between emoluments in respect of services as a director and other emoluments.[40] Finally, in this context, disclosure of information relating to directors and chairmen need only be made where the information is contained in the company's books and papers or where the company has the right to obtain it from the persons concerned.[41]

Higher paid employees   All companies are required to show the number of employees who are "remunerated at higher rates." For these purposes, employees are regarded as being higher paid if they earn in excess of £30,000. The numbers of such employees are to be shown according to the income band into which they fall. The income bands are:

£30,001 — £35,000
£35,001 — £40,000
£40,001 — £45,000

and continuing to go up in bands of £5,000.[42]

Employees for these purposes do not include directors and

---

[35] *Ibid.* para. 31.
[36] *Ibid.* para. 30.
[37] *Ibid.* para. 31.
[38] *Ibid.*
[39] *Ibid.* para. 32.
[40] See p. 90 above.
[41] Companies Act 1985, Sched. 5, para. 34.
[42] *Ibid.* para. 35.

those employed during the financial year (whether throughout that year or not) whose work was performed wholly or mainly outside the United Kingdom.[43]

The emoluments of higher paid employees will include:

(a) any sum paid to or receivable by him from the company, the company's subsidiary and any other person in respect of his services as an employee of the company or a subsidiary of it or as a director of a subsidiary of the company (except sums to be accounted for to any member of the group);

(b) fees and percentages;

(c) any sums paid by way of expenses allowance, which are subject to United Kingdom income tax; and

(d) the estimated money value of any other benefits received by a person otherwise than in cash.

If it is to be taken into account, an emolument must have been receivable during or in respect of the financial year, and in this case it is irrelevant when it was paid. Where sums are not receivable in respect of a period, the sums paid during that year should be disclosed.[44] An example of the latter category would be a payment made to an employee to compensate him for having to move house at the company's request, as it relates to a specific event, rather than to a period.

It has been seen that where an employee is liable to account for emoluments which have been paid to or are receivable by him, whether in respect of services to his employer or to another member of the group of companies to which his employer belongs, these sums are not included in calculating his emoluments. If, however, the liability is wholly or partly released or it is not enforced within a period of two years, then the amount which has not been accounted for must be disclosed at the first opportunity. The same applies to any sum which is paid to an employee by way of expenses allowance and which is charged to United Kingdom income tax after the end of the financial year.[45]

Depreciation

In formats 2 and 4 there are specific subheadings for "Depreciation and other amounts written off tangible and intangible fixed assets," which do not appear in formats 1 and 3. Instead this information must appear in the notes to the accounts when the latter two formats are used.[46] The rules governing depreciation are covered in Chapter 7.

Supplementary information

The details on the topics set out below must be given to supplement the information contained in the profit and loss account, whichever format is chosen.

[43] *Ibid.*
[44] *Ibid.* para. 36.
[45] *Ibid.*
[46] *Ibid.* Sched. 4, para. 8, note 17 to the profit and loss account.

Charges   The amount of interest payable or similar charges. These amounts must be shown in respect of bank loans and overdrafts, and other loans made to the company. The interest or similar charges on such borrowings needs to be disclosed in the following circumstances:

    (i) if repayment, otherwise than by instalment, is to be made before the end of the period of five years beginning with the day next following the end of the financial year;

    (ii) when a loan or overdraft is payable by instalment, the last of which falls due for payment before the end of that period, then the interest or similar charge must be disclosed; or

    (iii) interest or charges of any other kind payable by the company.

It is irrelevant for these purposes, whether the borrowing has been made on the security of debentures or not. Interest or charges on loans to a company from other members of the group to which it belongs must be shown separately.[47]

Share capital   The amounts set aside for redeeming share capital or loans. These must also be shown separately.[48]

Listed investments   Income from listed investments. SSAP 8, "The Treatment of Taxation under the Imputation System in the Accounts of Companies," requires that the amount to be shown under this heading is the amount of cash received or receivable plus the related tax credit. The amount of the tax credit will then be shown under U.K. corporation tax as "Tax attributable to franked investment income." Income from shares in group companies and from shares in related companies are disclosed under the relevant heading in all the profit and loss formats.

Rents   The amount of rents from land, after deduction of ground rent, rates and other outgoings. Only companies where such rents form a substantial part of their revenue need disclose this information.[49]

Hire   The amount charged to revenue for the hire of plant and machinery.[50]

Auditors   The amount of the auditors' remuneration. This sum will include any sums paid by the company in respect of the auditors' expenses.[51]

Particulars of tax

Detailed information relating to tax is required both by the Act and by accounting standards. The Act provides for the following particulars to be shown:

    (a) the basis on which the charge for United Kingdom corporation tax and income tax has been computed;

    (b) any special circumstances which affect the charge for tax

---

[47] *Ibid.* para. 53.
[48] *Ibid.*
[49] *Ibid.*
[50] *Ibid.*
[51] *Ibid.*

on profits, income or capital gains for the financial year to which the profit and loss account relates or for succeeding financial years;

(c) the amount of the charge for United Kingdom corporation tax. If this amount has been reduced by relief for double taxation, the amount which would have been charged, but for the relief, must be shown;

(d) the amount of the charge for United Kingdom income tax; and

(e) the amount of the charge for taxation imposed outside the United Kingdom of profits, income and, so far as charged to revenue, capital gains.

Items (c), (d) and (e) must be shown in respect of the tax on profit or loss on ordinary activities and the tax on any extraordinary profit or loss.[52] The latter is disclosed separately under the heading "Extraordinary items" which is discussed below.

In addition, SSAP 8 requires that the particulars on corporation tax include the charge for corporation tax on the income of the year. If any material transfers have been made between the deferred taxation account and the profit and loss account in respect of corporation tax, these must be disclosed separately. The Standard further provides that tax attributable to franked investment income,[53] the total amount of overseas taxation together with any double taxation relief and that part of the unrelieved overseas taxation which relates to the payment or the proposed payment of dividends, and the amount of irrecoverable ACT must be disclosed. SSAP 8 deals with the accounting treatment of ACT related to proposed dividends generally and this is supplemented by SSAP 15, "Accounting for Deferred Tax," regarding the carry forward of ACT.

SSAP 15 also deals with other matters relating to deferred tax and requires disclosure of:

(a) the amount of deferred tax relating to a company's ordinary activities;

(b) any amounts of deferred tax not provided for in the year, showing the main components which make up this sum;

(c) where earnings are retained overseas and there has been no provision for deferred tax, this should be stated in the notes to the accounts; and

(d) any deferred tax which relates to an extraordinary item of profit or loss.

Extraordinary and exceptional items

Extraordinary items

The Act requires disclosure of any extraordinary income or charges arising in the financial year, the effect of any transaction which is exceptional and the effect of any amount relating to any preceding financial year which is included in any item in the profit or loss account.[54]

[52] *Ibid.* para. 54.
[53] See p. 95 above.
[54] Companies Act 1985, Sched. 4, para. 57.

The term "extraordinary" is not defined by the Act, but SSAP 6, "Extraordinary Items and Prior Year Adjustments," states that it relates to those items that derive from event or transaction outside the ordinary activities of business. Such items must also be material and not expected to recur either frequently or regularly. From this definition, it will be seen that whether an item can be classified as "extraordinary" will depend upon the particular circumstances of a company. SSAP 6 does, however, give certain examples of what might be treated as an extraordinary item, *inter alia*, the discontinuance of a significant business segment either through termination or disposal, the sale of an investment that was not acquired with the intention of resale (such as the disposal of a significant tangible fixed asset, an investment in a subsidiary or in an associated company) and the expropriation of assets.

Extraordinary items appear under four headings in the profit and loss account formats, namely, "Extraordinary income," "Extraordinary charges," "Extraordinary profit or loss" and "Tax on extraordinary profit or loss." A single item "Extraordinary profit or loss" will therefore have to be expanded upon in the notes to the accounts.

Exceptional items
"Exceptional" transactions are defined by the Act as any transactions which are exceptional by virtue of size or incidence though they fall within the ordinary activities of the company.[54] They should be included in the appropriate heading of the selected profit and loss account and details disclosed in the notes thereto. The revised version of SSAP 6, which was issued in August 1986, contains a similar definition:

> "Exceptional items are material items which derive from events or transactions that fall within the ordinary activities of the company and which need to be disclosed separately by virtue of their size or incidence if the financial statements are to give a true and fair view."

The Standard gives examples of transactions which might fall within this definition; these include redundancy costs which relate to continuing business segments (if the business segment was not continuing, such costs might be classified as extraordinary items), amounts transferred to employee share schemes and profits or losses on the disposal of fixed assets. Details of such exceptional items should be given in notes to the accounts, but where it is necessary to give a true and fair view by showing the profit before exceptional items, then they should be disclosed as a separate item on the face of the profit and loss account.

Dividends

Although there is not a separate heading for dividends in any of the profit and loss formats, the Schedule does require that the aggregate amount of any dividends paid and proposed be shown separately in the profit and loss account.[55] The Act therefore

---

[55] *Ibid.* para. 3.

leaves it open as to where they should appear. The revised SSAP 6 requires that dividends should be shown after, and be deducted from, the profit or loss for the financial year.

The Stock Exchange rules provide that listed companies also disclose any arrangements under which a shareholder has either waived or agreed to waive any dividends.[56]

Earnings per share

The disclosure of a figure for earnings per share is not statutory provision but is to be found in SSAP 3, "Earning per Share," which requires, *inter alia*, listed companies to show this information on the face of the profit and loss account. The Standard also lays down rules for the calculation of the figure.

---

[56] See p. 52 above.

11 DISTRIBUTABLE PROFITS

Introduction

The declaration of dividends was once a matter solely for company decision or in rare cases, a matter of the directors' discretion if they had been given such power by the Articles of Association. Normally, the directors were given authority to recommend the amount of the dividend to be declared and this would then be sanctioned by the company in general meeting. The rules governing what profits were available for distribution were quite wide: it was possible to distribute the profit made from the disposal of a fixed asset at more than its book price[1] and the unrealised gain on a bona fide revaluation, by competent valuers, of capital assets if they were not subject to short term fluctuations.[2] Whilst the way in which dividends are declared has not been altered by statute, the profits from which they can be paid is now defined by legislation and this affects not only the payment of dividends but also any other distribution, as the Act clearly states that "A company shall not make a distribution except out of profits available for the purpose."[3]

All companies

Distributions For present purposes, distributions are defined as any distribution of a company's assets to its members, except:

"(a) an issue of shares as fully or partly paid bonus shares;
(b) the redemption or purchase of any of the company's own shares out of capital (including the proceeds of any fresh issue of shares) or out of unrealised profits in accordance with (The Companies Act 1985);
(c) the reduction of share capital by extinguishing or reducing the liability of any of the members on any of the company's shares in respect of share capital not paid up, or by paying off paid up share capital, and
(d) a distribution of assets to members of the company on its winding up."[4]

Although the rules governing distributable profits apply to both private and public companies, there are additional requirements placed upon public companies. The first question which must be answered, however, is which profits can be distributed and this will involve not only an examination of the nature of those profits, but also the type of accounts from which the profit figure is derived.

---

[1] *Lubbock* v. *British Bank of South America* [1892] 2 Ch. 198.
[2] *Dimbula Valley (Ceylon) Tea Co. Ltd.* v. *Laurie* [1961] 1 All E.R. 769.
[3] *Ibid.* s.263(1).
[4] *Ibid.* s.263(2).

Distributable profits

The profits which a company may distribute are defined by the Act as:

"its accumulated, realised profits, so far as not previously utilised by distribution or capitalisation, less its accumulated realised losses, so far as not previously written off in a reduction or reorganisation of capital duly made."[5]

Realised profits

The term "realised profits" is further expanded by the statute which states that they are:

"such profits of the company as fall to be treated as realised profits for the purposes of (the company's) accounts in accordance with principles generally accepted with respect to the determination for accounting purposes of realised profits at the time when those accounts are prepared."[6]

Relevant items

In calculating a company's distributable profits, the following items from that company's accounts must be taken into consideration:

(a) profits, losses, assets and liabilities;
(b) any provision for depreciation or diminution in value of assets, or for liabilities and charges; and
(c) share capital and reserves, including undistributable reserves.[7]

These items are referred to as the "relevant items" below.

Development costs

If development costs are shown as an asset in the company's accounts, they must be treated as a realised loss[8] for these purposes. There are two exceptions to this rule. Any amount included in development costs which represents an unrealised profit made on revaluation of those costs should not be regarded as a realised loss. Secondly, if the directors are justified in deciding that due to the company's special circumstances, development costs should not be treated as a realised loss, they need not be treated as such. If development costs have not been treated as a realised loss for this reason, this fact must be recorded in a note to the accounts, with an explanation of the special circumstances on which the directors based their decision.[9]

Depreciation, diminution in value, etc.

In determining distributable profits, provisions for depreciation, diminution in value of assets, liabilities and for charges are to be treated as realised losses. An exception is made for provisions for diminution in value of a fixed asset appearing on a revaluation of all a company's fixed assets, or all of its fixed assets other than goodwill.[10]

Where a fixed asset has been revalued and this results in it being shown in the accounts at a higher figure than previously, an unrealised profit will have been made. If the depreciation charge in respect of that asset is then increased on or after the revaluation, the amount by which the depreciation charge

[5] *Ibid*. s.263(3).
[6] *Ibid*. Sched. 4, para. 91.
[7] *Ibid*. s.270(2).
[8] *Ibid*. s.269(1).
[9] *Ibid*. s.269(2).
[10] *Ibid*. s.275(1).

increases may be treated as a realised profit.[11] Where the original cost of a revalued asset is unknown, because either there is no record of its original cost or it would be too costly or time consuming to produce such a record, the cost to be used when calculating whether a profit or loss has been made on the revaluation of that asset is the value ascribed to it in the earliest available record of its value, made on or after its acquisition by the company.[12]

A revaluation for these purposes may be the directors' consideration of the value of the asset concerned at any particular time.[13] This rule will only apply if the directors are satisfied that the aggregate value of any assets which they have valued at the time in question is not less than the aggregate amount at which the assets are, for the time being, stated in the company's accounts.[14]

There is, however, a proviso which applies when the accounts used for the calculation of distributable profits, whether they be a company's annual accounts or interim or initial accounts, are required to be properly prepared.[15] In this case, certain particulars must be stated in those accounts, if a directors' consideration as to the value of a fixed asset, which falls into any category of relevant items,[16] is to be effective in determining whether a difference in depreciation charges can be treated as a realised profit.[17] The particulars which are required to be disclosed in a note to the accounts are that:

(a) the directors are responsible for having considered the value at any time of any fixed assets of the company, without actually revaluing those assets;
(b) the directors are satisfied that the aggregate value of those assets at the time in question is or was not less than the aggregate amount at which they are, or were for the time being, stated in the company's accounts; and
(c) the assets which are the subject of the directors' consideration appear in the accounts used for determining the company's distributable profit at the value given to them by the directors.[18]

Distributions in kind   Should a company make a distribution in kind, or a distribution which includes a non-cash asset, and that asset has been included in the accounts used by a company for the determination of its distributable profits then the following provision applies. If any part of the amount of that asset, which has been included in those accounts, represents an unrealised profit, that profit may be treated as realised for the purpose of the distribution. The amount may also be taken to the profit and loss account but only for the purpose of making the distribution.[19]

Accounts   The accounts from which the relevant items are generally

---

[11] *Ibid.* s.275(2).
[12] *Ibid.* s.275(3).
[13] *Ibid.* s.275(4).
[14] *Ibid.* s.275(5).
[15] See pp. 102, 104 below.
[16] See p. 100 above.
[17] Companies Act 1985, s.275(6).
[18] *Ibid.*
[19] *Ibid.* s.276.

derived are a company's last annual accounts.[20] Interim or initial accounts may be substituted if their use is necessary to enable a reasonable judgment to be made as to the amounts of the relevant items set out on page 100 above. Interim or initial accounts will be necessary in the following circumstances:

(a) where the distribution would not be legal if reference were made only to the company's last annual audited accounts; in this case, interim accounts may be substituted for the last annual accounts; or

(b) where the distribution is proposed to be declared during the company's first accounting reference period, or before any accounts are laid in respect of that period, in which case initial accounts may be used instead.[21]

Properly prepared   If a company's last annual audited accounts are used, they must have been properly prepared in accordance with the Act. Alternatively, if the Act has not been followed, any deviation from it must not be material for the purposes of determining the relevant items. In relation to the relevant items, the true and fair test applies.[22]

Further, the annual accounts must have an unqualified audit report. If the report has been qualified, the company's auditors are required to give a written statement, setting out:

(a) whether in their opinion, their qualification materially affects a relevant item; and

(b) whether the distribution would be in breach of the Act.

A copy of the auditors' statement must have been laid before the company in general meeting.[23] It has been held that the need for an auditor's statement in the event of a qualified audit report being given is not merely a procedural matter which can be waived or dispensed with by the company members entitled to vote; it is an important part of the procedure established for the protection of creditors as well as members. Thus in the case of a company which subsequently went into liquidation, the lack of auditor's statement and its necessary approval by the company in general meeting, could not be rectified once the company was in liquidation, even though the distribution, when it was made, would have been lawful but for the omissions with regard to the auditor's statement.[24]

Once the auditors have made their statement, it may be used in connection with, not only the distribution contemplated at the time the statement was made, but also any other distribution which is to be made out of distributable profits calculated from the same annual accounts.[25]

Summary   To sum up so far, a company's distributable profits are therefore its realised profits less its realised losses, those figures being calculated from its last annual audited accounts, unless it is entitled to use interim or initial accounts.

---

[20] *Ibid.* s.270(3).
[21] *Ibid.* s.270(4).
[22] *Ibid.* s.271(2).
[23] *Ibid.* s.271(4).
[24] *Precision Ltd.* v. *Precision Marketing Ltd.* [1985] 3 W.L.R. 812.
[25] Companies Act 1985, s.271(5)

Public companies

There are additional requirements placed upon public companies in relation to both the profits available for distribution and the accounts used to determine those profits.

Distributable profits   A public company may distribute any profits which represent its realised profits less its realised losses, but in addition to this it will have to ensure that the distribution does not adversely affect its capital. Such a company may only make a distribution if, at the time it is made, the amount of the company's net assets is not less than the aggregate of its called-up share capital and undistributable reserves. Furthermore, the distribution can only be made to the extent that it does not reduce the amount of those assets to less than that aggregate.[26]

Net assets   The terms "net assets" and "undistributable reserves" are explained by the Act. "Net assets" are the aggregate of the company's assets less the aggregate of its liabilities.[27] In calculating a public company's assets any uncalled share capital may not be included as an asset in any accounts which are used for the calculation of distributable profits.[28] The term "liabilities" will include any provision for liabilities and charges.[29]

Undistributable reserves   "Undistributable reserves" are defined as:

"(a) the share premium account,
(b) the capital redemption reserve,
(c) the amount by which the company's accumulated, unrealised profits, so far as not previously utilised by capitalisation . . . exceed its accumulated, unrealised losses (so far as not previously written off in a reduction or reorganisation of capital duly made), and
(d) any other reserve which the company is prohibited from distributing by any enactment (other than one contained in (Part VIII of the Act)) or by its memorandum or articles";

Paragraph (c) applies to every description of capitalisation except a transfer of profits of the company to its capital redemption reserve on or after December 22, 1980.[30]

Accounts   As with private companies, a public company should use its last annual audited accounts in order to determine its distributable profits, or, in the same limited circumstances as are available to private companies, interim or initial accounts.[31] Where a public company uses its last annual audited accounts, those accounts must be properly prepared.[32] Unlike a private company, if a public company uses interim or initial accounts, it is obliged to ensure that these have been properly prepared. If they are not so prepared, the deviation must not materially affect the relevant items.[33]

---

[26] *Ibid.* s.264(1).
[27] *Ibid.* s.264(2).
[28] *Ibid.* s.264(4).
[29] *Ibid.* s.264(2).
[30] *Ibid.* s.264(3).
[31] *Ibid.* s.270(3)(4).
[32] See p. 102 above.
[33] Companies Act 1985, ss.272(1)(2), 273(1)(2).

Properly prepared   Properly prepared means, in the context of both interim and initial accounts, that:

>   (a) the accounts comply with the Act wherever possible,
>   bearing in mind that they are not annual accounts;
>   (b) the balance sheet has been signed, on behalf of the board,
>   by two directors; and
>   (c) the accounts present a true and fair view.[34]

Where interim accounts have been used, a copy of those accounts must have been delivered to the Registrar of Companies. The Registrar should also be furnished with a translation of the accounts, certified as being a correct translation, should the accounts not be in English.[35]

In the case of initial accounts, not only must the accounts and any relevant translation have been delivered to the Registrar of Companies, but the accounts must be accompanied by a report made by the company's auditors.[36] The auditors' report must state whether:

>   (a) in their opinion, the accounts have been properly
>   prepared; and if not
>   (b) in their opinion, the qualification materially affects a
>   relevant item; and
>   (c) the distribution is within the Act.[37]

If the auditors' report is not in English, a translation, properly certified, must also be sent.[38]

Successive distributions

Where a company, whether it be private or public, has already made one or more distributions, a further distribution will only be legal if the proposed distribution, together with the earlier distributions meets the criteria discussed above. This rule, however, will not apply to distributions, the legality of which, is not determined by reference to the same accounts.[39]

Certain forms of distribution are specifically included as being within this rule, *inter alia*, lawful financial assistance given out of distributable profits,[40] certain unlawful financial assistance,[41] and certain payments made by a company in respect of the purchase of its own shares.[42]

Investment and   The Act makes certain provision for investment companies
insurance   and insurance companies with long term business[43] which,
companies   because of their specialised nature, are not examined here. For these purposes, an investment company is, in general terms, a

---

[34] *Ibid.* ss.272(3), 273(3).
[35] *Ibid.* s.272(4)(5).
[36] *Ibid.* s.273(6)(7).
[37] *Ibid.* s.273(4)(5).
[38] *Ibid.* s.273(7).
[39] *Ibid.* s.274(1).
[40] *Ibid.* s.274(2)(3). See also p. 124ff below.
[41] *Ibid.* s.274(2)(3).
[42] *Ibid.* for purchase of own shares see p. 128ff below.
[43] *Ibid.* ss.265, 268.

public company which has given notice to the Registrar of Companies of its intention to carry on business as an investment company and an insurance company is one to which Part II of the Insurance Companies Act 1982 applies.[44]

CCAB guidance

The statutory rules governing distributable profits have proved problematical; apart from anything else the deceptively simple terms "realised profits" and "realised losses" are a minefield. In attempt to solve some of the difficulties, the Consultative Committee of Accountancy Bodies (CCAB) issued two technical releases, T.R. 481—The determination of realised profits and the disclosure of distributable profits in the context of the Companies Acts 1948 to 1981 and T.R. 482—The determination of distributable profits in the context of the Companies Acts 1948 to 1981. Whilst these releases deal with the pre-consolidation understanding of company legislation, they are still relevant to the interpretation of the 1985 Act. The full text of the two releases, amended to show the references to the 1985 Act, is given in Appendix III.

In the calculation of distributable profits, statute requires that principles generally accepted for the determination of realised profits must be taken into consideration.[45] Among those generally accepted principles will be the accounting principles set out in the Act itself. Further guidance is set out in SSAP 2, "Disclosure of accounting policies."[46] It is generally recognised that Statements of Standard Accounting Practice should be included as a source of guidance.[47] When any revision of an existing SSAP is undertaken or a new Standard published, the Accounting Standards Committee (ASC) has said that guidance, where necessary, will be given as to whether a profit should be treated as realised or unrealised.

Since the publication of T.R. 481, the ASC have started to publish Statements of Recommended Practice (SORPs).[48] Members of the CCAB bodies are expected to follow these Statements, whereas compliance with SSAPs is mandatory. While SSAPs will probably be regarded as highly persuasive when considering what are generally accepted principles, SORPs will not be as persuasive, although they may still be relevant.

Illegal distributions

Members' liability If a company should make a distribution in contravention of the statutory provisions, and the member to which it is made either knows or has reasonable grounds for believing that it is so made, that member will be liable to repay to the company the element of that distribution which is illegal. If the distribution is of non-cash

[44] *Ibid.* ss.266, 268.
[45] *Ibid.* Sched. 4, para. 91.
[46] See p. 39ff above.
[47] *Ibid.*
[48] See. p. 47ff above.

assets, the member will be under an obligation to pay the company a sum equal to the value of the illegal distribution.[49] This is without prejudice to any obligation apart from section 277 on a member to repay an unlawful distribution. The obligation to repay an unlawful distribution which is imposed by section 277 does not apply in relation to:

(a) unlawful financial assistance[50]; or
(b) any payment made by a company in respect of the redemption or purchase by the company of its own shares.[51]

---

[49] Companies Act 1985, s.277(1).
[50] See p. 124ff.
[51] Companies Act 1985, s.277(2).

12 DIRECTORS' REPORT

Introduction

One element of a company's annual accounts is the directors' report.[1] Some companies also include a chairman's statement but there is no legal obligation to do so and its content is a matter for individual chairmen. The directors' report, however, is governed by statute and must include information upon specific topics. One of the purposes of this report is to provide details, set out in narrative form, which is supplementary to the accounts.

Content

The directors of a company must prepare a report in respect of each financial year,[2] which includes information on the subjects detailed below.

Fair review of business development   A fair review should be given of the development of the business of the company and its subsidiaries during the financial year and of their position at the end of it.[3] This requirement is couched in general terms, thereby allowing the directors considerable discretion in their approach. The only restricting factor is that the auditors will check that the report is not inconsistent with the company's annual accounts.[4]

Dividends   The amount of any dividend which the directors have recommended must be stated, along with the amount (if any) which they propose to carry to reserves.[5]

Directors' names   The names of the persons who, at any time during the financial year, were directors of the company must be given.[6]

The company's principal activities   The report should set out the principal activities of the company and its subsidiaries in the course of the year. Any significant change in those activities during the year must also be noted.[7]

Significant changes in fixed assets   If any significant changes in the fixed assets of the company or of any of its subsidiaries have occurred during the financial year, particulars of the changes must be given in the report. Should the asset involve an interest in land and the market value of the asset, as at the end of the financial year, differs substantially from the amount at which it is

---

[1] Companies Act 1985, s.239.
[2] *Ibid.* s.235(1).
[3] *Ibid.*
[4] *Ibid.* s.237(6).
[5] *Ibid.* s.235(1).
[6] *Ibid.* s.235(2).
[7] *Ibid.*

included in the balance sheet, the directors must report on the difference with such degree of precision as is practicable. A report on any such difference need only be made, however, when the directors believe that the difference is of such significance as to require that the attention of company's members or debenture holders should be drawn to it.[8]

Directors' interests in shares or loans　Detailed information is required regarding the directors' interests in shares or debentures of the company or any member of the group to which the company belongs. Only those interests held by directors who were in office at the end of the financial year need be disclosed. The information to be given is:

(a) whether a director was, at the end of the financial year, interested in any shares or debentures of the company, or of any other member of a group to which the company belongs; this information should be taken from the register which the company keeps of directors' interests in such shares or debentures, in accordance with sections 324 to 328 of the Act; and if a director was so interested then the following particulars must be given;

(b) the number and amount of shares in and debentures of each body, according to the register at the end of the financial year; each body in which such an interest is held should also be specified;

(c) whether or not the director was at the beginning of that year interested in the shares or debentures; when a director has joined the board after the start of the financial year under consideration, it must be stated whether or not he held the interest at the time he became a director; the information should, once again, be taken from the register of directors' interests; and

(d) the number and amount of shares or debentures which the director held at the beginning of the financial year, or at the time he became a director, as the case may be.

It is possible to disclose this information in notes to the accounts instead of the directors' report.[9]

Political and charitable gifts　These disclosure requirements apply to those companies which were not wholly owned subsidiaries of a company incorporated in Great Britain. If money has been given for political or charitable purposes and the amount given for both these purposes exceeds £200 in aggregate, then the directors' report must show:

(a) the amount of money given for each purpose, showing the gifts to political causes separately from charitable contributions;

(b) in case of political gifts, where an individual gift exceeds £200, the name of each person to whom money has been given and the amount given. Where a donation or a subscription to a political party has been made which

---

[8] *Ibid.* Sched. 7, para. 1.
[9] *Ibid.* para. 2.

exceeds £200, then the identity of that party must be disclosed along with the amount of money given.

In the case of a group, the holding company's directors' report need only give the required information for the group as a whole, and then only if the total gifts of the group to both political and charitable causes exceeds £200.[10]

A political gift will be a donation or subscription to either:

(a) a political party of the United Kingdom or any part of it; or
(b) a person, who, to the company's knowledge, is carrying on any activities which can, at the time at which the donation or subscription was given, reasonably be regarded as likely to affect public support for a political party of the United Kingdom or any part of it.

In this context, "charitable purposes" means purposes which are exclusively charitable. In Scotland, the term "charitable" is to be defined according to the definition given in the Income Tax Acts. A charitable gift to a person who, when it was given, was ordinarily resident outside the United Kingdom is not to be taken into account for these purposes.[11]

Post balance sheet events Particulars must be given of any important events affecting the company or any of its subsidiaries which have occurred since the end of the financial year.[12] SSAP 17, "Accounting for Post Balance Sheet Events," imposes similar requirements. This Standard requires the disclosure of events occurring after the balance sheet date and the date on which the financial statements are approved by the board of directors, whether they are favourable or unfavourable. If material events occur after the directors' approval has been given to the financial statements, directors are advised to consider publishing the relevant information, in spite of the fact that the Standard does not apply in this situation, in order to avoid users of the financial statements being misled.

In contrast to the Act, SSAP 17 requires that disclosure should be by way either of adjustment to the financial statements or in the notes thereto. Important post balance sheet events which merit adjustments to the financial statements, are classified as "adjusting events" by the Standard. Such an event will be one which provides additional evidence relating to conditions that existed at the balance sheet date or which indicates that the going concern concept can no longer be applied to either the whole or a material part of the company. Among events which would normally require adjustments to the financial statements are a property valuation which evidences a permanent diminution in value, evidence received which shows that a previous estimate of accrued profit on a long term contract was materially inaccurate or the insolvency of a debtor. Certain post balance sheet events will be treated as requiring adjustments to be made because of statutory provisions or customary accounting practice. Proposed dividends, amounts appropriated to reserves and the effects of

[10] *Ibid.* paras. 3, 4.
[11] *Ibid.* para. 5.
[12] *Ibid.* para. 6.

changes in taxation are among the events included in this category.

If a company follows the practice laid down in SSAP 17 and discloses in the notes to the accounts details of adjustable events, rather than disclose the information in the directors' report in accordance with the Act, a cross reference should appear in the document in which the information is not given. A company may of course show the information as required by both the Act and the Standard.

A non-adjustable event is a material post balance sheet event which does not require adjustment to be made in the financial statements. Disclosure of such an event should be made in a note to the accounts. A non-adjusting event can arise in one of two ways. The first possibility is that such an event arises after the balance sheet date and concerns conditions which did not exist at the financial year end. As the event did not exist before the balance sheet date, there are no adjustments which can be put through the accounts, but its materiality will be such that not to disclose details of the event would result in the financial statements giving a misleading impression. In order to determine whether such an event is of sufficient materiality to require disclosure, the Standard advises that regard should be had to all matters, which will affect the ability of the users of the financial statements to assess the company's financial position. The second possibility is that the event is either a reversal or a maturity after the year end of a transaction entered into before the year end, and the substance of that transaction was primarily to alter the appearance of the company's balance sheet.

Examples of events which are usually treated as non-adjustable would be the issue of shares or debentures after the balance sheet date, the opening of new trading activities or the extension of existing ones after that date and the occurrence of strikes and other labour disputes, also after the balance sheet date.

Where a post balance sheet event is of the non-adjustable type, the notes to the accounts should disclose the nature of the event and an estimate of its financial effect. Should it not be possible to give an estimate, that fact should be noted.

Likely future developments   The directors' report must give an indication of likely future developments in the business of the company and of its subsidiaries.[13] The wording of the Act gives directors freedom to interpret this requirement as they wish, although, as the auditors are required to consider whether the directors' report is consistent with the annual accounts,[14] there is a check on extravagant forecasts. Listed companies should pay particular heed to how this section of their directors' report is phrased, for if it can be construed as a profits forecast, the Stock Exchange will require an accountants' report upon it. Also, the Stock Exchange's Continuing Obligations state that if the forecast differs materially from actual performance, the difference should be explained in the following year's financial statements.[15] In

---

[13] *Ibid.*
[14] *Ibid.* s.237(6).
[15] See pp. 49–50 below.

1975, the Stock Exchange advised that it would consider that a profits forecast had been made whenever it became possible, by using the wording of any statement "in conjunction with published data, to arrive at an approximate figure for future profits by an arithmetical process."

Research and development   An indication must be given in the directors' report of any activities of the company and its subsidiaries in the field of research and development.[16] As the Act does not specify what information should be disclosed under this heading, a broadly worded review of research and development projects could be given so as to avoid disclosing too much information to competitors.

There is no statutory definition of the terms "research" or "development." SSAP 13, "Accounting for Research and Development," however, uses three broad categories, namely:

"(a) Pure (or basic) research: original investigation undertaken in order to gain new scientific or technical knowledge and understanding. Basic research is not primarily directed towards any specific practical aim or application;

(b) Applied research: original investigation undertaken in order to gain new scientific or technical knowledge and directed towards a specific practical aim or objective;

(c) Development: the use of scientific or technical knowledge in order to produce new or substantially improved materials, devices, products, processes, systems or services prior to the commencement of commercial production."

Expenses related to the locating or exploitation of mineral deposits would not be classified as research and development expenditure, nor would expenditure which was reimbursable by third parties.

The Standard requires disclosure, but not necessarily in the directors' report, of the movements on deferred development expenditure and the amount carried forward at the beginning and the end of the financial period. Deferred development should be disclosed separately and not included in current assets. In addition to this, the accounting policies applied to research and development will have to be shown in the financial statements.[17]

Acquisition of own shares   Disclosure is required in the following situations where a company acquires its own shares by:

(a) purchase;

(b) forfeiture or surrender in lieu of forfeiture, gift or in a reduction of capital duly made or by order of the court;

(c) retention of a beneficial interest in its own shares which have been acquired by a nominee of the company;

(d) retention of a beneficial interest in its own shares, which have been acquired by a person with the financial assistance of the company;

---

[16] Companies Act 1985, Sched. 7, para. 6.
[17] See also p. 59ff above.

(e) the subjecting of its shares to a lien or other charge permitted by statute.[18]

Where a company has purchased its own shares during the financial year, the directors' report must disclose:

(a) the number and nominal value of shares which the company has purchased during the year;
(b) the aggregate amount of the consideration paid for such shares; and
(c) the reasons for the company's purchase.[19]

Where the shares have been acquired by the company as set out in (b) to (d) above, the information required is:

(a) the number and nominal value of shares acquired during the financial year;
(b) the maximum number and nominal value of shares acquired, whether or not during that year, which are held at any time by the company or other person during that year;
(c) the number and nominal value of shares acquired, whether or not during that year, which are disposed of by the company or another person on the company's behalf, or cancelled by the company during that year; and
(d) where any shares have been disposed of by the company of the person who acquired them for money or money's worth, the amount or value of the consideration in each case.[20]

In respect of shares over which the company has exercised a lien or otherwise charged, the information to be shown is:

(a) the number and nominal value of the shares charged during the financial year;
(b) the maximum number and nominal value of shares, which having been so charged, are held at any time by the company during that year; it is not necessary for this requirement to apply for the shares to have been charged during the financial year to which the directors' report relates;
(c) the number and nominal value of the shares so charged, whether or not during that year, which are disposed of or cancelled by the company during that year; and
(d) the amount of the charge in each case.[21]

Where the above disclosure requirements provide for the number and nominal value of shares of any particular description to be given, the percentage of the called-up share capital, which shares of that description represent, must also be shown.[22]

Under the Stock Exchange's rules, a listed company must also give particulars of any shareholders' authority for the purchase by the company of its own shares existing at the end of the year. Where such purchases have been made or are proposed

---

[18] Companies Act 1985, Sched. 7, para. 7.
[19] *Ibid*. para. 8.
[20] *Ibid*.
[21] *Ibid*.
[22] *Ibid*.

to be made otherwise than through the market or by tender or partial offer to all shareholders, then the names of the sellers of such share purchased or proposed to be purchased by the company during the year must be disclosed. Further, if a company has purchased its own shares since the end of the financial year, or entered into any option or contract to make such purchases after that date, then equivalent information to that required by the Act should be given.[23]

Employee information   Information regarding the employment of disabled persons, arrangements for the health, safety and welfare at work of the company's employees and details of employee involvement in company must be given in the directors' report. In the case of group accounts, only the holding company need give this information, although in practice, many companies give these details for the whole group.

Employment of disabled persons   Where the average number of a company's employees exceeds 250, the directors must disclose the policy which the company has applied during the financial year towards the job applications received by them from disabled persons, having regard to the applicant's particular aptitudes and abilities. Also the policy regarding the continuing employment and training of those who become disabled whilst employed by the company and regarding the training, career development and promotion of other disabled employees must be detailed. Only disabled persons employed by the company to work wholly or mainly inside the United Kingdom are covered by these requirements, and for these purposes, "disabled persons" means the same as in the Disabled Persons (Employment) Act 1944.[24]

Health, safety and welfare at work   Directors are obliged to report on the arrangements in force in the financial year for "securing the health, safety and welfare at work of employees of the company and its subsidiaries." Information must also be given concerning the steps taken to protect "other persons against risks to health and safety ensuing out of or in connection with the activities at work of these employees." It is impossible to say what information will be necessary to satisfy these requirements as to date these provisions have not yet been brought into effect. When they are, the Secretary of State will specify those classes of company which have to supply information in their directors' reports under this heading, and any exemptions or modifications to the disclosure requirements. Transitional provisions may also be included.[25]

Employee involvement   Only companies whose employees on average exceed 250 in each week during the financial year must comply with the duty to include in their directors' report a statement concerning employee involvement. Where a company is obliged to give such a statement, the directors must describe

---

[23] See p. 53 above.
[24] Companies Act 1985, Sched. 7, para. 9.
[25] *Ibid.* para. 10.

the action that has been taken during the financial year to introduce, maintain or develop arrangements aimed at:

"(a) providing employees systematically with information on matters of concern to them as employees;

(b) consulting employees or their representatives on a regular basis so that the views of employees can be taken into account in making decisions which are likely to affect their interests;

(c) encouraging the involvement of employees in the company's performance through an employee's share scheme or by some other means;

(d) achieving a common awareness on the part of all employees of financial and economic factors affecting the performance of the company."

In the context of statements on employee involvement, the term "employee" does not include a person employed to work wholly or mainly outside the United Kingdom.[26]

Average number of employees

It will be seen that the disclosure requirements regarding disabled persons and employee involvement only apply to those companies employing an average of more than 250 employees. The average number of employees is calculated by adding together the number of employees employed in each week of the financial year (whether they were employed throughout a particular week or not), and dividing that total by the number of weeks in the financial year.[27]

Companies listed on the Stock Exchange are required to disclose additional information which is usually shown in their directors' reports. These requirements are set out on pages 49 to 53 above.

Audit

Whilst not subject to a full audit the directors' report must be consistent with the company's annual accounts. The auditors are required to check that this is so and to state in their report if they find any inconsistencies.[28]

Penalties

In the event of a directors' report not giving the necessary information, every person who was a director immediately before the end of the time limit for laying and delivering the accounts[29] will be guilty of an offence and liable to a fine. It will be a defence for a director who was in office at the requisite time to prove that he took all reasonable steps for securing compliance with the requirements in question.[30]

[26] *Ibid.* para. 11.
[27] *Ibid.* paras. 9, 11.
[28] *Ibid.* s.237(6) and p. 119 below.
[29] See p. 14ff above.
[30] Companies Act 1985, s.235(7).

13 AUDIT

Introduction

An auditors' report must be included with the accounts which are laid before the company in general meeting and delivered to the Registrar of Companies.[1] The report should be addressed to the members of the company[2] and it is, therefore, to them that the auditors owe their primary duty. It will, however, for reasons of practicality, be with the directors or officers of the company that the auditors consult regarding decisions affecting the accounts. In some instances, such as any change of formats,[3] legislation specifically gives the decision to the directors, but directors who are not expert in accounting matters could usefully call upon the experience of their auditors when deciding such questions.

Auditors' qualifications

Professional qualifications

Auditors are governed by law and by the rules of their professional bodies. To qualify as an auditor of a company, a person must be a member of one of the bodies listed below:

> Institute of Chartered Accountants in England and Wales
> Institute of Chartered Accountants of Scotland
> Chartered Association of Certified Accountants
> Institute of Chartered Accountants in Ireland.[4]

There is another group of people also entitled to act as auditors, namely those who have been so authorised by the Secretary of State.[5] This is, in effect, a residual category.

Independence

In addition to membership of one of the four accountancy bodies, a person who has certain close links with a company cannot act as its auditor. Such relationships are:

(a) an officer or servant of the company (an auditor of a company is not regarded as an officer or servant of it for these purposes);
(b) a person who is a partner of or in the employment of an officer or servant of the company; and
(c) a body corporate.[6]

If a person falls within the barred relationships, then not only may he not audit the company's accounts, but he is further disqualified from acting as auditor for any member of the group of companies of which the first company forms part.[7] Should a

---

[1] Companies Act 1985, s.239.
[2] *Ibid.* s.236(1).
[3] See p. 27 above.
[4] Companies Act 1985, s.389(1)(3).
[5] *Ibid.* s.389(1).
[6] *Ibid.* s.389(6).
[7] *Ibid.* s.389(7).

person become disqualified to act as auditor during the course of his appointment, he must vacate his post at once.[8]

A person who acts or continues to act as an auditor when he knows that he is not qualified so to do, will be guilty of an offence. An offence will also be committed if an auditor fails, without reasonable excuse, to give notice of vacating his office for reasons of disqualification. A person found guilty of either of these offences will be liable to a fine. Continued default will result in the imposition of a daily default fine.[9]

The professional bodies also require their members who act as auditors to have a greater degree of independence than that laid down by statute, for example, their members may not act as auditors of a company in which they hold shares.

Appointment of auditors

First auditors

The directors are entitled to appoint the company's first auditors at any time before the company's first general meeting at which accounts are laid and the auditors so appointed will hold office until the end of that meeting.[10] Failure of the directors to appoint auditors in this way will entitle the general meeting to make the appointment.[11]

Subsequent appointments

Subsequently, a company's auditors are normally recommended by the directors and appointed or re-appointed, as the case may be, by every general meeting at which accounts are laid. The auditors' appointment will then run from the end of that meeting to the end of the next general meeting at which accounts are laid.[12]

Casual vacancies

To take account of vacancies occurring in mid-term, the directors or the company in general meeting may fill any casual vacancy. The surviving or continuing auditor will continue to act during any vacancy.[13] Any appointment made mid-term will, in due course, be voted on at the next general meeting at which accounts are laid, when it can either be confirmed or new auditors appointed.

Failure to appoint

If a general meeting, at which auditors should be appointed, fails to make such an appointment, the Secretary of State may appoint a person to fill the vacancy. A company is under a duty to inform the Secretary of State of the failure of a general meeting to appoint an auditor within one week of the meeting at which the appointment should have been made. Failure to notify is an offence resulting in the company and any officer in default being liable to a fine and for continuing contravention to a daily default fine.[14]

Remuneration

Having appointed its auditors, the company in general meeting must decide upon the amount of remuneration to be paid to them.[15] As it is possible for the company in general meeting to

[8] *Ibid.* s.389(9).
[9] *Ibid.* s.389(10).
[10] *Ibid.* s.384(2).
[11] *Ibid.* s.384(3).
[12] *Ibid.* s.384(1).
[13] *Ibid.* s.384(4).
[14] *Ibid.* s.384(5).
[15] *Ibid.* s.385(1).

decide on an alternative method of arriving at the auditors' remuneration, the directors of a company could be given authority in the company's Articles of Association to decide this question. For these purposes, remuneration will include expenses.[16] If, however, the auditors were appointed by the directors, statute authorises the directors to fix their remuneration, or the Secretary of State may do so, in the rare cases in which he makes the appointment.[17] The amount of the auditors' remuneration, however it is arrived at, must be disclosed in a note to a company's profit and loss account. In this case also, remuneration will include the amount of any expenses paid by the company to its auditors.[18]

Auditors' duties

Audit report The function of the auditors is set by statute and it is to:

> "report to the members on the accounts examined by them and on every balance sheet and profit and loss account, and on all group accounts, copies of which are to be laid before the company in general meeting during the auditors' tenure of office."[19]

The auditors' report must contain the auditors' opinion on the following topics:

(a) whether the balance sheet, profit and loss account and group accounts (if any) have been properly prepared in accordance with the Companies Act 1985;

(b) whether the balance sheet gives a true and fair view of the state of the company's affairs at the end of the financial year;

(c) whether the profit and loss account (if not presented as a consolidated account) gives a true and fair view of the company's profit or loss for the financial year; and

(d) whether the group accounts (if any) give a true and fair view of the state of affairs and profit or loss of the holding company and its subsidiaries dealt with by those accounts, so far as concerns the members of the holding company.[20]

The phrase "true and fair" is central to the auditors' report and has been discussed in Chapter 5. Auditors who are members of the professional bodies which belong to the Consultative Committee of Accountancy Bodies are also obliged to ensure that the best accounting practice as set out in the Statements of Standard Accounting Practice has been followed. In the case of significant departures from the Standards, the onus is on the auditors to ensure that such departures are disclosed and where they concur with the departures, either expressly or impliedly, they must justify them.

When an auditor is satisfied that statutory and non statutory

[16] *Ibid.* s.385(3).
[17] *Ibid.* s.385(2).
[18] *Ibid.* Sched. 4, para. 53.
[19] *Ibid.* s.236(1).
[20] *Ibid.* s.236(2).

provisions have been met, the audit report will be drafted.
Should an auditor find himself unable to report affirmatively on
all the above matters, his report will be qualified if the matter in
doubt is material.

A qualification will generally result either from uncertainty
or from an auditors' disagreement with the way in which the
financial statements have been prepared or with their contents.
Where uncertainty prevents an auditor from forming an opinion
on a matter, the qualification may be a "subject to" opinion. If
the matter is material but not fundamental, or if it is a
fundamental issue, the qualification will take the form of a
disclaimer of opinion. In a "subject to" opinion, an auditor
effectively disclaims an opinion on a particular matter which is
not fundamental, whereas in a disclaimer of opinion, he will state
that he is unable to form an opinion as to whether the financial
statements give a true and fair view. In the event that an auditor
does not agree with the way in which the financial statements
have been prepared and the matter is not rationalised by
discussion with the company's directors, the qualification will
either be an "except" opinion where the matter is material but
not fundamental, or an adverse opinion where it is fundamental.
An "except" opinion is one in which an auditor expresses an
adverse opinion on a particular matter; whereas, in an adverse
opinion, he will state that in his opinion, the financial statements
do not give a true and fair view.

The auditor has further responsibilities placed upon him by
statute and these responsibilities in their turn impose certain
duties upon the company whose accounts are being audited.
Those responsibilities and duties are set out below.

Accounting records investigation   An auditor must carry out such investigations as are
necessary for him to form an opinion as to whether:

(a) the company has kept proper accounting records and that
proper returns adequate for his audit have been received
from branches not visited by him, and

(b) the company's balance sheet and (if not consolidated) its
profit and loss account are in agreement with the
accounting records and returns.

If his investigations reveal failure by the company in any or all of
these respects, the auditor is required to state the fact in his
report.[21]

Access to papers   In carrying out his work, the auditor has the right of access
at all times to the company's books, accounts and vouchers.
Should he require further information or explanation then the
auditor may question the company's officers. It is for the auditor
to decide what information is required and not for the company's
officers to supply what they consider to be necessary. The auditor
has to decide what, to the best of his knowledge and belief, is
needed for the purposes of his audit. Any failure to obtain all the
necessary information and explanation has to be disclosed by the
auditor in his report.[22] It is an offence for an officer of the
company to knowingly or recklessly make a statement to the
auditor which is misleading, false or deceptive in a material

---

[21] *Ibid*. s.237(1)(2).
[22] *Ibid*. s.237(3)(4).

particular. An officer found guilty of such an offence will be subject to imprisonment or a fine, or both.[23]

Where the accounts of a group of companies is being audited, any group subsidiary which is incorporated in Great Britain is under the duty to give the auditor of the holding company such information and explanation as he may reasonably require for the purposes of his duties as auditor of the holding company. The subsidiary's own auditor is also required to provide such information. The auditor of the holding company may require the holding company to take any reasonable steps to obtain from a subsidiary such information and explanation as he requires.[24] Failure by a subsidiary or its holding company to comply with these requirements will render the company and any officer of it who is in default, guilty of an offence and liable to a fine. An auditor of a subsidiary who fails to assist the holding company's auditor will also be guilty of an offence and liable to a fine.[25]

Particulars of employees and directors

An auditor is under an obligation to report if a company's accounts fail to give the required particulars regarding:

(a) the chairman's and directors' emoluments, pensions and compensation for loss of office[26];
(b) higher paid employees[27]; and
(c) directors' and officers' loans and certain other transactions.[28]

If these items have not been included, the auditor is obliged to give those particulars so far as he is able.[29]

Directors' report

A further duty of an auditor is "to consider whether the information given in the directors' report for the financial year for which the accounts are prepared is consistent with those accounts . . . "[30] Two matters should be noted with regard to this duty. First, that an auditor is not required to check the accuracy of the directors' report but only *its consistency with the accounts* to which it is attached and secondly, that an auditor is only required to report on any inconsistencies he finds. Thus, for example, the fact that the directors misreported the degree of employee involvement in the company would not strictly have to be reported by the auditor as there is nothing in the accounts with which it could be said to be inconsistent. How far, however, directors could be over optimistic in their forecasts of the company's future would be question of degree for the auditor's discretion as to when the accounts could not be said to support a wildly optimistic view of the future.

General meetings

In addition to his right to receive what information he thinks necessary for the carrying out of his work, an auditor is also entitled to attend any general meeting of the company. At the meeting, he may speak on any part of the business of the meeting which concerns him as auditor. When sending out any papers

[23] *Ibid.* s.393.
[24] *Ibid.* s.392(1).
[25] *Ibid.* s.392(2).
[26] See p. 89ff above.
[27] See p. 93ff above.
[28] See Chap. 15.
[29] Companies Act 1985, s.237(5).
[30] *Ibid.* s.237(6).

relating to general meetings, such as notices of those meetings, the company should also send them to its auditor.[31] As the auditors also have the right of access to the company's minute books,[32] they should be fully informed as to the proceedings of directors' meetings (and of managers' meetings if any) as minutes of these meetings are required to be kept by the company.[33]

Detection of fraud   Another task of an auditor which is at present under much discussion is the detection of fraud. It is not a statutory requirement that an auditor should carry out his investigation in such a way as to discover fraud and the courts have said, in this respect, that an auditor should be likened to a watch dog and not to a bloodhound.[34] The Government is, however, keen that auditors should take a more active role in uncovering fraud. At present, the usual course of action is to report any fraudulent act noted to the company's directors, or in extreme cases, where proof of a crime is available, and the directors refuse to act, report may be made to the company in general meeting, as well as to the police.

Change of auditors

Removal by company   A company may remove its auditor before the expiration of his term of office by means of an ordinary resolution to that effect,[35] although special notice of the resolution must be given.[36] A company may remove its auditor notwithstanding anything to the contrary in any agreement between him and the company.[37] An auditor is not, therefore, guaranteed security of appointment but if any contract which he has with the company is broken, he may of course seek compensation for the breach.[38] He may not insist upon re-appointment.

A company which does remove its auditor mid-term must, within 14 days of passing the requisite resolution, notify the Registrar of Companies of the fact, in the prescribed form. The company and any officer who fails to meet this requirement is liable to a fine and, for continued contravention, to a daily default fine.[39]

On receiving the special notice of the resolution proposing his removal, an auditor may make written representations, of a reasonable length, to the company. These representations must then be circulated to company members by the company[40] or, where this is not possible, the representations may be read to the meeting at which the auditors' removal is considered.[41]

The company is protected from an auditor who seeks to abuse his rights in order "to secure needless publicity for

---

[31] Companies Act 1985, s.387(1).
[32] See p. 118 above.
[33] Companies Act 1985, s.382(1).
[34] *Re Kingston Cotton Mill Co.* (No.2) [1896] 2 Ch. 279.
[35] Companies Act 1985, s.386(1).
[36] *Ibid.* s.388(1).
[37] *Ibid.* s.386(1).
[38] *Ibid.* s.386(3).
[39] *Ibid.* s.386(2).
[40] *Ibid.* s.388(2)(3).
[41] *Ibid.* s.388(4).

defamatory matter." In these circumstances, the company or any other person claiming to be aggrieved may apply to the court for an order that notification of the existence and contents of the auditor's representations need not be issued and the court may further order that the whole or part of the company's costs be paid by the auditor.[42]

Resignation   Apart from being removed by the company, an auditor's relationship with a company may be ended by the auditor's resignation. Written notice of his resignation must be deposited by the auditor at the company's registered office and it will take effect from the date it is deposited, unless a later date is specified in the notice. The notice must state whether or not there are circumstances connected with the resignation which should be brought to the attention of the company's members and if there are any, details of such circumstances.[43] The company then has 14 days within which to send a copy of the notice to the Registrar of Companies and to copy any relevant information about the resignation to those members entitled to receive copies of the accounts.[44] Once again, the court has power to stop publication if it is satisfied that the auditor is abusing his rights. The company and any officer in default will be liable to a fine and for continuing contravention, to a daily default fine, if they fail to notify the Registrar of Companies or the company's members of the auditor's resignation as necessary. This also applies should the company breach any order the court may make as to the circulation of a statement setting out the effect of any ruling it gives.[45]

When a resigning auditor believes that there are matters about which company members ought to know, he may also requisition an extraordinary meeting of the company, for the purpose of considering the circumstances of his resignation. He may then prepare a written statement of reasonable length setting out the reasons for his resignation which the company must circulate before any general meeting when it is is proposed to appoint a replacement auditor or the general meeting convened by the auditor himself.[46] The company must then inform the members that such a statement has been issued and send a copy of the statement to members who are entitled to receive a notice of meeting. The company is relieved from this obligation if the auditor's statement is received too late for the company to comply with the requirements.[47] The company then has 21 days from the deposit of the auditor's requisition to call a meeting, which must be held within 28 days of the notice convening the meeting. Every director who does not take all reasonable steps to meet these requirements is liable to a fine.[48] A resigning auditor has similar rights to those of an auditor removed by the company to be informed of and to attend a meeting at which his resignation is to be considered. He may also put his reasons for resigning to

---

[42] *Ibid*. s.388(5).
[43] *Ibid*. s.390(1)(2).
[44] *Ibid*. s.390(3).
[45] *Ibid*. s.390(4)(5)(7).
[46] *Ibid*. s.391(1)(2).
[47] *Ibid*. s.391(3).
[48] *Ibid*. s.391(4).

that meeting. The Court may order his silence if he is abusing these rights.[49]

Non approval   An auditor will cease to act as auditor where he has been appointed by the directors and his appointment has not been approved by the general meeting. In this case the meeting should agree the appointment of an alternative auditor, or in the absence of such agreement, notify the Secretary of State of its failure to make an appointment, where upon the Secretary of State may nominate an auditor instead.[50]

Dormant companies

As has been seen, it is the general rule that all companies must produce annual accounts, which must then be audited. There is, however, a special exemption with regard to the audit requirement for companies which have been dormant during a financial year. The right not to appoint an auditor, where a
Special resolution   company is dormant must be exercised by special resolution passed by the company at the general meeting at which its accounts for that year are laid.[51] Once the resolution has been passed, it does not have to be renewed annually. If, however, the dormant period ends, an auditor will have to be appointed.[52] If the company has been dormant since its incorporation, the resolution should be passed at its first general meeting.[53]

Qualifying conditions   Those companies which wish to claim exemption from audit must, in addition to passing the requisite resolution, meet certain conditions. Public companies and special category companies, however, even if they can comply with the conditions, are not permitted to take advantage of these provisions.[54] The qualifying conditions are as follows:

(a) the financial year for which the exemption from audit is sought must not be a year for which directors are required to lay group accounts[55];

(b) the directors must be entitled to deliver modified accounts[56] for that financial year if they so wish; if a company meets the conditions enabling it to deliver modified accounts but is prevented from so doing because it is a member of an ineligible group, it may still take advantage of the dormant company rules[57];

(c) the company has been dormant since the end of the financial year.[58]

Dormant   For these purposes, a company will be classified as dormant if no significant accounting transaction has occurred during the requisite period. A significant accounting transaction is one

[49] *Ibid*. s.391(5)(6)(7). See pp. 120–121 above.
[50] *Ibid*. s.384(5).
[51] *Ibid*. s.252(1)(2).
[52] *Ibid*. s.252(6).
[53] *Ibid*. s.252(3).
[54] *Ibid*. s.252(4). For special category companies see p. 3 above.
[55] *Ibid*. s.252(2).
[56] See p. 30ff above.
[57] Companies Act 1985, s.252(2).
[58] *Ibid*.

which must be entered in the company's accounting records.[59] This will include any sum of money received or expended by the company, but a transaction whereby a subscriber to the memorandum of a company takes shares in pursuance to an undertaking of his in the memorandum, will not be classed as a significant transaction.[60]

Re-appointment of auditors

Any period of dormancy will end with the occurrence of a significant accounting transaction and the company will then have to appoint an auditor for that financial year.[61] An auditor will also have to be appointed if the company fails to meet any of the other conditions during that period.[62] When the exemption is lost, the directors must appoint an auditor before the next company meeting at which the accounts are to be laid or, if they fail to do so, the company in general meeting may make such an appointment.[63]

Audit report

Where a company meets the criteria in respect of any one financial year and passes a special resolution sanctioning the non appointment of auditors, it follows that an audit report need not be included with the accounts laid before the company in general meeting or delivered to the Registrar of Companies.[64] The directors, however, must include a statement in the balance sheet, placed immediately above their signatures, to the effect that the company was dormant throughout the financial year.[65] If the company is delivering modified accounts[66] to the Registrar of Companies, the directors' statement relating to those accounts, as well as the auditors' special report, may be omitted.[67]

Directors' statement

---

[59] For accounting records, see pp. 6–8 above.
[60] Companies Act 1985, s.252(5).
[61] *Ibid.* s.252(5)(6).
[62] *Ibid.* s.252(6).
[63] *Ibid.* s.252(7).
[64] *Ibid.* s.253(1)(2).
[65] *Ibid.* s.253(3).
[66] See p. 30ff above.
[67] Companies Act 1985, s.253(3).

14 FINANCIAL ASSISTANCE AND A COMPANY'S ACQUISITION OF ITS OWN SHARES

Introduction

Companies may not as a general rule give financial assistance to a third party who intends using that money to acquire shares in the company. The original purpose of this prohibition was to prevent certain forms of asset stripping but the form of the prohibition proved to be too wide and was amended by the Companies Act 1981 and subsequently consolidated in the 1985 Act. While companies may not still provide financial assistance enabling a third party to purchase the company's shares, certain types of transaction which are deemed to be of an acceptable nature are permitted.

The Companies Act 1981 also saw the introduction of provisions allowing companies to acquire their own shares, whether by redemption or purchase. Before this, companies were restricted to issuing redeemable preference shares where it was wished to reduce the capital base at some future date. A company wishing to acquire its own shares will have to comply with detailed conditions which are ensuring that the company's solvency will not be adversely affected by the acquisition. In addition, members of the company are given the opportunity to challenge the acquisition if they so desire.

Financial assistance

General prohibition There is a general prohibition on companies providing financial assistance to a person who is acquiring or who is proposing to acquire shares in that company, whether that assistance is given directly or indirectly. Where a person is acquiring shares in a holding company, a subsidiary of that holding company is also prohibited from assisting financially with such an acquisition.[1] In addition, companies or their subsidiaries are not allowed to discharge or reduce a person's obligation to pay for such shares **Penalties** once the acquisition has taken place.[2] A company which contravenes these rules, or an officer of it who is in default, will be liable to a fine. A defaulting officer will also be liable to imprisonment, which may be in addition to a fine.[3]

---

[1] Companies Act 1985, s.151(1).
[2] *Ibid.* s.151(2).
[3] *Ibid.* s.151(3).

Definition   "Financial assistance" is defined in wide terms by the Act, and may be given by way of gift, guarantee, security or indemnity, loan or other similar arrangement. The definition also includes any other financial assistance which reduces the donor company's net assets to a material extent or any financial assistance given by a company which has no net assets.[4]

This wide definition would catch all manner of acceptable transactions, such as a declaration of dividends, were it not for the fact that certain exemptions to the rule have been made. The exemptions fall into two categories, general and specific. The **General** general exemption permits any company to give financial **exemptions** assistance for the purpose of any acquisition of shares in it or its holding company if:

    (a) the purpose in giving the assistance was not the main objective but an incidental part of some larger purpose; and

    (b) the assistance was given in good faith in the interests of the company.[5]

Specific   The specific exemptions relate to various arrangements **exemptions** which are of an acceptable nature. These include a lawful declaration of dividends, the allotment of bonus shares and the giving of financial assistance where shares have been acquired in accordance with an employees' share scheme.[6]

Any company may enter into any of the activities within the **Public companies** specific exemptions but a public company may only take advantage of certain of these exemptions, for example, the acquisition of shares under an employees' share scheme, if its net assets are not thereby be reduced. If those assets are reduced by such transaction, the assistance must be provided out of distributable profits.[7] For these purposes, "net assets" means the amount by which the aggregate of the company's assets exceeds the aggregate of its liabilities. The term "liabilities" also includes contingent liabilities. The amount of both assets and liabilities must be taken from the company's accounting records immediately before the financial assistance is given. This will mean that a public company may not necessarily use its last audited balance sheet in order to see whether or not it complies, but must bring the amounts of its assets and liabilities up to date if financial assistance is to be given after the last audited balance sheet date.[8]

Private companies   In addition to the general and specific exceptions set out above, a private company is given considerable freedom to provide financial assistance for the acquisition of its own shares, or shares in its holding company if that company is also a private company. Where that holding company is a subsidiary of another company, that other must also be a private company. The power to provide financial assistance can only be exercised by a private company if it complies with certain conditions.[9] Those conditions are aimed at ensuring that the company's capital is not adversely

---

[5] *Ibid.* s.153(1)(2).
[6] *Ibid.* s.153(3)(4).
[7] *Ibid.* s.154(1); for distributable profit see Chap. 11.
[8] *Ibid.* s.154(2).
[9] *Ibid.* s.155(1)(3).

affected by the provision of such financial assistance and that the company's members have an opportunity to vote on the matter. The details of these conditions are set out in the following paragraphs.

Protection of capital

The company's net assets must not be reduced by the provision of financial assistance. If they are reduced, the amount thereby reduced must be provided for out of distributable profits. The term "net assets" bears the same meaning as in page 125 above.[10]

Members' approval

The provision of financial assistance must be sanctioned by special resolution of the company in general meeting. This condition does not apply if the company giving the financial assistance is a wholly owned subsidiary.[11]

Where the financial assistance is for the acquisition of shares in a company's holding company, the company wishing to provide the assistance must pass the necessary special resolution. A special resolution must also be passed by the holding company and any other intermediate holding company which stands between the company providing the assistance and the holding company in which the shares are to be acquired. Only wholly-owned subsidiaries need not pass the requisite resolution.[12]

Timing of approval

If a special resolution is required in order to approve the provision of financial assistance, it must be passed on the date on which the directors make their statutory declaration (see below). Alternatively, the resolution must be passed within one week of that date.[13]

Effective approval

A special resolution will only be effective if the directors' statutory declaration and the auditors' report which must be annexed to it (see below), are open to inspection by the company's members at the meeting at which the resolution is passed.[14]

The resolution may, however, be challenged in court and if the court orders its cancellation, it will not then be effective.[15] In order to institute such a challenge, the holders of not less in aggregate than 10 per cent. in nominal value of the company's issued share capital, or any class of it, must apply to the court. In the case of a company not limited by shares, the requirement is for the application to be made by 10 per cent. of the company's members. A person who has consented to or voted for the resolution may not be included among those making the application. The application must be made within 28 days of the passing of the resolution and the requirements which govern the challenging of special resolutions generally, such as the duty placed upon a company to notify the Registrar of Companies of the application to the court, also apply.[16]

Directors' declaration

The directors of the company providing the assistance are required to make a statutory declaration. Where shares are to be acquired in the company's holding company, the directors of that holding company and of any intermediate holding company are

[10] *Ibid.* s.155(2).
[11] *Ibid.* s.155(4).
[12] *Ibid.* s.155(5).
[13] *Ibid.* s.157(1).
[14] *Ibid.* s.157(4)
[15] *Ibid.*
[16] *Ibid.* s.157(2)(3).

also obliged to make such a declaration.[17] No exception is made for the directors of wholly owned subsidiaries. The statutory declaration must give particulars of the assistance to be given and of the business of the company of which they are directors, as well as the identity of the person to whom the financial assistance is to be given.[18] The declaration must also state that the directors have formed the following opinions:

(a) that immediately following the date on which the assistance is proposed to be given, there will be no ground on which the company could then be found to be unable to pay its debts; and either

(b) if it is intended to commence the winding up of the company within 12 months of the date on which the assistance is proposed to be given, that the company will be able to pay its debts in full within 12 months of the commencement of the winding up; or

(c) in any other case, that the company will be able to pay its debts as they fall due during the year immediately following that date; in other words, that the company will remain solvent for a year after the assistance has been granted.[19]

In determining whether or not a company is able to pay its debts as they fall due, the directors must consider the same liabilities as are relevant when deciding in a winding up by the court, whether or not a company can pay its debts. These liabilities include contingent and prospective liabilities.[20]

Penalties   Any director who makes the statutory declaration without having reasonable grounds for the opinion expressed in it, will be liable to imprisonment, a fine or both.[21]

Auditors' report   An auditors' report, addressed to the directors, must be annexed to the directors' declaration. In their report, the auditors must state that they have inquired into the affairs of the company and that they are unaware of anything which indicates that any part of the directors' statement is unreasonable in all the circumstances.[22]

The directors' statutory declaration, along with the auditors' report must then be delivered to the Registrar of Companies.
Filing of documents   These documents should be accompanied, where appropriate, by a copy of any special resolution which has been passed approving the grant of financial assistance. A copy of the special resolution is required to be registered with the Registrar of Companies in any event under section 380 of the Act. Delivery of these papers must take place within 15 days of the special resolution being passed or if a special resolution is not required, within 15 days of the directors' declaration.[23]

Penalties   If the Registrar of Companies is not furnished with copies of the requisite documents, the company and every officer of it who

---

[17] *Ibid.* s.155(6).
[18] *Ibid.* s.156(1); see also S.I. 1985 No. 854.
[19] *Ibid.* s.156(2).
[20] *Ibid.* s.156(3).
[21] *Ibid.* s.156(7).
[22] *Ibid.* s.156(4).
[23] *Ibid.* s.156(5).

is in default will be liable to a fine. Continuing contravention will lead to a daily default fine being imposed.[24]

Time limits   Financial assistance must be given within certain time limits. Where a special resolution approving the provision of such assistance is needed, the assistance may not be given until four weeks has expired, beginning with the date on which the special resolution was passed. If more than one such resolution is passed, the four weeks will run from the date on which the last of them was passed. The assistance may be given before the four week limit if the resolution, or each resolution, as the case may be, was passed unanimously.[25] The purpose of this requirement is to allow any dissident shareholders to bring their complaints before the court. Where members of the company have applied to the court, challenging the special resolution regarding the provision of financial assistance, the assistance may not be given before the final determination of the application or until such time as the court may order.[26] The financial assistance must then be given within eight weeks of:

(a) the date on which the directors of the company providing the assistance made their statutory declaration;

(b) where more than one statutory directors' declaration is required, the date on which the earliest of those declarations is made; or

(c) the failure of an application to the court to quash a special resolution approving the financial assistance, or any other date which the court orders.[27]

If the above conditions are met, a company may give financial assistance for the purchase of its own shares or of the shares of its holding company.

Acquisition by a company of its own shares

A company, which is limited by shares or limited by guarantee and having a share capital, may either redeem or purchase its own shares if it complies with certain conditions. The conditions common to both the redemption and purchase of a company's own shares are set out below.

Authorisation   The company must be authorised by its articles of association to redeem or purchase its own shares.[28] In the case of the purchase of shares, the authority should include the purchase of any redeemable shares. Companies which have adopted, unamended, the Table A articles of association introduced in 1985, will have authority to purchase their own shares, including any redeemable shares, already included.[29] Those companies which adopted the Table A set out in the Companies Act 1948 will not have such authority included in their articles of association. These articles should be amended accordingly if such power is required.

---

[24] *Ibid.* s.156(6).
[25] *Ibid.* s.158(1)(2).
[26] *Ibid.* s.158(3).
[27] *Ibid.* s.158(1)(4).
[28] *Ibid.* ss.159(1), 162(1).
[29] S.I. 1985 No. 805 as amended by S.I. 1985 No. 1052.

Remaining shares   A company may not acquire its own shares if, as a result of the acquisition it would have no other shares left or only redeemable shares.[30]

Fully paid up shares   The shares which are to be acquired must be fully paid.[31] The terms of the redemption or purchase must include provision for payment on acquisition.[32] Only certain funds are available to meet the cost of acquisition. This is discussed in more detail below.

Cancellation of shares   On acquisition, the shares acquired must be treated as cancelled. The nominal value of the shares will then have to be deducted from the company's issued share capital, but this will not reduce the amount of the company's authorised share capital. Where a company is about to acquire its own shares, it may issue shares up to the nominal value of the shares acquired, as if those shares had never been issued.[33]

Available funds   **Funds from which the acquisition may be made**   A company is only allowed to acquire its own shares if it can do so without adversely affecting its remaining capital. This is achieved by restricting the funds from which the acquisition may be made. Private companies are, however, given more discretion in this matter than public companies. These rules do not affect the acquisitions of shares in the event of the company being wound up before the acquisition is completed.[34]

Companies, both private and public, may acquire their own shares from their distributable profits for acquisition purposes or from the proceeds of a fresh issue of shares made for the purpose of the acquisition.[35] In addition to this, a private company may use its capital to fund an acquisition, and this is discussed below.

Share premiums   Any premium payable on acquisition must be paid out of distributable profits.[36] If the shares were originally issued at a premium, any premium payable on acquisition may also be funded out of the proceeds of a fresh issue of shares made for the purposes of acquisition but only up to a certain amount. That amount is the lesser of either, the aggregate of the premiums received by the company on the issue of the shares to be acquired, or the current amount of the company's share premium account. Any amount transferred to that account in respect of premiums on the new shares may also be used. An equivalent of the amount paid from the proceeds of a fresh issue of shares in respect of any premium payable on the acquired shares must be deducted from the company's share premium account.[37]

Capital redemption reserve   When a company redeems or purchases its own shares, a capital redemption reserve must be created. Where the acquisition has been made wholly out of the company's distributable profits, an amount representing the nominal value of the shares which have been cancelled as a result of the

---

[30] Companies Act 1985, ss.159(2), 162(3).
[31] *Ibid.* ss.159(3), 162(2).
[32] *Ibid.*
[33] *Ibid.* ss.160(4)(5), 162(2).
[34] *Ibid.* ss.160(1), 162(2).
[35] *Ibid.*
[36] *Ibid.*
[37] *Ibid.* ss.160(2), 162(2).

acquisition must be transferred to that reserve.[38] If the proceeds of a fresh issue of capital are used for the acquisition and the aggregate amount of those proceeds is less than the aggregate nominal value of the shares acquired, the amount of the difference must be transferred to the capital redemption reserve. Where the proceeds of a fresh issue are used in addition to a payment out of capital, this transfer need not be made, as separate provisions regarding the amount to be transferred in such an event apply.[39]

Payment out of capital

When a private company wishes to acquire its own shares, it may also fund the acquisition by a payment out of capital. In order to take advantage of this option, a company must be authorised by its articles of association to make a payment out of capital.[40] Once it has this authority, it would appear that a company must first use any available profits, before it makes a payment out of capital. This would seem to be the consequence of the statutory method of calculating the payment, which is referred to as the permissible capital payment.

Permissible capital payment

The permissible capital payment is defined as the difference between any available profits of the company, together with the proceeds of any fresh issue of shares made for the purposes of the acquisition and the acquisition price, thus suggesting that a company must first use its available profits before applying its capital.[41] For these purposes, a company's available profits are its distributable profits, although in order to calculate those profits, the following rules apply, rather than the provisions normally governing distributable profits which are set out in Chapter 11.[42]

The amounts which are to be used in calculating a company's available profits are its profits, losses, assets, liabilities, provisions for depreciation or diminution in value of assets, provisions for liabilities or charges and its share capital and reserves. In this context, a company's reserves includes its undistributable reserves. These amounts are to be taken from the

Relevant accounts

company's relevant accounts.[43] To classify as relevant accounts, the accounts must have been prepared as at any date within a three month period ending with the date on which the directors make their statutory declaration. Full annual accounts do not need to be prepared, only such accounts as are necessary to enable a reasonable judgment to be made as to the amounts comprising a company's available profits.[44] Should a company make a lawful distribution after the relevant accounts have been prepared but before the directors have made their statutory declaration, then the amount of available profit must be reduced accordingly.[45]

Qualifying conditions

Once a company has calculated its permissible capital payment, it must comply with certain conditions before the payment can lawfully be made. These conditions, which are set out in the following paragraphs, are aimed at ensuring that the

[38] *Ibid.* s.170(1).
[39] *Ibid.* s.170(2)(3); see also pp. 83–84 above.
[40] *Ibid.* s.171(1).
[41] *Ibid.* s.171(3).
[42] *Ibid.* s.172(1).
[43] *Ibid.* s.172(2).
[44] *Ibid.* s.172(3)(6); for directors' statutory declaration see p. 131 below.
[45] *Ibid.* s.172(4).

payment will not adversely affect the company's solvency. They also allow the company's members to vote on the matter.

Directors'
declarations

The company's directors are required to make a statutory declaration which specifies the amount of the permissible capital payment. They must state that they have made full inquiry into the affairs and prospects of the company which enables them to form an opinion on the following matters:

(a) that immediately following the date on which the permissible capital payment is proposed to be made, there will be no grounds on which the company could then be found unable to pay its debts, and

(b) that for the year immediately following that date, the company will be able to continue to carry on business as a going concern throughout that year.

In forming their opinion as to the solvency of the company in the year following the permissible capital payment, the directors are required to take into consideration their intentions regarding the management of the company's business during that year, and to the amount and character of the financial resources which will in their view be available to the company during that period.[46] In assessing the amount and character of the company's financial resources, a statement of the source and application of funds will be an important tool.[47]

Penalties

The directors should ensure that they have reasonable grounds for their opinion expressed in the statutory declaration. A director who does not have such grounds will have committed an offence and be liable to imprisonment, a fine, or both.[48]

Auditors' report

An auditors' report, addressed to the directors, must be annexed to the directors' statutory declaration. The auditors must report on the fact that they have inquired into the company's state of affairs. They must also state that, in their opinion, the permissible capital payment has been properly calculated in accordance with the statutory rules and that they are not aware of anything to indicate that the opinion expressed by the directors in their statutory declaration is not reasonable in all the circumstances.[49]

Members'
approval

The payment out of capital must be approved by special resolution of the company.[50] This resolution should be passed, either on the date on which the directors make their statutory declaration, or within the week immediately following that date.[51] Any member who holds shares to which the resolution relates should not vote on the resolution, the reason being that, if the resolution is only passed because of his vote, it will be ineffective.[52] The resolution will also be ineffective if the directors' statutory declaration and the auditors' report are not available for inspection by members at the meeting at which the resolution is passed.[53]

[46] *Ibid.* s.173(3)(4).
[47] See pp. 46–47 above.
[48] Companies Act 1985, s.173(6).
[49] *Ibid.* s.173(5).
[50] *Ibid.* s.173(2).
[51] *Ibid.* s.174(1).
[52] *Ibid.* s.174(2).
[53] *Ibid.* s.174(4).

Publicity
A company making a payment out of capital is further required to publicise the payment nationally, thereby allowing creditors the opportunity of objecting to the payment if they so wish. A notice giving details of the payment must appear in the Gazette and in a national newspaper within the week immediately following the date of the resolution. As an alternative to the requisite information being published in a national newspaper, the company may send a written notice containing the same information as would have otherwise been published, to each of its creditors.[54] The details which must be published are:

(a) the fact that the company has approved a payment out of capital for the purpose of acquiring its own shares; the notice should also specify whether the shares are to be purchased or redeemed or both, as the case may be;
(b) the amount of the permissible capital payment;
(c) the date on which the resolution was passed;
(d) the fact that the directors' statutory declaration and the auditors' report are available for inspection at the company's registered office; and
(e) the fact that any creditor of the company may challenge the making of the order in court, as long as the application to the court is made within the five weeks immediately following the date of resolution approving the payment.[55]

Filing of documents
In addition to the requirement to give national publicity to the payment out of capital, a copy of the directors' statutory declaration and of the auditors' report must be delivered to the Registrar of Companies. These documents must be filed, at the latest, by the day on which the company first publishes the required notice either in the Gazette or a national newspaper, whichever is the earlier.[56]

Inspection of documents
The statutory declaration and the auditors' report must then be kept at the company's registered office and open to inspection during business hours by any member or creditor of the company without charge. These documents must be so kept and available for inspection from the date that a payment out of capital was first publicised nationally until five weeks after the passing of the resolution approving the payment.[57] Failure to allow proper inspection of the statutory declaration and the auditors' report will result in the company and every officer of it who is in default being liable to a fine. In the event of continued contravention, a daily default fine will be imposed.[58] It is also within the court's power to order immediate inspection of the declaration or report when necessary.[59]

Time limits
Once the conditions relating to making a payment out of capital have been satisfied, a payment will only be valid if it is made within a specified period. That period is between five and seven weeks after the date of the resolution approving the payment.[60]

[54] *Ibid.* s.175(1)(2)(3).
[55] *Ibid.* s.175(1).
[56] *Ibid.* s.175(4)(5).
[57] *Ibid.* s.175(6).
[58] *Ibid.* s.175(7).
[59] *Ibid.* s.175(8).
[60] *Ibid.* s.174(1).

Objections   **Objections to payment out of capital** Any member who did not vote in favour of the resolution approving the payment out of capital and any creditor of the company has the right to apply to the court for the cancellation of the resolution. The application must be made within five weeks of the date on which the resolution was passed.[61] When such an application is made, the company must notify the Registrar of Companies of the fact and deliver an office copy of any subsequent court order to him. Failure to notify the Registrar as required will result in the company and any officer of it who is in default being liable to a fine, and to a daily default fine if the contravention continues.[62]

Capital   Where a payment out of capital is made, the company's
redemption capital redemption reserve may be affected. No adjustments to
reserve this reserve will be necessary if the amount of the payment is equivalent to the nominal amount of the shares acquired. If this is not the case, however, and the payment out of capital is less than the nominal amount of those shares, a sum representing the amount of the difference must be transferred to the capital redemption reserve.[63] Should the payment be greater than the nominal amount of the shares acquired, the following may be reduced by the difference between those two amounts:

(a) the capital redemption reserve, share premium account or fully paid share capital of the company, and

(b) any unrealised profits of the company for the time being standing to the credit of any existing revaluation reserve.

It is possible to reduce amounts in both these categories, but the aggregate of the reductions must not exceed the amount of the difference between the payment and the nominal amount of the shares acquired.[64] In the event of a company acquiring its own shares out of the proceeds of a fresh issue and a payment out of capital, these proceeds of the fresh issue must be added to the payment out of capital when calculating whether or not there is a difference between the payment out of capital and the nominal amount of the shares acquired.[65]

Payments other   The rules so far discussed have dealt with the funds which
than purchase are available to meet the acquisition cost of the shares. Certain
price payments, however, apart from the purchase price, must be made out of a company's distributable profits. Those payments are consideration for:

(a) the acquisition of any right with respect to the purchase of any of its own shares under a contingent purchase contract[66];

(b) the variation of an off-market or a contingent purchase contract[67]; or

(c) the release of any of the company's obligations with respect to the purchase of any of its own shares under a

---

[61] *Ibid.* s.176(1).
[62] *Ibid.* s.176(3)(4).
[63] *Ibid.* s.171(4).
[64] *Ibid.*s.171(5); for revaluation reserve see also pp. 83–84 above.
[65] *Ibid.* s.171(6).
[66] For contingent purchase contract see p. 136 below.
[67] For off-market and market purchase see p. 134 above.

contingent purchase contract or under a off-market or market contract.[68]

If distributable profits are not used in respect of these transactions, purchases in pursuance of a contingent purchase contract or in pursuance of a variation of an off-market or market contract will not be lawful. Any purported release of a company's obligations will be void.[69]

Purchase by a company of its own shares

Off-market purchase Where a company purchases its own shares, specific rules will apply depending on whether the purchase is an "off-market" or "market" purchase. A purchase will be regarded as "off-market" if

> "the shares either:
> (a) are purchased otherwise than on a recognised stock exchange, or
> (b) are purchased on a recognised stock exchange but are not subject to a marketing arrangement on that stock exchange."

Shares will be subject to a "marketing arrangement" if they are listed on that stock exchange, or if dealings in the shares can take place at any time on that stock exchange without the prior permission of the authority governing the exchange for individual transactions.[70]

Market purchase A "market" purchase of shares will be one which is made on a recognised stock exchange, other than a purchase of shares which are subject to a marketing arrangement. A purchase of shares on a recognised stock exchange which are subject to a marketing arrangement will, of course, be an off-market purchase.[71]

Off-market purchases

Members' approval Before a contract for an off-market purchase of shares is entered into, its terms must be authorised by a special resolution.[72] That authority may then be varied, revoked or from time to time renewed by special resolution.[73] The authority given to a public company, however, must specify the date on which it expires. The expiry date must not be later than 18 months after the date on which the resolution is passed. If the authority is subsequently renewed by special resolution, it can not be renewed for more than 18 months from the date on which the special resolution giving renewed authority passed.[74]

Anyone holding shares which are to be purchased by the company should not vote, either in person or by proxy, on any resolution which confers, varies, evokes or renews authority for the purchase, for if the resolution would not have been passed had he not voted, the resolution will be ineffective. This rule

---

[68] Companies Act 1985, s.168(1).
[69] *Ibid.* s.168(2).
[70] *Ibid.* s.163(1)(2).
[71] *Ibid.* s.163(3).
[72] *Ibid.* s.164(2).
[73] *Ibid.* s.164(3).
[74] *Ibid.* s.164(4).

applies whether or not such a shareholder votes in respect of the shares to be purchased on a poll or not.[75]

Inspection of contract

A resolution will also not be effective unless a copy of the proposed contract has been available for inspection by members of the company, at the company's registered office, for at least 15 days before the meeting at which the resolution is to be passed. A copy of the contract must also be available for inspection at the meeting itself. If the contract is not in writing, then members must have the chance to inspect a memorandum of its terms. The contract or the memorandum must specify the names of the holders of the shares which it is proposed to purchase or a written memorandum listing the names omitted from the contract itself must be annexed to the copy of the contract made available for inspection by members.[76]

Variation of contract

Once a contract has been approved by the company's members, it may only be varied if the members approved the variation before the revised contract is agreed. The same procedure for approving the original authority should be followed when the authority for the variation is sought, the only difference being that members should be able to inspect not only a copy of the altered terms, but also a copy of the original contract at least 15 days before the meeting at which the variation is to be approved, and at the meeting itself.[77]

Market purchase Members' approval

As with off-market purchases, a market purchase must also be authorised by the company in general meeting before the shares are bought.[78] The resolution granting authority need not, however, be a special resolution.

The resolution may either give general authority to make a market purchase or it may limit the authority to the purchase of shares of a particular class or description. Further, the resolution may, if required, impose conditions upon the exercise of that authority.[79]

Whether or not the authority given is general or limited, conditional or unconditional, the resolution must contain certain details. Those details are:

(a) the maximum number of shares authorised to be acquired;
(b) the maximum and minimum prices which may be paid for the shares must be set out in the resolution; and
(c) the date on which the authority is to expire, which date must not be more than 18 months after the date on which the resolution is passed.[80]

The requirement to state the maximum and minimum prices which may be paid for the shares may be satisfied either by specifying a particular sum, or by providing a basis or formula for calculating those accounts. If a basis or formula is given for the calculation, it must not involve reference to any person's discretion or opinion.[81]

If it is envisaged that a company might wish to purchase its

[75] *Ibid.* s.164(5).
[76] *Ibid.* s.164(6).
[77] *Ibid.* s.164(7).
[78] *Ibid.* s.166(1).
[79] *Ibid.* s.166(2).
[80] *Ibid.* s.166(3).
[81] *Ibid.* s.166(6).

own shares after the expiry date of the authority has passed, the terms of the authority should include permission for the company to make a contract of purchase which would or might be executed wholly or partly after its expiration. A purchase of shares after the expiry date would then be effective if the contract for the shares was concluded before that date.[82]

A company in general meeting may vary, revoke or from time to time renew the authority for the purchase of its own shares. Any subsequent authority should contain the same details as the original concerning the number of shares to be purchased, the maximum and minimum prices to be paid and the date on which the authority is to expire. The expiry date must not be later than 18 months after the passing of the resolution approving the market purchase.[83]

A resolution which confers authority on a company to purchase its own shares, or which varies, revokes or renews that authority should be sent to the Registrar of Companies within 15 days of the resolution being approved by the company.[84]

Contingent purchase contract   A contract, which does not amount to an agreement to purchase shares, but which confers rights on a company to purchase its own shares or obliges it so to do, is termed a contingent purchase contract.[85] A company wishing to enter into such a contract will have to obtain the approval of its members, as if it were a contract of purchase. If this is not done, the company will not be able to purchase its own shares in pursuance of the contract.[86]

Assignment   The rights of a company under a contract for the purchase of its own shares, whether it be an off-market or market purchase, or under a contingent purchase contract may not be assigned by **Release agreements** the company.[87] Any agreement by a company to release its rights under an off-market purchase or a contingent purchase contract must be approved in advance by a special resolution of the company before the agreement is entered into. Approval for a proposed release agreement must be given in the same way as approval for a proposed variation of an existing contract.[88]

Disclosure

Directors' report   When a company purchases its own shares certain disclosure obligations are placed upon it. First, details of the purchase must **Listed companies** be given in the directors' report.[89] Where a company is listed on the Stock Exchange, the disclosure obligations with which it must comply are wider than those imposed by statute.[90]

Return to Registrar   Secondly, a return must be made to the Registrar of Companies within the period of 28 days beginning with the date

---

[82] *Ibid.* s.166(5).
[83] *Ibid.* s.166(4).
[84] *Ibid.* s.166(7).
[85] *Ibid.* s.165(1).
[86] *Ibid.* s.165(2).
[87] *Ibid.* s.167(1).
[88] *Ibid.* s.167(2).
[89] See pp. 111–113 above.
[90] See pp. 53, 112–113 above.

on which any shares purchased by the company are delivered to it. The return must state the number and nominal value of each class of shares purchased and the date on which shares of each class were delivered to the company.[91] In the case of a public company the return must also show the aggregate amount paid by the company for the shares; and the maximum and minimum prices paid in respect of shares of each class purchased.[92] It is possible to include in a return particulars of share delivered to the company on different dates and under different contracts. Where this is done, the aggregate amount paid for the shares will be the aggregate amount paid for all the shares included in the return.[93]

Penalties

If a return is not made to the Registrar in compliance with the Act, every officer of the company who is in default will be liable to a fine. Continued contravention will result in a daily default fine being imposed.[94]

Retention of copy contracts

Where a company enters into a contingent purchase contract or an off-market or market purchase contract, a copy of the contract must be kept at the company's registered office. If the contract is not in writing, a memorandum of its terms must be kept instead. Companies are obliged to keep either a copy of the contract or a memorandum of its terms for a period of ten years, beginning with the date on which the purchase of all of the shares, which are the subject of the contract, is completed. Alternatively, the contract itself may determine the length of time which is to apply in this respect. These rules also apply to any variation of a contract, where a copy of that contract, or a memorandum of its terms, is required to be kept.[95]

Inspection

While either a copy of the contract (or any variation of it) or a memorandum of terms is kept at a company's registered office, it must be available for inspection by any member of the company and, if it is a public company, by any other person. The documents should be open for inspection during business hours free of charge.[96]

Penalties

If a company fails to keep the requisite copies or memoranda of their terms, as the case may be, at its registered office for the required period, or does not allow inspection according to the statutory provisions, the company and every officer of it who is in default will be liable to a fine. In the event of continuing contravention, a daily default fine will be imposed.[97] Should a person being refused the right to exercise his power of inspection, the court may order immediate inspection of the document concerned.[98]

Stamp duty

Where shares are issued in place of any shares acquired, stamp duty may be levied if the actual value of the new issue exceeds the value of the shares acquired at the date of the acquisition.[99]

---

[91] Companies Act 1985, s.169(1).
[92] *Ibid.* s.169(2).
[93] *Ibid.* s.169(3).
[94] *Ibid.* s.169(6).
[95] *Ibid.* s.169(4)(9).
[96] *Ibid.* s.169(5).
[97] *Ibid.* s.169(7).
[98] *Ibid.* s.169(8).
[99] *Ibid.* ss.161, 162(2).

Failure to acquire own shares

Where a company has, on or after June 15, 1982, either issued redeemable shares or agreed to purchase any of its own shares, it will not be liable in damages if it subsequently fails to acquire those shares.[1] This does not, however, affect any other right which a shareholder may have against the company, although the court may not order specific performance of a contract if the company is able to show that it is unable to meet the cost of the acquisition out of its distributable profits.[2]

If a company is wound up before it is able to acquire its own shares, the terms of the acquisition agreement may be enforced against the company. In the event of the acquisition agreement being enforced, any shares which are redeemed or purchased in pursuance of it must then be treated as cancelled.[3] Any consideration due to be paid by the company under the agreement will rank after all other debts and liabilities of the company (other than any to members in their character as such) and this will include any interest on the company's debts and liabilities which would otherwise have been due after the payment of all the company's other debts. If other shares carry rights (whether as to capital or income) which are preferred to the rights as to capital attaching to the shares which are the subject of the acquisition agreement, any amount due in satisfaction of those preferred rights will have priority over consideration due for the acquisition.[4] If, however, either the terms of the agreement provided for the acquisition to take place at a date later than that of the commencement of the winding up, or if the company, between the date on which the acquisition should have taken place and the beginning of the winding up, could not lawfully have made a distribution equal to the consideration due to be paid for the shares, then the agreement will not be enforced.[5]

[1] *Ibid.* s.178(1)(2).
[2] *Ibid.* s.178(3).
[3] *Ibid.* s.178(4).
[4] *Ibid.* s.178(6).
[5] *Ibid.* s.178(5).

15 TRANSACTIONS INVOLVING DIRECTORS AND OFFICERS

Introduction

Generally, a company may engage in any activity which is authorised by its objects clause. Statute has, however, sought to restrict a company's use of its resources for the benefit of its directors, so as to afford members and creditors of the company some protection from possible abuse. In addition to this, legislation requires disclosure of certain transactions involving directors and officers, so that the users of a company's accounts will be aware of how the company assets are being employed. For present purposes, this area is examined under three main headings:

— directors' loans, quasi-loans and credit transactions;
— other contracts and transactions involving directors; and
— officers' transactions.

Directors' loans, quasi-loans and credit transactions

In recent years, there has been an increase in the restrictions placed upon directors using their company's money for their own purposes. The present law, which is complex and far reaching, not only restricts the circumstances in which a director may use his company's funds but also requires disclosure of the particulars of transactions involving directors. The law on loans, quasi-loans and credit transactions applies both to directors and to shadow directors.[1] A shadow director is a person in accordance with whose directions or instructions the directors of a company are accustomed to act, other than a person who provides advice in a professional capacity.[2] It should also be noted that the Act talks in terms of a company granting a director, for example, a loan. Thus, should a company make a loan to a manager, who subsequently becomes a director, that loan will not become illegal merely because the borrower is now a director; although after the manager's appointment to the board, any alteration to the terms of that loan would be a contravention of the Act.

Prohibitions   There are three basic categories of transaction which are prohibited, although the prohibitions do not necessarily affect all companies. Those categories are loans, quasi-loans and credit transactions.

[1] Companies Act 1985, s.330(5).
[2] *Ibid.* s.741(2).

Loans

Loans are not defined by the Act. In *Champagne Perrier SA v. Finch Ltd* the court had to consider the meaning of the word "loan" as used in a company's articles of association. Walton J. took the dictionary meaning of the word and held that it meant "A sum of money lent for a time to be returned in money or money's worth."[3] It would seem unlikely that a different meaning would be given to the term in the present context and a loan can therefore be regarded as being used in its usual sense of one person lending money to another on the understanding that it will be repaid.

Quasi-loans

Quasi-loans are one step removed from loans. A quasi-loan is a transaction under which one party, who is known as the creditor, agrees to pay, or pays otherwise than in pursuance of an agreement, a sum for another, the borrower. It also covers an agreement to reimburse, or reimbursement made otherwise than in pursuance of an agreement, expenditure incurred by another party for the borrower.[4] The aim in restricting a company from entering into such an arrangement is to prevent the company getting round the prohibition on loans by arranging for the director to receive financial support from a third party. Thus if a company agrees to pay a director's house insurance and that director is under an obligation to repay the company in full within a year, then that would fall within in the definition of a quasi-loan. Another example would be where a director used his company's credit card to purchase items for himself and was then required to reimburse the company.

The definition of a quasi-loan is wide enough to encompass both the situation where the director is obliged to repay the company and also where he pays or reimburses an amount "otherwise than in pursuance of an agreement." Where repayment is made without the director being contractually obliged to do so, in order for there to be a quasi–loan the expenditure must be incurred by the company for the director "in circumstances giving rise to a liability on the (director) to reimburse the (company)."[5]

Credit transactions

The third category of prohibited arrangements is credit transactions. A credit transaction is defined as:

"a transaction under which one party ("the creditor")—
   (a) supplies any goods or sells any land under a hire purchase agreement or a conditional sale agreement;
   (b) leases or hires any land or goods in return for periodical payments;
   (c) otherwise disposes of land or supplied goods or services on the understanding that payment (whether in a lump sum or instalments or by way of periodical payments or otherwise) is to be deferred."[6]

A conditional sale agreement in this context bears the same meaning as in the Consumer Credit Act 1974.[7]

The term "understanding" in the third branch of the definition is particularly wide. No further guidance is given as to

---

[3] [1982] 3 All E.R. 713, 717.
[4] Companies Act 1985, s.331(3).
[5] *Ibid.*
[6] *Ibid.* s.331(7).
[7] *Ibid.* s.331(10).

how this term is to be interpreted, so it would be reasonable to assume that it is to be given its usual meaning and thus include an element of consensus between two parties. This would mean that where there is no discussion as to payment it could be argued that a transaction otherwise within this part of the definition would not be prohibited.

Peripheral transactions   In addition to the prohibitions on loans, quasi-loans and credit transactions, there are certain other transactions which are peripheral to the three central categories of prohibition. The first of these peripheral transactions is the giving of any guarantee or the provision of any security in connection with one of the prohibited transactions. For these purposes, "guarantee" includes an indemnity.[8]

Secondly, there are the "catch all" provisions designed to prevent companies circumventing the main prohibitions. Under these provisions, a company is not permitted to arrange for the assignment to it, or assumption by it, of any rights, obligations or liabilities under a transaction, which if the company had entered into itself would have been illegal.[9] Also, a company may not take part in any arrangement whereby another person enters into a transaction which would have been illegal for the company itself to enter into, and that other person, as a result of the arrangement, has obtained or is to obtain any benefit from any member of the group of which the company is a member.[10]

Application of prohibitions
Relevant company   Certain prohibitions apply to all companies and there are also restrictions on a category of company referred to as "relevant" companies. A "relevant company" is a company which is either a public company or a member of a group of companies which includes a public company amongst its number.[11]

All companies   All companies are prohibited from making loans to their directors or to the directors of their holding companies. Further they may not enter into any guarantee or provide any security for such a loan.[12] A company may not avoid these prohibitions by entering into any of the transactions described in the "catch all" provisions.[13]

Relevant companies   A relevant company, in addition to being prevented from entering into a loan for its directors or a director of its holding company, may not enter into the following transactions:

(a) a loan to a person connected with its director or a director of its holding company;
(b) quasi-loan to its director or a director of its holding company or to a person connected with such a director;
(c) a credit transaction for such a director or connected person;
(d) a guarantee or provision of security connected with any of the transactions set out in (a) to (c) above; and
(e) any transaction falling within the "catch all" provisions.[14]

---

[8] *Ibid.* s.331(2).
[9] *Ibid.* s.330(6).
[10] *Ibid.* s.330(7).
[11] *Ibid.* s.331(6).
[12] *Ibid.* s.330(2).
[13] *Ibid.* s.330(6)(7).
[14] *Ibid.* s.330(3)(4)(6)(7).

Connected person   The definition of "connected person" is complicated. The following persons are deemed to be connected with a director:

(a) the director's spouse, child or step-child; an illegitimate child of the director will be within this category, but any person who has attained the age of 18 is excluded;

(b) except where the context requires otherwise, a company with which the director is associated; the ways in which a director will be associated with a company are examined below;

(c) a person acting in his capacity as trustee of any trust (other than an employees' share scheme or a pension scheme) if the beneficiaries of that trust include:
   (i) the director, his spouse of any children or step-children of his; "children" and "step-children" bear the same meaning as in (a) above; or
   (ii) a company with which he is associated;

(d) a person acting in his capacity as a trustee of any trust (other than an employees' share scheme or a pension scheme) whose terms confer a power on the trustees that may be exercised for the benefit of the directors or persons connected with him by virtue of (a) above;

(e) a partner of the director or any person who falls within (a) to (d) above; or

(f) a Scottish firm in which the director, or persons connected with him by virtue of (a) to (d) above are partners; a fellow partner of the director in a Scottish firm or a partner of such connected persons is also included.[15]

"Associated with"   A director is deemed to be associated with a company if, but only if, he and the persons connected with him together are either interested in at least 20 per cent. of the nominal value of the company's equity share capital or are entitled to exercise or control the exercise of more than 20 per cent. of the voting power at any general meeting of the company.[16]
A director will be regarded as controlling a company if:

(a) the director or any person connected with him is interested in any part of that company's equity share capital; or

(b) he or any person connected with him is entitled to exercise or control the exercise of any part of the voting power at any general meeting of that company.

In both cases, the interests of the director, the persons connected with him and his fellow directors, must exceed more than 50 per cent. of that company's share capital. Alternatively, they must be entitled to control more than half of the voting power.[17] Thus, for example, a director will be associated with a company, if the director and any person connected with him together control the exercise of more than 20 per cent. of the voting power of that company through an intermediate company.
     Where a director would be deemed to be associated with another company as a result of the above provisions, that

[15] *Ibid.* s.346(2)(3).
[16] *Ibid.* s.346(4).
[17] *Ibid.* s.346(5).

company will not be treated as being connected with him unless it is also connected with him by virtue his being a trustee or a partner, within (c) or (d) on page 142 above. Further, where the beneficiaries of a trust, which either includes or may include a company, a trustee of that trust will not be treated as connected with a director of that company by reason of that fact alone.[18]

The all embracing effect of this definition has been mitigated by the introduction of various exemptions which are designed at freeing legitimate business transactions from the prohibitions discussed above.

Exemptions
There are four exemptions of which all companies may take advantage. First, small loans where the relevant amount does not exceed £2,500.[19] Secondly, loans made by a subsidiary at the behest of its holding company. This exemption also includes the provision of a guarantee or security in connection with such a loan.[20] Thirdly, the provision of funds to a director for the purpose of business expenditure.[21] The aggregate of the relevant amounts under this exemption must not exceed £10,000. Furthermore, the company in general meeting must approve the expenditure or the funds must be provided on the basis that they will be repaid in the event of the company failing to give its approval.[22] Finally, loans made or guarantees given by a money lending company. A relevant company may only use this exemption where the aggregate of the relevant amounts does not exceed £50,000. This provision does not, however, apply to recognised banks. Further, there are specific rules which apply when a money lending company lends money to its own director or to a director of its holding company, and that money is to be used in connection with the director's residence.[23]

The following exemptions are also available to relevant companies: short term quasi-loans where the relevant amount does not exceed £1,000,[24] intercompany loans or quasi-loans within the same group,[25] minor and business transactions[26] and quasi-loans and credit transactions entered into by a subsidiary at the behest of its holding company.[27]

Relevant amounts
In determining whether a transaction falls within the exemptions for small loans, minor transactions, business transactions, director's expenditure or is a loan or quasi-loan made by a money lending company (these are referred to as the "relevant exemptions"), it is necessary to calculate what are termed "relevant amounts" to ensure that the transaction is within the financial limit imposed in respect of the particular exemption. In calculating what are relevant amounts, the basic rule is that the value of the proposed transaction and any other transactions already made under the particular exemption must be aggregated.[28] Where a proposed transaction is either a loan or

[18] *Ibid*. s.346(6).
[19] *Ibid*. s.334.
[20] *Ibid*. s.336.
[21] *Ibid*. s.337(1)(2).
[22] *Ibid*. s.337(3)(4).
[23] *Ibid*. s.338.
[24] *Ibid*. s.332.
[25] *Ibid*. s.333.
[26] *Ibid*. s.335.
[27] *Ibid*. s.336.
[28] *Ibid*. s.339.

quasi-loan which is to be made by a recognised bank in connection with a director's residence, any other transaction which has been made for the director under the general exemption set out on page 143 above need not be taken into consideration when calculating the relevant amount for these purposes.[29] Finally, where Company A enters into a transaction when it is a subsidiary of Company B which is to make the transaction, or it is a subsidiary of Company B's holding company, that transaction will not have to be included in the calculation of the relevant amount if at a later date Company A is no longer such a subsidiary. That later date is the time when it is necessary to decide whether a proposed transaction or arrangement falls within any relevant exemption.[30]

Consequences of breach

If a company enters into one of the prohibited transactions or arrangements, the nature of the consequences will depend upon whether or not it is a relevant company. All companies will face civil liability, but criminal penalties will only be imposed upon relevant companies.

Civil liability

Where a company breaches the prohibition provisions, the transaction or arrangement will be voidable at the instance of the company. The company will lose the right to avoid the transaction or arrangement in three situations:

(a) where restitution of any money or any other asset which is the subject matter of the transaction or arrangement is not possible;

(b) where a third party has acquired any rights under the agreement, bona fide for value and without actual notice of the contravention; or

(c) where a company has been indemnified for any loss or damage suffered by it.[31]

It may also be established that, without prejudice to any other liability they may have those responsible for the company entering into the transaction or arrangement and those for whom it was made, are liable to account to the company for any gain made directly or indirectly by the arrangement or transaction. They may also be jointly and severally liable to indemnify the company for any resulting loss or damage. The persons who are so liable are:

(a) a director of the company or its holding company, for whom the agreement was made;

(b) a person connected with such a director, where applicable; and

(c) any other director of the company who authorised the transaction or arrangement.[32]

Where a company and a person connected with a director of the company or its holding company has entered into a prohibited transaction or arrangement, that director will not be liable if he can show that he took all reasonable steps to secure the company's compliance with the Act.[33] A person connected with

---

[29] *Ibid.* s.339(4).
[30] *Ibid.* s.339(5).
[31] *Ibid.* s.341(1).
[32] *Ibid.* s.341(2)(3).
[33] *Ibid.* s.341(4).

the director, or a director who authorised the prohibited agreement will have a defence if he can show that at the time of the transaction or arrangement was entered into, he did not know the relevant circumstances constituting the contravention.[34]

Criminal liability   A breach of the prohibition provisions by a relevant company will result in an offence being committed by the following persons:

(a) a director of the relevant company who authorises or permits the company to enter into the prohibited transaction or arrangement; that director must either know or have reasonable cause to believe that the company is thereby in contravention of the Act;

(b) the relevant company entering into such a transaction or arrangement for one of its directors or for a director of its holding company; it will not be guilty of an offence, however, if it can show that, at the time of the transaction or arrangement was entered into, it did not know the relevant circumstances; and

(c) a person who procures a relevant company to enter into such a transaction or arrangement but only if that person knows or has reasonable cause to believe that the company was thereby in contravention of the Act.

Any such person found guilty of an offence is liable to imprisonment or a fine, or both.[35]

Disclosure   In addition to prohibiting certain loans, quasi-loans and credit transactions, statute also requires that disclosure of these transactions and arrangements, whether or not they are prohibited.[36] Disclosure should be made in the notes to the accounts and reference to directors in the context of disclosure should be read as including shadow directors.[37]

For disclosure purposes, it is irrelevant whether or not the director was a director at the time the transaction or arrangement was made, or in the case of a transaction or arrangement made for a person connected with such a director, whether that person was so connected at that time. It is sufficient that the director was a director at some time during the financial year, or the person so connected at some time during that period. Where disclosure is required of a subsidiary's transactions or arrangements, the fact that the company was a subsidiary for part of the financial year will necessitate disclosure.[38]

Exemptions   Disclosure will not have to be made in the following three situations. First, where the transaction, arrangement or agreement is made between one company, Company A, and another, Company B, and a director of Company A, or of its subsidiary, is interested only by virtue of his being a director of Company B.[39] Secondly, where the transaction, arrangement or agreement was not entered into during the financial year and did not subsist at any time during that period.[40] Finally, particulars

---

[34] *Ibid.* s.341(5).
[35] *Ibid.* s.342.
[36] *Ibid.* Sched. 6, para. 6.
[37] *Ibid.* s.232.
[38] *Ibid.* Sched. 6, para. 6.
[39] *Ibid.* para. 5.
[40] *Ibid.*

are not required to be given in the accounts prepared by a company which is, or is the holding company of, a recognised bank. For this exemption to apply the recognised bank must be party to such a transaction, arrangement or agreement.[41]

Loans   The disclosure requirements relate to the following transactions or arrangements which involve loans:

(a) loans made by a company to a person who was a director of that company or its holding company, at any time during the financial year;

(b) the provision of a guarantee or security in connection with a loan made by any person to such a director;

(c) transactions of the type described in (a) and (b) but entered into for a person connected with a director of the company or its holding company;

(d) an agreement to enter into transactions covered by the three categories above; and

(e) an arrangement within the "catch all" provisions.[42]

A holding company is also obliged to give particulars of any transaction, arrangement or agreement falling into the above categories which is entered into by any of its subsidiaries.[43]

Quasi-loans and credit transactions   The transactions or arrangements which must be disclosed involve quasi-loans or credit transactions namely:

(a) a quasi-loan to or credit transaction for any person who was, at any time during the financial year, a director of the company or of its holding company;

(b) a quasi-loan to or credit transaction for a person connected with such a director;

(c) a guarantee or the provision of any security in connection with a quasi-loan or a credit transaction made by any other person for such a director or a person so connected;

(d) an agreement by the company to enter into any of the transactions or arrangements in (a) to (c) above made for a person who at any time during the financial year was a director of the company or its holding company or who was connected with such a director; and

(e) an arrangement within the catch all provisions.[44]

A holding company will also have to disclose any transaction, arrangement or agreement which falls into the above categories and which was entered into by any of its subsidiaries.[45]

Required details to be disclosed   The principal terms of any loan, quasi-loan or credit transaction coming within the above categories must be disclosed along with the following details:

(a) a statement showing that the transaction, arrangement or agreement was either made or subsisted during the financial year; and

(b) the name of the person for whom it was made; where it was made for a person connected with a director of the

---

[41] *Ibid*. para. 4.
[42] *Ibid*. para. 2.
[43] *Ibid*. para. 1
[44] *Ibid*. para. 2
[45] *Ibid*. para. 1

company or its holding company, the name of that director must be included.[46]

Further details are required depending upon the nature of the transaction, arrangement or agreement. In respect of a loan, an agreement for a loan or one of the catch all transactions relating to a loan, the following details must also be shown:

(a) the amount of the liability of the person to whom the loan was or was agreed to be made, in respect of principal and interest, at the beginning and at the end of the financial year;

(b) the maximum amount of that liability during that year;

(c) the amount of any interest which, having fallen due, has not been repaid; and

(d) the amount of any provision made in respect of any failure or anticipated failure by the borrower to repay the whole or part of the loan or any interest thereon.[47]

In the case of quasi-loans and credit transactions, an agreement for either a quasi-loan or a credit transaction or an arrangement within the catch all provisions which relates to either a quasi-loan or a credit transaction, the additional information to be shown is the value of the transaction. In the case of an agreement for either a quasi-loan or a credit transaction, the value of the transaction or arrangement to which the agreement relates should be shown.[48]

Value of the transaction   The term "the value of the transaction" is a term which bears different meanings according to the type of transaction.

(a) **Loans and quasi-loans**   The value of a loan is the amount of its principal and the value of a quasi–loan is the amount or the maximum amounts which the person to whom the quasi-loan is made is liable to reimburse the creditor.

(b) **Guarantees of securities**   The value of either of these transactions is the amount guaranteed or secured.

(c) **Catch all transactions**   The value of one of the catch all transactions is the value of the transaction to which the arrangement relates less any amount by which the liabilities under the arrangement or transaction of the person for whom the transaction was made have been reduced.

(d) **Other transactions**   The value of any other transaction is the price which it is reasonable to expect could be obtained for the goods, land or services supplied.

Should the value of a transaction or arrangement be incapable of being expressed as a specific sum of money, it will be deemed to exceed £50,000 thus encouraging companies to ascertain its value wherever possible.[49]

Where a company has given a guarantee or provided security in respect of a loan, quasi-loan or credit transaction, additional particulars are required. This information will also have to be

---

[46] *Ibid.* para. 9.
[47] *Ibid.*
[48] *Ibid.*
[49] *Ibid.* s.340

shown in respect of any arrangement under which the company purports to assign to it any rights obligations or liabilities under a transaction which it otherwise would have been unlawful for it to have entered into. The additional particulars which are required to be disclosed are:

(a) the amount for which the company was liable under the guarantee or in respect of the security both at the beginning and at the end of its financial year;
(b) the maximum amount for which the company may become so liable; and
(c) any amount paid and any liability incurred by the company for the purpose of fulfilling the guarantee or discharging the security (including any loss incurred by reason of the enforcement of the guarantee or security.[50]

Exemptions   The additional information related to specific types of transaction need not be given if the following criteria are met:

(a) the transaction, arrangement or agreement is a loan or quasi-loan;
(b) the loan or quasi-loan was made or agreed to be made by a company to or for another company; and
(c) the company making the loan or quasi-loan is a member of a group of companies and the parties to the loan or quasi-loan are members of the same group and are either the holding company and a wholly owned subsidiary or are both wholly owned subsidiaries; and
(d) disclosure would not have had to be made, if the company making the loan or quasi-loan had not been associated with a director of that company at any time during the financial year.[51]

No disclosure at all is required for certain transactions, where the aggregate value of the transaction or arrangement is small. This exemption applies to credit transactions, guarantees provided or security entered into in connection with a credit transaction, catch all arrangements related to credit transactions and agreements to enter into a credit transaction if:

(a) the transaction, arrangement or agreement was made by the company or a subsidiary of it;
(b) the transaction, arrangement or agreement was made for a person who at any time during that financial year was a director of the company or of its holding company, or was connected with such a director; and
(c) the aggregate of the values of each transaction, arrangement or agreement did not at any time during the financial year exceed £5,000; in calculating whether or not this sum has been exceeded, any amount by which the liabilities of the person for whom the transaction or arrangement was made has been reduced should be deducted from the aggregate amount.[52]

---

[50] *Ibid*. para. 9.
[51] *Ibid*. para. 10.
[52] *Ibid*. para. 11.

Transactions of material interest

The disclosure provisions introduce a new category of transaction or arrangement which may be freely entered into but details of which must be given in a company's annual accounts. Disclosure under this heading is necessary when a person, who at any time during the financial year was a director of the company or its holding company, has a material interest in any transaction or arrangement with the company or a subsidiary of it. That interest may either be direct or indirect. The information required to be given must be shown in the group accounts, where the company is a holding company, or in the individual accounts of any other relevant company.[53]

Interest   Any transaction or arrangement made between a company and a director of it or of its holding company will be deemed to be one in which the director is interested, as will one between a company and a person connected with such a director.[54] Whether **Material** or not such a transaction or arrangement is material will depend upon the opinion of the board of directors. The director involved in the dealings under scrutiny may not take part in determining whether his interest in a transaction or arrangement is material. This decision should be taken by the directors who are responsible for the preparation of the company's annual accounts. A majority decision will be sufficient.[55]

No further assistance is given in the Act with regard to the meaning of "material." A director could have a material interest in a transaction because that transaction involved a large sum for him personally, but in the company's terms, it could be insignificant. On the other hand, the interest might be material to the director because it is material to the company to which he is a director. A third possible interpretation is that the director might be materially interested because the transaction could influence shareholders. It is up to the particular board to decide what criteria should be used in determining whether an interest is material or not.

Penalties   The Act does not lay down any penalties in the case of a board misusing its discretion but directors of a company will be liable under section 245 of the Act if defective accounts are laid before the company in general meetings or delivered to the Registrar of Companies. In addition to this there are indirect penalties in such an event. First, the directors involved in the decision might be in breach of their duties towards the company. In the event of the company becoming insolvent, such a decision might be a ground for disqualifying a director and making him personally liable for the company's losses.[56] Finally, a perverse decision might lead to the company's accounts being qualified if the transaction was material to the company, as the auditors are under a duty to see that the company has complied with the accounting provisions of company law. Whilst it remains uncertain what the true meaning of "material" is in this context, the safest course of action is probably, if in doubt, disclose.

[53] *Ibid.* paras. 1(*c*), 2(*c*).
[54] For connected person see pp. 142–143 above.
[55] Companies Act 1985, Sched. 6, para. 3.
[56] Company Directors Disqualification Act 1986, s.9, Sched. 1.

Disclosure of any transaction or arrangement in which a director has a material interest will be necessary even if the person for whom it was made was not a director of the company at the time it was made. A holding company will also have to disclose such transactions or arrangements entered into by its subsidiary even though the subsidiary was not a member of the group at the time the transaction or arrangement was made. It is sufficient that the company became a subsidiary during the financial year.[57]

Required details   The particulars which must be disclosed are:

(a) a statement of the fact that the transaction or arrangement was made or subsisted during the financial year;
(b) the name of the director or of the person connected with a director, for whom it was made; in the latter case, the name of the director with whom that person is connected must also be given;
(c) the nature of that director's interest; and
(d) the value of the transaction or arrangement to which the agreement relates.[58]

Exemptions   As with the other disclosure requirements for transactions involving directors, there are exemptions to the rule that all transactions and arrangements in which a director is materially interests must be disclosed. These exemptions are discussed in the following paragraphs.

Directorships   Particulars need not be disclosed of a transaction or arrangement between one company, Company A, and another, Company B, in which a director of Company A or of a company in the same group as Company A is interested only by virtue of his being a director of Company B.[59]

Contracts of service   A contract of service between a company and one of its directors or a director within the same group need not be disclosed under these provisions. The disclosure requirements which relate to this particular type of contract are discussed on pages 152–154 below.[60]

Financial year   Where a transaction or arrangement was not entered into during the financial year and did not subsist at any time during that period, no disclosure is necessary.[61]

Inter group transactions   A holding company need not disclose certain inter group transactions where the parties to the transaction or arrangement are members of the same group of companies. The transaction or arrangement must be entered into at arm's length and in the ordinary course of business. In addition to this, its terms must not be more favourable than the terms that would have been granted to a person other than a director.[62]

Director's association   Disclosure will not be required merely because of a director's association with the company if the following conditions are met:

(a) the reporting company is a member of a group of companies; and

---

[57] Companies Act 1985, Sched. 6, para. 6.
[58] *Ibid.* paras. 9, 14. For 'value of the transaction' see p. 147 above.
[59] *Ibid.* para. 5.
[60] *Ibid.*
[61] *Ibid.*
[62] *Ibid.* para. 7.

(b) either the company is a wholly owned subsidiary or no member of the group to which that company belongs (other than the reporting company or its subsidiary) was party to the transaction or arrangement; and

(c) the director in question was at some time during the financial year in question associated with the company; and

(d) the material interest of that director would not have arisen if he had not been associated with the company at any time during the relevant period.[63]

Minor transactions

This exemption applies to a transaction or arrangement in which a director has a material interest and which was entered into during the financial year for which the accounts are being prepared. Disclosure need only be made if the value of that transaction or arrangement, together with the value of any similar transaction or arrangement which was entered into before the beginning of the financial year under consideration, did not exceed £1,000 during that year. If the aggregate amount did exceed £1,000, the exemption will still apply if the aggregate amount did not exceed £5,000 or one per cent. of the value of the net assets of the company as at the end of the financial year, whichever is the less. In calculating the financial limits, the amount of any reduction made to the liabilities of the person for whom the transaction or arrangement was made should be deducted from the value of the transaction.[64]

Other transactions involving directors

Disclosure of a different sort is required in respect of other contracts or transactions in which a director is interested. These are general contracts in which a director is interested, contracts of service and substantial property transactions.

General contracts

A director who is interested in any way, whether directly or indirectly, in a contract or proposed contract to which the company is or will be a party, is bound to declare his interest and

Disclosure

the nature of his interest at the first board meeting at which it is possible so to do.[65]

The disclosure obligation will be satisfied if a director gives a general notice to his fellow directors which states that he is a member of a specified company or firm and is to be regarded as interested in any contract which may, after the date of the notice, be made with that company or firm. Alternatively, if the director is likely to enter into any contract with persons who are connected with him, he may give a general notice to the board of directors which states that he is to be regarded as interested in any contract which may, after the date of the notice, may be made with such persons. A general notice in either form must be given at a meeting of directors for it to be an effective declaration of interest.[66] If it is not so given, the director should take

[63] *Ibid.* para. 8.
[64] *Ibid.* paras. 12, 14. For 'value of the transaction' see p. 147 above.
[65] *Ibid.* s.317(1)(2).
[66] *Ibid.* s.317(3).

reasonable steps to secure that it is brought up and read at the next board meeting after it is given.[67]

Contract A contract in which a director is interested need not be a contract in the legal sense, but includes any transaction or arrangement made or entered into after December 22, 1980.[68] A transaction or arrangement which falls within the categories discussed on pages 139–141 above will always be a transaction or arrangement in which the director is interested.[69]

Shadow directors A shadow director is also required to declare his interest in contracts with a company in the same way as directors, although in the case of a shadow director, the declaration of interest must be given in writing. A notice of interest may be specific, in which case the timing of the notice will depend upon whether the contract is proposed or has already been made. Alternatively, general notice of interest may be given. The requirements in respect of a general notice are the same as for directors, except that a written notice must be given.[70]

Penalties A director or shadow director who fails to declare his interest in a contract with the company will be guilty of an offence and liable to a fine.[71]

These provisions do not prejudice the operation of any rule of law which restricts a company director from having an interest in contracts with the company.[72]

Service contracts A copy of a director's or a shadow director's contract *of service*, or a memorandum of its terms if it is not in writing, must be kept by the company. A holding company is also obliged to keep a copy of the contract of service of any of its directors who is employed by a subsidiary. If the contract is not in writing, a memorandum of its terms should be kept instead. As the following rules apply to shadow directors as they do to directors, all references to directors will also include shadow directors.[73]

Employment outside the U.K. If a director's employment with the company, or if he is employed by a subsidiary, with that company, is wholly or partly outside the United Kingdom, then a copy of his contract of service or a memorandum of its terms need not be kept. Instead the company must keep a memorandum which gives the director's name and the provisions of the contract regarding its duration. In the case of a director employed by a subsidiary, the memorandum should set out the same details, as well as the name and place of incorporation of the subsidiary.[74]

Penalties It is an offence not to keep the requisite copy of a director's contract of service or, a memorandum of its terms, where the contract is not in writing or the director is employed wholly or partly outside the United Kingdom. The company and every officer of it who is in default will be liable to a fine, and, for continued contravention, to a daily default fine.[75]

---

[67] *Ibid.* s.317(4).
[68] *Ibid.* s.317(5).
[69] *Ibid.* s.317(6).
[70] *Ibid.* s.317(8).
[71] *Ibid.* s.317(7).
[72] *Ibid.* s.317(9).
[73] *Ibid.* s.318(1)(6).
[74] *Ibid.* s.318(5).
[75] *Ibid.* s.318(8).

Place of keeping   The documents which a company is required to keep in relation to the contracts of service of its directors should be kept at the company's registered office or at the place where its register of members is kept, if that place is other than its registered office. Another alternative is for the copy or memorandum to be kept at the company's principal place of business, provided that that place is situated in that part of Great Britain in which the company was registered.[76] In other words if the company is registered in England and Wales, the copy or memorandum may not be kept at the company's principal place of business in Scotland, instead it would have to be kept at its registered office or at the place where its register of members was kept, where applicable. Whichever location is chosen, all copies and memoranda should be kept at the same place.[77]

In the event of a company choosing a place of keeping other than its registered office, the Registrar of Companies must be notified of that place. If the place of keeping is subsequently changed, the change must also be notified to the Registrar.[78]

Penalties   Failure to notify the Registrar in either event within 14 days will result in the company and every officer responsible for the failure being liable to a fine. For continued contravention a daily default fine will be imposed.[79]

Inspection   Every copy or memorandum which a company is obliged to keep under these provisions must be open to inspection by any member of the company and no charge may be levied for

Penalties   inspection.[80] If inspection is refused, the company and any officer of it who is in default will be liable to a fine and, for continued contravention, to a daily default fine. The court may also order an immediate inspection.[81]

The above rules also apply to a variation of a director's contract of service, as they apply to the original contract.[82] They do not, however, apply to a contract, or its variation, which only has less than 12 months to run, or which may be terminated by the company, without payment of compensation, within the next ensuing 12 months.[83]

Listed companies   In addition to the right of inspection under the Companies Act, a company listed on the Stock Exchange is obliged to make available for inspection, for a limited period, all directors' service contracts of more than one year's duration. Where a service contract is not written, a memorandum of its terms must be made available. The contracts or memoranda should be available for inspection by all interested parties at the company's registered office or its transfer office.

Contracts of five   years or more   Special rules apply to both directors' contracts *of* service and to contracts *for* services which are of more than five years duration. These rules require the company in general meeting to approve such contracts and as part of the requirements, the contractual terms may be inspected by the company members.

---

[76] *Ibid.* s.318(3).
[77] *Ibid.* s.318(2).
[78] *Ibid.* s.318(4).
[79] *Ibid.* s.318(8).
[80] *Ibid.* s.318(7).
[81] *Ibid.* s.318(8)(9).
[82] *Ibid.* s.318(10).
[83] *Ibid.* s.310(11).

These provisions apply to the service contracts of both directors and shadow directors.[84]

Substantial property transactions

A company may only enter into an arrangement under which non-cash assets are acquired or are to be acquired from or by:

(a) a director of the company or of its holding company,
(b) a shadow director of the company or of its holding company (for these purposes all future references to directors includes shadow directors), or
(c) a person connected with such a director,

if the arrangement is first approved by a resolution of the company in general meeting. A resolution should also be passed by a holding company where the director is a director of the holding company or the connected person, who is party to the contract, is connected with such a director.[85]

Exemptions

The acquisition of non-cash assets which, at the time of the arrangement, are valued at less than £1,000, but subject to that, exceed £50,000 or 10 per cent. of the company's asset value, need not be approved in the above manner. The asset value of a company is to be taken as the value of the company's net assets, which must be calculated using the annual accounts of the last preceding financial year in respect of which such accounts were laid. Where no accounts have been prepared and laid before that time, the amount of the company's called up share capital must be substituted for its net asset value.[86]

Approval is not required if:

(a) the company is a wholly owned subsidiary of any company, wherever incorporated[87];
(b) the ownership of the asset is going to move from a holding company to any of its wholly owned subsidiaries or vice versa[88];
(c) the ownership of the asset is to be transferred between wholly owned subsidiaries in the same group[89]
(d) the arrangement is entered into by a company which is being wound up; this exemption does not apply in the event of a members' voluntary winding up[90]; or
(e) the asset is to be acquired by a member of the company, who is acting in his capacity as member.[91]

Penalties

Where approval is required but not obtained, the transaction will be voidable at the option of the company, unless restitution of money or any other asset which has passed under the arrangement is no longer possible or the company has been indemnified for any loss or damage suffered by it. The acquisition of any rights under the transaction by a third party who acted in good faith without actual knowledge of the contravention will also be a bar to the company avoiding the transactions; as will the affirmation of the transaction within a

---

[84] *Ibid.* s.319.
[85] *Ibid.* s.320(1)(3).
[86] *Ibid.* s.320(2).
[87] *Ibid.* s.321(1).
[88] *Ibid.* s.321(2).
[89] *Ibid.*
[90] *Ibid.*
[91] *Ibid.* s.321(3).

reasonable period by the company or by its holding company where the director involved is a director of that holding company.[92]

In addition to this, liability will also be imposed upon the director of the company or its holding company who was a party to the transaction, any person connected with such a director, who entered into an arrangement with the company and any director who authorised the transaction. Such a person will be liable to account to the company for any gain which he has made directly or indirectly by the arrangement or transaction and liable to indemnify the company for any loss or damage resulting from the arrangement or transaction.[93]

A director of the company who is connected to a person who is a party to the transaction or arrangement with that company will have a defence to liability if he can show that he took all reasonable steps to secure the company's compliance with the statutory provisions.[94] A director who authorised the transaction, or who was a party to the transaction or arrangement and a person who was connected with such directors, and who was a party to it, will not be liable if he can prove that, at the time the transaction or arrangement was entered into, he did not know the relevant circumstances constituting the contravention.[95]

Officers' transactions

In addition to the disclosure rules relating to directors, certain transactions involving a company's officers, other than its directors, must also be disclosed.[96] These are disclosure requirements only and a company is not prohibited from entering into such transactions. The Act states that "officer" includes a director, manager or secretary of the company, but as the definition is not exhaustive, disclosure should be considered where transactions involve others who play an important role within the company.[97] Auditors, for example, may be regarded as officers for these purposes.

If a person is or was an officer of a company at any time during the financial year for which accounts are being prepared and the company or its subsidiary enters into certain transactions, arrangements or agreements, then disclosure must be made, in the notes to the accounts. In the event of a holding company not preparing group accounts, disclosure should be made in its individual accounts.[98] The disclosure requirements apply to the following classes of transactions, arrangements and agreements:

(a) loans of a kind which are prohibited to companies and relevant companies;

---

[92] *Ibid.* s.322(1)(2).
[93] *Ibid.* s.322(3).
[94] *Ibid.* s.322(5).
[95] *Ibid.* s.322(6).
[96] *Ibid.* s.233(1)(2).
[97] *Ibid.* s.744.
[98] *Ibid.* s.233(1)(2)(4)(5).

      (b) quasi-loans of a type into which relevant companies may not enter;

      (c) credit transactions of a type into which relevant companies may not enter;

      (d) guarantees or the provision of security relating to such loans, quasi-loans or credit transactions;

      (e) arrangements within the "catch-all" provisions; and

      (f) agreements to enter into any of the above transactions or arrangements.[99]

Exemption   A recognised bank which enters into any of the above transactions or arrangements for its officers or for any officer of its holding company is not required to comply with the disclosure requirements.[1]

Disclosure   The aggregate amounts which are outstanding at the end of the financial year must be disclosed separately for each of the above categories, along with the numbers of officers for whom they were made. Transactions, arrangements and agreements do not have to be disclosed if the aggregate amount outstanding for a particular officer does not exceed £2,500.[2]

Penalties   No specific penalties are imposed for breach of these disclosure requirements, although where defective current accounts are laid before the company in a general meeting or delivered to the Registrar of Companies, a director of the company will be liable to a fine. A defence is available to the directors who can show that they took all reasonable steps to secure compliance with the requirements.[3] Further, accounts which do not comply with the statutory requirements may receive a qualified audit report where the amount involved is material.[4]

---

[99] *Ibid.* Sched. 6, para. 15. For "relevant company" and "catch-all" provisions see p. 141 above.

[1] *Ibid.* s.233(3).

[2] *Ibid.* Sched. 6, para. 16.

[3] *Ibid.* s.245.

[4] For audit reports see pp. 117–118 above.

16 GROUP ACCOUNTS

Introduction

Accounts for groups of companies, as with individual company accounts, are the subject of British companies legislation. They are also governed by the EC Seventh Directive, which has been adopted by the European Communities. This Directive, however, has not yet been incorporated into the law of the United Kingdom; member states have until the end of 1987 to incorporate the Directive into their own legislation and until January 1, 1990 to implement it. Any law which is enacted in connection with the Seventh Directive on Group Accounts is not expected to affect to any great extent the present U.K. law on the subject as it already conforms to many of the Directive's requirements.

The Companies Act 1985 requires that any company, which, at the end of the financial year, has one or more subsidiaries, should produce group accounts, as well as individual accounts for that year.[1] Before examining further the nature of group accounts, the definition of a "subsidiary" and of a "holding company" must be considered.

Subsidiary   The Act deems a company (Company A) to be the subsidiary of another company (Company B) in three situations only. First, Company B will be the holding company of Company A, which will therefore be its subsidiary, if Company B is a member of Company A and controls the composition of its board of directors.[2] Control of Company A's board may result from the fact that Company B has sufficient shares to control voting at Company A's general meeting, or from special rights given to it by Company A's articles of association.

Company A's board will thus be deemed to be controlled by Company B if (but only if) Company B can, of its own initiative, appoint or remove the holders of all or a majority of the directorships.[3] Company B will be deemed to have power to appoint to a directorship if it is not possible to appoint a director to Company A without Company B's approval, or if a person's appointment to the directorship follows necessarily from his appointment as director of Company B. Finally, if the directorship is held by Company B itself or by a subsidiary of it, then Company B will also be deemed to have power to appoint directors to Company A.[4]

Secondly, Company A will be the subsidiary of Company B if Company B holds more than half in nominal value of the equity share capital of Company A.[5] A company's equity share capital is its issued share capital, other than that capital which has no right to participate beyond a specified amount in a distribution, whether that distribution be of dividends or capital.[6]

[1] Companies Act 1985, s.229(1).
[2] *Ibid.* s.736(1).
[3] *Ibid.* s.736(2).
[4] *Ibid.* s.736(3).
[5] *Ibid.* s.736(1).
[6] *Ibid.* s.744.

Thirdly, where Company A is the subsidiary of any company which is Company B's subsidiary, Company A will be Company B's subsidiary also.[7] Thus, for example, Company A is the subsidiary of Company C which is the subsidiary of Company B, Company C will be Company A's holding company, but Company B may be Company A's ultimate holding company, as well as Company C's holding company.

In determining whether Company A is a subsidiary of Company B, the following rules will also apply:

(a) any shares held or power exercisable by Company B's nominee or the nominee of Company B's subsidiary is deemed to be held or exercisable by Company B itself;

(b) where Company B, its nominee or the nominee of its subsidiary holds shares or exercises power in a fiduciary capacity, the shares will not be regarded as held or the power exercisable by Company B;

(c) where shares are held or power exercisable under the provision of any of Company A's debentures or of a trust deed securing any such debentures, the shares held or power exercisable may be disregarded; and

(d) if, in the ordinary course of business, Company B lends money and shares are held or power exercisable by Company B, its nominee or the nominee of its subsidiary, by way of security only for the purposes of a transaction entered into in the ordinary course of business, then those shares are not deemed to be held or the power exercisable by Company B.[8]

Holding company   Company B will be deemed to be the holding company of Company A if, but only if, Company A is its subsidiary. If Company A has no members except Company B, Company B's wholly owned subsidiaries and Company B's nominees or the nominees of Company B's subsidiary, then Company A will also be deemed to be Company B's wholly owned subsidiary.[9]

Individual accounts of holding companies and subsidiaries

General   A holding company, whilst it is obliged to prepare group accounts, must also prepare its own individual accounts, as must each of its subsidiaries.[10] The individual accounts will follow the same formats as used by companies which are not members of a group, except that certain information relating to the other group members will have to be given, for example, under "Fixed assets" in the balance sheet format 1, there are the subheadings "Investments—shares in group companies" and "Investments— loans to group companies."

A company preparing its own accounts must, under each relevant section of the formats show the aggregate amounts relating to:

[7] *Ibid.* s.736(1).
[8] *Ibid.* s.736(4).
[9] *Ibid.* s.736(5).
[10] *Ibid.* ss.227(1), 229(1).

(a) amounts attributable to dealings with or interests in any holding company or fellow subsidiary of the company; and

(b) amounts attributable to dealing with or interests in any subsidiary of the company.

These amounts should be shown separately, either by way of subdivision of the relevant item in the balance sheet itself or in a note to the company's accounts.[11] A company is a fellow subsidiary of another company if both are subsidiaries of the same company, but neither is a subsidiary of the other.[12]

Amounts owed to other companies within the group must be shown separately from amounts owed by those companies to the reporting company, as it is not permissible to set off these amounts.[13] Amounts owed to a company by a member of the same group, or amounts owed by it to other members of the group, will need to be analysed between amounts due or payable within one year of balance sheet date and these due or payable after that, under the normal disclosure requirements relating to debtors and creditors.[14] The directors need to establish their intended action with regard to payment or collection of debts within the group to the best of their knowledge and belief at the date of signing the accounts. This will not necessarily bind the parties to these terms of payment. The fact that directors may review the terms under which intra group debts are made and are not, therefore, committed to previously agreed terms results from the control exercised by a holding company over its subsidiaries and thus enables it to require subsidiaries to agree to any alterations deemed necessary.

A holding company is further required to disclose in a note to its own accounts, the number, description and amount of the shares in and debentures of the company held by its subsidiaries or their nominees. This information, however, need not be disclosed where the subsidiary is concerned only as personal representative or as trustee. In the latter case, disclosure is not required provided that the subsidiary is not beneficially interested under the trust. If the subsidiary does have a beneficial interest the information need not be given if that interest is by way of security only for the purposes of a transaction entered into by it in the ordinary course of business, which must include the lending of money.[15]

Holding company disclosure Where a company has subsidiaries, it must disclose details of each subsidiary and of its shareholding in it. The information specifically required is:

(a) the name of the subsidiary[16];

(b) where the subsidiary is incorporated outside Great Britain, the country of its incorporation[17];

(c) where a subsidiary is registered in England and Wales, but the holding company is registered in Scotland, or vice

---

[11] *Ibid.* Sched. 4, para. 59.
[12] *Ibid.* para. 80.
[13] *Ibid.* para. 5.
[14] See pp. 71, 72 above.
[15] Companies Act 1985, Sched. 4, para. 60.
[16] *Ibid.* Sched. 5, para. 1.
[17] *Ibid.*

versa, the part of Great Britain in which it is registered must be given[18];

(d) in relation to shareholdings in the subsidiary, the identity of each class of share held, and the proportion of the nominal value of the allotted shares of each class represented by the shares held; where any shares are held by a nominee this fact and the extent of the nominee's shareholding must also be disclosed[19]; and

(e) the aggregate amount of the capital and reserves of the subsidiary as at the end of the financial year.[20]

In respect of the information relating to a subsidiary's capital and reserves, if its financial year end is the same as that of its holding company, the information should relate to that financial year. In the unusual circumstances that the two companies do not share the same year end, then the information should be given in respect of the subsidiary's financial year ending last before the holding company's year end.[21]

Exemptions   Compliance with the disclosure requirements set out above will not be necessary in certain circumstances. In relation to items (a) to (d), those circumstances are where:

(a) the subsidiary is a subsidiary of an intermediate company and is incorporated outside the United Kingdom[22]; or

(b) such a subsidiary is incorporated in the United Kingdom, but carries on business outside it, and in the opinion of the directors of the holding company, disclosure would be harmful to the business of any member of the group; where a company seeks to take advantage of this provision, it will be necessary for the Secretary of State to approve the directors' decision[23]; or

(c) the directors of the holding company are of the opinion that the particulars which are required to be disclosed would be of excessive length; where, however, a subsidiary carried on business which, in the directors' opinion, principally affects the group's profitability or the amounts of its assets, then disclosure must be made in respect of that subsidiary.[24]

If disclosure is not made because the particulars required would be of excessive length, a note to the accounts should be included which states that the information which have been given only relates to subsidiaries whose business principally affects the group's profit or loss or its assets. In addition to this, the information disclosed and that omitted must be included in the company's next annual return.[25]

In respect of the information relating to a subsidiary's capital and reserves, disclosure is not necessary where:

(a) the holding company is not obliged to prepare group

[18] *Ibid.*
[19] *Ibid.* paras. 1 and 2.
[20] *Ibid.* paras. 14 and 16.
[21] *Ibid.*
[22] *Ibid.* para. 3.
[23] *Ibid.*
[24] *Ibid.* paras. 4 and 5.
[25] *Ibid.* para. 5.

accounts because it is a wholly owned subsidiary of another company[26];

(b) the holding company prepares group accounts and either the accounts of the subsidiary are included as an appendix to the group accounts package or the holding company's investment in the subsidiary's shares have been shown in the group accounts by way of the equity method of valuation[27] (this method of valuation is discussed on page 165 below);

(c) the information is not material[28]; or

(d) disclosure would, in the opinion of the holding company's directors, result in particulars of excessive length being given; the same conditions apply in this case as are set out in relation to (c) on page 160 above.[29]

Subsidiary's disclosure
The accounts of a subsidiary company must include the name of the company which the directors regard as being their company's ultimate holding company, and if known to them, the country in which it is incorporated.[30] A company which carries on business outside the United Kingdom need not disclose this information about its ultimate holding company if its directors are of the opinion that such disclosure would be harmful to any company within the group and the Secretary of State agrees that the information need not be disclosed.[31]

Group accounts

Group accounts are accounts or statements which deal in aggregate with the state of affairs and the profit or loss of the holding company and its subsidiaries.[32] A company which has subsidiaries will not have to prepare group accounts if it is itself a wholly owned subsidiary of another company.[33]

Year ends
In order to facilitate comparison between the results of the holding company and those of its subsidiaries, the directors of the holding company are under an obligation to ensure that the financial year of each of its subsidiaries coincides with that of the holding company. If the directors, however, are of the opinion that there are good reasons for members of the group to have differing year ends, then they are permitted to allow this.[34] This requirement is echoed in SSAP 14, "Group Accounts," which states that, where practicable, all companies within a group should have their financial statements prepared to the same accounting date and for the identical accounting periods as the holding company.

Where a holding company and its subsidiary share the same year end, their group accounts will deal with the same period.

---

[26] *Ibid.* para. 17.
[27] *Ibid.*
[28] *Ibid.*
[29] *Ibid.* para. 18.
[30] *Ibid.* para. 20.
[31] *Ibid.* para. 21.
[32] *Ibid.* s.229(1).
[33] *Ibid.* s.229(2).
[34] *Ibid.* s.227(4).

Where the year ends differ, the group accounts must deal with the subsidiary's state of affairs as at its relevant financial year end and with its profit or loss for that year. The relevant "financial year" is the last financial year ending of the subsidiary before the end of the financial year of the holding company dealt with in the group accounts.[35] For example, if the financial year of Company A, a subsidiary of Company B, is December 31, 1986, and Company B's year end is March 31, 1987, the group accounts will include figures from Company A for the year ending December 31, 1986, aggregated with the figures from Company B for the year ending March 31, 1987.

Where the financial years of companies within a group do not coincide, both statute and SSAP 14 require that the notes to the group accounts must disclose certain details in relation to each subsidiary which has a different financial year, whether or not that subsidiary is dealt with in any group accounts prepared by the company. Those details are the reasons why the directors of the holding company consider that the group should have differing financial years, together with the dates on which the relevant financial years end or the earliest and latest of those dates.[36] SSAP 14 further requires that if the principal subsidiary's accounting period is of a different length from that of the holding company, this accounting period should also be stated.

Laying and delivering

When a holding company prepares group accounts, they form part of its annual accounts. It will, therefore, be necessary to lay them before the company in general meeting and deliver them to the Registrar of Companies.[37]

Omission of subsidiaries

Group accounts should include the results of all members of the group. A subsidiary may, however, be excluded from the group accounts if the directors of the holding company are of the opinion that:

"(a) it is impracticable, or would be of no real value to the company's members, in view of the insignificant amounts involved, or

(b) it would involve expense or delay out of proportion to the value to members, or

(c) the result would be misleading, or harmful to the business of the company or any of its subsidiaries, or

(d) the business of the holding company and that of the subsidiary are so different that they cannot reasonably be treated as a single undertaking."[38]

If a subsidiary is excluded because the directors are of the opinion that disclosure would be harmful or that the group cannot be treated as a single undertaking due to the diversity of businesses within the group, then the approval of the Secretary of State must be obtained before any subsidiary is omitted from the accounts.[39]

It is possible that the directors of the holding company could reach the opinion that each and every subsidiary should be

---

[35] *Ibid*. s.230(7).
[36] *Ibid*. Sched. 4, para. 70.
[37] *Ibid*. s.239; for laying and delivering accounts see p. 14ff above.
[38] *Ibid*. s.229(3).
[39] *Ibid*. s.229(4).

omitted on one or other of the above grounds. If this is the case, group accounts do not have to be prepared.[40]

When a subsidiary is excluded under any of the above exemptions, or the holding company does not prepare group accounts the following information should be given in the notes to the holding company's accounts, or to the consolidated financial statements if these have been prepared:

(a) the reason why the subsidiary is not dealt with in group accounts;

(b) where the subsidiary's accounts have been qualified by their auditors, a statement setting out the qualifications; the subsidiary's accounts in this context refer to the accounts covering the period that ends with or during the holding company's financial year and only those qualifications which have not been included in the holding company's own audit report need be shown here, and only if they are material from the point of view of the holding company's shareholders; and

(c) the aggregate amount of the total investment of the holding company in the shares of the subsidiaries by way of the equity method of valuation (the equity method of valuation is discussed on p. 165) below.

Where the holding company is a wholly owned subsidiary of another company, the information in (c) above need not be given. This dispensation may be applied only if the holding company's directors hold certain opinions. The directors must consider that the shares it holds in its subsidiary and the amounts owing to it (whether on account of a loan or otherwise) from that subsidiary are not less than the aggregate of the amounts at which those assets are stated or included in the company's balance sheet. A statement of the directors' opinion should be included in a note to the holding company's accounts.[41]

If any of the information set out above is not obtainable, then the notes to the holding company's accounts must include a statement to that effect.[42]

The information required to be given when a subsidiary is not included in group accounts may be omitted if the Secretary of State, on the application or with the consent of the company's directors, so directs. Alternatively, he may require that disclosure be made in a modified form.[43]

Forms of group accounts

Consolidated accounts
Group accounts will normally take the form of consolidated accounts. These will comprise a consolidated balance sheet dealing with the state of affairs of the company and all the subsidiaries to be dealt with in the group accounts, and a consolidated profit and loss account dealing with the aggregate

[40] *Ibid.* s.229(3).
[41] *Ibid.* Sched. 4, para. 69.
[42] *Ibid.*
[43] *Ibid.*

Exceptions profit or loss of the company and those subsidiaries.[44] If, however, the directors of the holding company are of the opinion that the same or equivalent information could be presented in a better form, which would be readily understood by the company's members then it may use another method.[45] When another form of group accounts is used then the same or equivalent information as would have appeared in any **Listed companies** consolidated accounts must be given.[46] Companies, however, which are listed on the Stock Exchange, are required under their continuing obligations to prepare group accounts in consolidated form. Consolidated financial statements are also regarded by **SSAP 14** SSAP 14 as the most usual form of group accounts. The Standard defines this term as a form of group accounts that presents the information contained in the separate financial statements of a holding company and its subsidiaries as if they were a single entity's financial statements. When consolidated financial statements are prepared, the Standard requires them to include a statement describing the bases on which those statements have dealt with subsidiary companies.

Other forms   For companies which can adopt a form of group accounts other than consolidated, the Act suggests the following alternatives:

(a) more than one set of consolidated accounts dealing respectively with the company and one group of subsidiaries together with a set of consolidated accounts dealing with other groups of subsidiaries;

(b) separate accounts dealing with each of the subsidiaries;

(c) statements expanding the information about the subsidiaries in the holding company's individual accounts;

(d) any combination of (a) to (c); or

(e) group accounts wholly or partly incorporated in the holding company's individual balance sheet or profit and loss account.[47]

This list is not exhaustive.

     Should group accounts take a form other than consolidated accounts, SSAP 14 requires directors to state the reasons why they consider that the group accounts presented give a fairer view of the groups financial position than those statements would have done had they been presented as consolidated financial statements.

General rules   Group accounts, whatever their form, must give a true and fair view of the state of affairs and the profit or loss of the company and the subsidiaries dealt with by those accounts as a whole, so far as concerns the members of the holding company.[48] They must also follow the provisions of Schedule 4, insofar as those provisions relate to group accounts.[49] As with individual accounts, additional information may be shown if it is necessary in order to present a true and fair view. The true and fair override

[44] *Ibid.* s.229(5).
[45] *Ibid.* s.229(6).
[46] *Ibid.* Sched. 4, para. 68.
[47] *Ibid.* s.229(6)(7).
[48] *Ibid.* s.230(2).
[49] *Ibid.* s.230(1).

may also be used in circumstances which justify departure from the provisions of that schedule.[50] The Secretary of State, on the application of or with the consent of the directors, may order the modifications of the Schedule 4 requirements so as to adapt them to a particular company's circumstances.[51]

Preparation
In preparing group accounts, the starting point is to aggregate all the information contained in the separate balance sheets and profit and loss accounts of the holding company and of the subsidiaries dealt with in the group accounts. If they deem it necessary, the directors of the holding company may make adjustments to these combined financial statements.[52]

Equity method of accounting
In dealing with an investment by any member of the group in shares of any other company, the holding company may choose to use the "equity method of accounting" when preparing group accounts. It may only do this, if the directors of the holding company consider that the company in which the investment has been made is so closely associated with any member of the group as to justify the use of this method.[53] The Act does not provide a definition of what is meant by the terms the "equity method of accounting" or "closely associated."

Guidance in relation to the equity method of accounting is, however, to be found in SSAP 14. The Standard defines this method as:

"A method of accounting under which the investment in a company is shown in the consolidated balance sheet at:
(a) the cost of the investment; and
(b) the investing company or group's share of the post-acquisition retained profits and reserves of the company; less
(c) any amounts written off in respect of (a) and (b) above; and under which the investing company accounts separately in its profit and loss account for its share of the profits before tax, taxation and extraordinary items of the company concerned."

SSAP 1, "Accounting for Associated Companies," requires that the value of an investment treated under the equity method of accounting will be the total of:

"(a) The investing group's share of the net assets (other than goodwill) of the associated companies, stated, when possible, after attributing fair values to the net assets at the time the interests in the associated companies were acquired.
(b) The investing group's share of any goodwill in the associated companies' own financial statements.
(c) The premium paid (or the discount) on the acquisition of the interests in the associated companies, in so far as it has not already been written off or amortised."

Group accounts must show item (a) separately but (b) and (c) may be aggregated.

---

[50] *Ibid*. s.230(3)(4)(5); see also p. 24ff above.
[51] *Ibid*. s.230(8).
[52] *Ibid*. Sched. 4, para. 61.
[53] *Ibid*. para. 65.

Thus, while the aggregate value disclosed will be the same, SSAPs 1 and 14 differ on how it is achieved. Associated companies are governed by SSAP 1, so investments in companies other than associates (for example, subsidiaries) will use the SSAP 14 method.

The phrase "closely associated" has not been the subject of definition by an accounting standard, but it is thought that an associated company will fall within it.

Consolidated group accounts

Consolidated group accounts comprise the consolidated balance sheet and related notes, the consolidated profit and loss account and related notes,[54] the holding company's balance sheet and related notes,[55] the directors' report[56] and the auditors' report.[57] Under SSAP 10, "Statements of Source and Application of Funds," the group's statement of source and application of funds may also have to be included.[58] The auditors' report will cover all the above financial statements with the exception of the directors' report on which they are only obliged to report if it is inconsistent with the accounts.[59]

A holding company may choose not to include its own profit and loss account and related notes if it prepares consolidated accounts and the consolidated profit and loss account:

(a) complies with the provisions of the Act; and
(b) shows how much of the consolidated profit or loss for the financial year is dealt with in the company's individual accounts.

Where the holding company's profit and loss account is not included, this fact must be stated in a note to the group accounts.[60]

As with other forms of group accounts, a holding company preparing consolidated accounts need not include all its subsidiaries in the calculations if the directors are of the opinion that one of the statutory exemptions apply.[61] When subsidiaries have been excluded under the provisions of the Act, the group accounts must contain notes disclosing certain information and in the case of consolidated accounts, there must also be shown details of the inter-company balances with excluded subsidiaries and details of the investment held.[62]

Omission of subsidiaries   In addition to the statutory rules, SSAP 14 provides that subsidiaries must be excluded from consolidated accounts in certain circumstances. This requirement is mandatory, although the circumstances set out in the Standard, while being more

[54] *Ibid.* s.229(5).
[55] *Ibid.* s.228(1).
[56] *Ibid.* s.235(1).
[57] *Ibid.* ss.236(1), 239.
[58] See pp. 46–47 above.
[59] Companies Act 1985, ss.236(1), 237(6).
[60] *Ibid.* s.228(7).
[61] See p. 162 above.
[62] Companies Act 1985, Sched. 4, para. 67; see also p. 163 above.

restrictive than those in the Act, would fall within the categories provided by statute.

According to SSAP 14, subsidiaries must be excluded where:

(a) the subsidiary's activities are so dissimilar from those of the other companies that any consolidated financial statements which included that subsidiary would be misleading; in this case, the information relating to the subsidiary is better provided by presenting separate financial statements in respect of that subsidiary;

(b) the holding company does not exercise effective control of the subsidiary; effective control will not be exercised when the holding company, although it holds more than half of the subsidiary's equity share capital, does not control the voting power; alternatively, the holding company will not have effective control where it has contractual or other restrictions placed upon its ability to appoint the majority to the subsidiary's board of directors;

(c) the subsidiary operates under severe restrictions that significantly affect the holding company's control over the subsidiary's assets and operations and this situation is expected to continue for the foreseeable future;

(d) the holding company's control over the subsidiary is intended to be temporary.

The accounting treatment of a subsidiary which has been excluded from consolidated accounts will depend upon the reason for its exclusion. The rules applying to each of the four exceptions are set out below.

Dissimilar activities
In the case of a subsidiary being engaged in activities which are so dissimilar from those of the other members of the group, the consolidated accounts may include the separate financial statements for that subsidiary. The subsidiary's financial statements should then include details of the holding company's interest, particulars of intra-group balances, the nature of the subsidiary's transactions with the rest of the group and a reconciliation with the amount included in the consolidated financial statements for the group's investment in the subsidiary. The group's investment in the omitted subsidiary should be stated under the equity method of accounting.[63] In the case of more than one subsidiary falling within this category, a combination of the financial statements of all the excluded subsidiaries would be possible where they were engaged upon similar activities.

Lack of effective control
A subsidiary over whom the holding company does not have effective control should be included in the consolidated group accounts under the equity method of accounting.[64] If it is an associated company or is an investment, at cost or valuation less any provision required, which is not an associate then the same basis of accounting should be employed. SSAP 1, "Accounting for Associated Companies," will apply in determining whether or not the omitted subsidiary is an associate.

Severe restrictions
Where the holding company's control over its subsidiary is severely restricted, the amount of the group's investment in the

[63] See p. 165 above.
[64] *Ibid.*

subsidiary should be stated in the consolidated balance sheet, at the amount at which it would have been included under the equity method of accounting,[65] at the date when the restrictions came into force. No further accrual should be made for its profits or losses after that date. Provision for losses should be made through the consolidated profit and loss account where the directors consider that there has been a permanent fall in the value of the investment; investments should be considered separately and not in the aggregate. The notes to group accounts should also give details of the subsidiary's net assets, its profits or loss for the period, and an amount included in the consolidated profit and loss account for dividends received or for the writing down of the investment.

Temporary control   In the case of a holding company's control over a subisdiary being temporary, the investment should be included in the consolidated balance sheet as a current asset at the lower of cost and net realisable value.

Disclosure   When subsidiaries have been excluded from consolidated accounts, the Standard requires that the following details should be given in addition to the statutory requirements:

(a) the reasons for excluding the subsidiaries from consolidation;
(b) the names of the principal subsidiaries excluded;
(c) any premium or discount on acquisition (determined by comparing the purchase consideration and the fair value of the assets acquired) to the extent that it has not been written off.

Uniform accounting policies   It is usual that in the preparation of consolidated group accounts uniform accounting policies will be applied throughout the group. Should a subsidiary follow different policies, SSAP 14 provides that appropriate adjustments should be made in the consolidated accounts. The need to make such adjustments should not be common, as all companies operating wholly within the United Kingdom are expected to follow SSAPs. On the acquisition of a new subsidiary which has employed different accounting policies from the rest of the group, the new subsidiary will normally change its policies and make prior year adjustment as is required by SSAP 6, "Extraordinary Items and Prior Year Adjustments."

Where, however, adjustments on consolidation are inappropriate, SSAP 14 permits subsidiaries to keep their individual accounting policies when preparing their own individual accounts. If different accounting policies are used, they must be generally acceptable and disclosure of the following information should be made in the group accounts:

(a) the different accounting policies used;
(b) an indication of the amounts of assets and liabilities involved and, where practicable, the effect which the use of the different policies has had on the group's results and net assets; and
(c) the reasons for the different treatment.

[65] *Ibid.*

Minority interests   Neither the statutory formats nor the rules supplementing them deal with the disclosure of minority interests thus allowing companies to choose where they show them in the balance sheet, with the exception that SSAP 14 provides that they should be disclosed as a separate amount in the consolidated balance sheet and not shown as part of shareholders' funds. This is in conflict with the EC Seventh Directive which requires minority interests to be shown as a separate item, under the heading "Shares held by persons outside the group" in the company's capital, reserves and results brought forward. It is thought, however, that this conflict will in fact be of little importance in practice, as minority interests are usually shown either as a deduction from net assets or as an additional item next to capital and reserves.

The profit or loss attributable to minority interests should be shown separately in the consolidated profit and loss accounts, after arriving at the group's profit or loss. This calculation must be shown after the deduction of tax but before extraordinary items, for example in format 1 this will be between "Profit or loss on ordinary activities after taxation" and "Extraordinary income." SSAP 14 further provides that the minority interest in extraordinary items should be either deducted from or added to the related amounts in the consolidated profit and loss account.

In the event of a loss being made, the minority interests' proportion of the debit should only be included in the consolidated accounts where there is a binding obligation on the minority shareholders to make good the losses incurred. Where this is the case, the minority's share of the losses should be provided for in the consolidated profit and loss account, and no amount added back in profit and loss account for the minority interest. When the subsidiary starts to make profits which can be attributable to the minority the process should be reversed.

Provisions inapplicable to group accounts

The following information need not be disclosed in group accounts, whether or not they are presented in the consolidated form:

(a) details of the aggregate shareholdings in companies other than subsidiaries;

(b) financial information about subsidiaries and other companies in which shares are held;

(c) details of the aggregate chairman's and directors' emoluments, pensions and compensation for loss of office; only those amounts relating to the chairman and directors of the holding company need be disclosed;

(d) particulars relating to the aggregate number of higher paid employees; only those details relating to employees of the holding company need be given; and

(e) particulars of loan and other transaction favouring directors and officers.[66]

---

[66] Companies Act 1985, Sched. 4, para. 63.

Acquisition or disposal of subsidiaries

The disclosure requirements necessary when changes are made to the composition of a group are set by SSAP 14 which provides that sufficient information about the results of the subsidiaries acquired or sold must be shown in consolidated accounts to enable shareholders to appreciate the effect which these results have had on the consolidated results. The effects of additions to and disposals from the group should also be shown in the statement of source and application of funds.

In calculating the group's profit or loss, the consolidated profit and loss account should take account of a newly acquired subsidiary's results from the date on which it was acquired by the group. On a material disposal, the consolidated profit and loss account should include the subsidiary's results up to the date of disposal and the gain or loss on the sale of the investment. The gain or loss will be the difference, at the time of the sale, between the sale proceeds and the holding company's share of the subsidiary's net assets, together with either any premium (less any amounts written off) or any discount on acquisition.

The date of disposal or sale is to be taken as the earlier of either the date on which consideration passes, or the date on which an offer becomes, or is declared, unconditional. When a decision is taken to sell a subsidiary before the holding company's year end, but the disposal does not take place until early in the next accounting period, then SSAP 17, "Accounting for Post Balance Sheet Events," requires that the subsidiary should still be included in the current year's consolidation. If the sale is material, the fact of the sale and its financial effect should be shown in the notes to the consolidated accounts. The subsidiary should not be excluded from consolidation even though the holding company's control could be said to be temporary.

Foreign currency translation

When a company has overseas subsidiaries, the question arises of how the results of that company are to be shown in the consolidated accounts. This subject is governed by SSAP 20, "Foreign Currency Translation," which also deals with the translation of the results of overseas associated companies and foreign branches. Normally a company should use the closing rate/net investment method for such translations. The Standard should be consulted for further details of the accounting treatment of the results of overseas companies connected with United Kingdom companies.

17 ACQUISITIONS, MERGERS AND GOODWILL

Introduction

The subject of the acquisition by one business of another or the merger of two businesses is a complex subject, and this chapter aims only to deal with some of the accounting issues which arise upon an acquisition or merger. Once a business has been acquired or there has been a merger, a balancing figure will probably appear either in the acquiring company's accounts or in the group accounts under the heading of "goodwill." Whilst it will appear under "Intangible assets," goodwill is unlike other types of intangible asset and special accounting rules will have to be applied to it.

Acquisitions and mergers

The accounting treatment of business combinations has caused the accountancy profession many headaches over recent years. The present position is that the Act lays down certain rules regarding merger relief for individual companies and SSAP 23, "Accounting for Acquisitions and Mergers," governs acquisition accounting and merger accounting in consolidated accounts.

Merger relief   The starting point for merger relief is section 130 of the Act which requires that when a company issues shares at a premium, whether that premium be for cash or not, a sum equal to the aggregate amount or value of the premiums on those shares must **Share premium** be transferred to a share premium account.[1] The use to which the **account** share premium account may be put is then restricted to the following applications:

(a) paying up unissued shares to be allotted to members as fully paid bonus shares;
(b) writing off the company's preliminary expenses;
(c) writing off the expenses of, or the commission paid or discount allowed on, any issue of shares or debentures of the company; or
(d) providing for the premium payable on redemption of debentures of the company.[2]

Subject to this, the share premium account may be treated as though it were part of the company's paid up share capital in the event of a reduction of the company's share capital.[3]

When one company is acquired by another, there are two possible methods of accounting for the acquisition. The normal

---

[1] Companies Act 1985, s.130(1).
[2] *Ibid*. s.130(2).
[3] *Ibid*. s.130(3).

Acquisition accounting accounting treatment, if the acquisition was on a share for share basis, is the acquisition method. Under this method, the shares transferred to the vendor company are recorded in that company's books at the value of the consideration given. Where the vendor company issued shares in exchange and these shares are given a value in excess of their nominal value, the excess is transferred to the share premium account, and is therefore only available for application in limited circumstances.

Merger accounting The alternative method, which prior to 1980 was only very occasionally used, is the merger method. Under this method, the shares transferred to the vendor company would be entered in that company's books at the nominal value of the shares that it issued in exchange. The only difference which would arise under the merger method was the difference between the nominal value of the shares issued as consideration and the nominal value of the shares transferred to the vendor company. The result of this accounting treatment of an acquisition was that the distributable reserves of both the companies involved in the transaction would still be available for distribution, whereas under the acquisition method, the acquired company's reserves would be treated as pre-acquisition reserves and thus undistributable.

The legality of the merger method of accounting for business combinations was always open to question, but the issue was finally decided in *Shearer* v. *Bercain Ltd*,[4] in which the court held that where shares were issued at a premium, whether for cash or otherwise, the premium had to be carried to the share premium account, with the result that it could, in future, only be applied in limited circumstances. The outcome of this case was in effect to make illegal the use of merger accounting and to prohibit the distribution of the pre-acquisition profits of the company which had been acquired. *Shearer* v. *Bercain* led to the introduction of certain provisions in the Companies Act 1981, now consolidated in the 1985 Act, which gave specific exemptions from the requirement to create a share premium account under what is now section 130 of the 1985 Act.

Qualifying conditions Merger relief, in other words, exemption from the need to transfer an amount representing the value of any share premium to a share premium account in the event of an issue of shares as part of a business combination, is available to a company (the issuing company), which acquires at least a 90 per cent. equity holding in another company (the acquired company), under the

Arrangement terms of an arrangement.[5] An arrangement is defined by the Act as "any agreement, scheme or arrangement" and includes an arrangement sanctioned under a company compromise with members and creditors or an arrangement whereby a liquidator accepts shares, etc., as consideration for the sale of company property.[6] The exemption from the requirement to transfer certain sums to a share premium account is not available if the acquired company is a member of the same group as the issuing company or, in other words, in the case of a group reconstruction.[7]

The arrangement to which the issuing and the acquired

---

[4] [1980] 3 All E.R. 295.
[5] Companies Act 1985, s.131(1).
[6] *Ibid.* s.131(7).
[7] *Ibid.* s.131(1).

companies are parties must provide for the allotment of equity shares in the issuing company in exchange for either the issue or transfer to the issuing company of equity shares in the acquired company, or for the cancellation of any such shares not held by the issuing company.[8] "Equity shares" are defined as shares comprised in the company's equity share capital,[9] and a transfer of shares will include the transfer of a right to appear in the company's register of members in respect of those shares, transfers of shares or by a company will include any transfers made by its nominees.[10] Where an arrangement of this type is made and at least 90 per cent. of the equity shares in the acquired company are held by the issuing company, any premium on the equity shares in the issuing company which have been allotted under the arrangement need not be transferred to a share premium account.[11]

Where an arrangement also provides for the allotment of any shares in the issuing company in consideration for either the acquisition of non-equity shares in the acquired company or the cancellation of any such shares not held by the issuing company, merger relief will extend to any shares in the issuing company which are allotted under the terms of such an arrangement.[12] "Non-equity shares" are shares of any class which do not form part of a company's equity share capital.[13]

When calculating the percentage of shares which the issuing company holds in the acquired company, the effect of the arrangement must be taken into account, so that where shares are acquired by the issuing company, these will be added to any equity share already held in the acquired company, or if shares are cancelled, the acquired company's nominal share capital should be reduced accordingly.[14] Shares held by a company which is a member of the same group as the issuing company, or held by nominee of either the issuing company or fellow group member, are deemed to be held by the issuing company for these purposes.[15] Where the acquired company has different classes of equity share capital, the conditions set out on page 172 above must be complied with in respect of each class of equity share.[16]

Merger relief will not apply where the issue of shares took place before February 4, 1981. Retrospective relief may, however, be available in these circumstances.[17]

Disclosure   When a company relies upon the merger relief provisions, it must disclose the following information in a notes to the accounts:

    (a) the name of the other company;
    (b) the number, nominal value and class of:
        (i) shares allotted; and

---

[8] *Ibid.*
[9] *Ibid.* s.131(7).
[10] *Ibid.* s.133(3).
[11] *Ibid.* s.131(2).
[12] *Ibid.* s.131(3).
[13] *Ibid.* s.131(7).
[14] *Ibid.* s.131(4).
[15] *Ibid.* s.131(6).
[16] *Ibid.* s.131(5).
[17] *Ibid.* s.131(8); see also p. 175 below.

(ii) shares in the other company that were issued, transferred or cancelled;

(c) details of the accounting treatment adopted by the company in its own accounts or in its group accounts; and

(d) where the company prepares group accounts, the extent to which and manner in which the group's profit or loss is affected by any profit or loss of the company or any of its subsidiaries which arose before the merger.

Where during a particular financial year or during either of the two preceding financial years, a company, Company A, has taken advantage of the merger relief provisions when allotting shares, further information must be shown in the following circumstances:

(a) the disposal by Company A or any of its subsidiaries of shares in the other company, Company B;

(b) the disposal by Company A or any of its subsidiaries of any fixed assets of Company B or any of Company B's subsidiaries which were assets at the time of the allotment; and

(c) the disposal by Company A or any of its subsidiaries of shares in a company, Company C, but only if the profit or loss on such a disposal is to some extent attributable to the fact that Company C or any of Company C's subsidiaries, at the time of the disposal, owned shares in Company B or fixed assets which were within (b) immediately above.

If a profit or loss is made by Company A or any of its subsidiaries on a disposal arising in any of the above circumstances, and that profit or loss is included in Company A's consolidated profit and loss account or, where such an account has not been prepared, its individual profit and loss account, the net amount of the profit or loss must be disclosed in a note to the accounts. An explanation of the transaction to which that information relates must also be given.[18] Similar disclosure requirements are set by SSAP 23.[19]

Group reconstructions

In *Shearer* v. *Bercain*, Walton J. also applied the rule against merger accounting to group reconstructions. The merger relief in these circumstances is governed by section 132 and is available only in limited situations.

Qualifying conditions

Merger relief can be claimed for group reconstructions if the following conditions are met:

(a) the issuing company is a wholly owned subsidiary of another company, the holding company;

(b) the issuing company allots shares to the holding company or to another wholly owned subsidiary of the holding company;

(c) the allotment of shares is in exchange for the transfer to the issuing company of assets, other than cash;

(d) the assets are transferred by any company (the transferor company) which is a member of the same group as the holding company and all its wholly owned subsidiaries; and

---

[18] *Ibid.* Sched. 4, para. 75.

[19] See p. 178 below.See p. 178 below.

(e) the issuing company's shares allotted under such an arrangement are issued at a premium.[20]

If these conditions are satisfied, the issuing company is not required to transfer any amount in excess of the "minimum premium value" to the share premium account.[21]

Minimum premium value

The "minimum premium value" is defined as "the amount (if any) by which the base value of the consideration for the shares allotted exceeds the aggregate nominal value of those shares."[22] To calculate the base value of the consideration for the shares allotted, the base value of the assets transferred and the base value of any liabilities of the transferor company assumed by the issuing company as part of the consideration for the assets transferred must be ascertained.[23] The "base value" of the assets transferred is:

(i) the cost of those assets to the transferor company, or
(ii) the amount at which those assets are stated in the transferor company's accounting records immediately before the transfer,

whichever is the less; and the "base value" of the liabilities assumed is the amount at which they are stated in the transferor company's accounting records immediately before the transfer.[24] The "base value" of the consideration for the shares allotted is then taken as the amount by which the base value of the assets transferred exceeds the base value of any liabilities of the transferor company assumed by the issuing company.[25]

Merger relief will not be available for a group reconstruction where the issue of shares took place before February 4, 1981.[26] Retrospective relief may, however, be available.

Retrospective relief

Where an issuing company has issued shares at a premium before February 4, 1981, retrospective relief from the need to transfer the value of any premium on the issued shares to a share premium account may be available.[27] The statutory provisions should be consulted for the details. The retrospective rules are wider than those governing merger relief under section 131 of the 1985 Act as, *inter alia*, the issuing company is not required to hold 90 per cent. or more of the acquired company's shares, nor does it have had to have allotted its own equity shares in exchange for the shares acquired in order to obtain relief.

Merger relief regulations

The Secretary of State is empowered to make regulations either extending or restricting merger relief, including retrospective relief, as appears to him to be appropriate.[28] Under this power the Secretary of State will be able to make any changes which need to be made to this area of law as a result of the implementation of the EC Seventh Directive on group accounts.

---

[20] Companies Act 1985, s.132(1).
[21] *Ibid.* s.132(2).
[22] *Ibid.* s.132(3).
[23] *Ibid.* s.132(4).
[24] *Ibid.* s.132(5).
[25] *Ibid.* s.132(4).
[26] *Ibid.* s.132(6)(7).
[27] Companies Consolidation (Consequential Provisions) Act 1985, s.12.
[28] Companies Act 1985, s.134 and Companies Consolidated (Consequential Provisions) Act 1985, s.12(6).

Accounting for acquisitions and mergers

Background   SSAP 23 was issued by the ASC after long debate, which began with the issue in 1971 of an Exposure Draft on accounting for mergers and acquisitions. This draft never became a Standard. A subsequent Exposure Draft was formulated and issued in 1982 in response to an indication from the Government, made during the passage of the merger relief provisions through Parliament, that guidance should be given to companies as to the accounting treatment which they should adopt where they obtained merger relief. The 1982 Exposure Draft was approved and became a Standard, SSAP 23, "Accounting for Mergers and Acquisitions." The Standard applies to financial statements beginning on or after April 1, 1985.

     SSAP 23, unlike the statutory merger relief provisions, only applies to the accounting treatment of acquisitions and mergers in consolidated accounts. The Standard stipulates when acquisition accounting should be used instead of merger accounting and vice versa.

Differing accounting treatment   The main difference between acquisition accounting and merger accounting arises from the fact that acquisition accounting only reflects the effect of the business combination in the group accounts after the date of the acquisition, whereas in merger accounting, the group accounts are presented as if the businesses had always been combined. Thus in merger accounting, even if the merger may have taken place during the year, the group accounts combines both companies full year's results and the previous years figures are drawn up on that basis also, although the merger had not then taken place.

Methods to be used   The main criterion which the Standard lays down for determining which method of accounting should be used is whether or not the combination is principally based on a share for share exchange. Where it is and the two groups of shareholders continue, or are in a position to continue, their shareholdings as before but on a combined basis, then merger accounting is considered to be an appropriate method. Where there is a transfer of the ownership of at least one of the combining companies and substantial resources leave the group as consideration for that transfer, then acquisition accounting

Choice of method   should be used. On that basis, SSAP 23 provides that a group may use either merger accounting or acquisition accounting if it can satisfy certain conditions. Where those conditions are not met, only acquisition accounting may be used.

Merger accounting conditions   The qualifying conditions which must be satisfied before merger accounting can be applied are:

(a) an offer must be made both to the holders of all the equity shares that the offeror does not already hold, and to the holders of all those voting shares that the offeror does not already hold;

(b) as a result of the offer, the offeror must secure a holding of at least 90 per cent. of each class of the offeree's equity shares (taking each class of equity separately), and must secure at least 90 per cent. of the offeree's votes;

(c) immediately before the offer, the offeror must not hold 20 per cent. or more of any class of the offeree's equity shares (taking each class of equity separately), or must not hold 20 per cent. or more of the offeree's votes; and

(d) the following cash limits must be met:

    (i) equity share capital must form not less than 90 per cent. of the fair value of the total consideration that the offeror gives for the offeree's equity share capital;

    (ii) equity share capital and/or voting non-equity share capital must form not less than 90 per cent. of the fair value of the total consideration that the offeror gives for the offeree's voting non-equity share capital.

The fair value of the total consideration that the offeror gives should include also the fair value of the consideration that the offeror gave for shares that it held before the offer.

For the purpose of compliance with the merger conditions, any convertible stock that is outstanding at the time of the offer should not be treated as forming part of the equity. The only exception to this rule is where the convertible stock is converted into equity as a result of, and at the time of, the business combination.

In relation to the merger conditions, the term "the offeror" includes the offeror itself, the holding company of the offeror, and a subsidiary or fellow subsidiary of the offeror. "Voting shares" refers to full voting shares, in other words, the term does not include shares which only carry votes in certain circumstances, for example when dividends are in arrears.

It will be seen that the conditions which must be satisfied before merger accounting is permitted are more restrictive than those governing the statutory merger relief. This may result in a holding company being able to obtain merger relief, while the group is required to use acquisition accounting on consolidation.

Merger accounting rules

If the conditions for merger accounting are satisfied, a group need not include the subsidiary's assets and liabilities at fair value in the consolidated accounts. It may use the figures recorded in the subsidiary's books before the combination. This may not, however, be possible where the acquired company's accounting policies differ from those of the group, as SSAP 14, "Group Accounts," requires that groups adopt uniform accounting policies. Unless it is not practicable to apply a uniform accounting policy, the amounts of the assets and liabilities should be restated in the books of the acquired company to reflect the change in accounting policy.

It has been seen that, where merger accounting is used, the results of both companies are included for the full year, regardless of when the combination actually took place. The corresponding amounts for the previous year will also be adjusted to show the combined results.

In the holding company's balance sheet, the holding company's investment in the subsidiary will be shown at the nominal value of the shares that the holding company issued as consideration. To this will be added the fair value of any additional consideration. Any difference which arises on consolidation between the value of the investment in the subsidiary which appears in the holding company's balance sheet and the nominal value of the subsidiary's shares acquired by the holding company should be adjusted through the consolidated reserves. If the difference arises because the value of the investment shown in the holding company's balance sheet is less than the nominal value of the shares acquired by the holding company and that difference is material, the Standard requires that the difference be treated as a separate reserve in order that a true and fair view is shown.

Disclosure   When a business combination is material, SSAP 23 lays down certain disclosure rules, which apply regardless of whether acquisition accounting or merger accounting is used. The

General information required information, which must be shown in the consolidated accounts for the period in which the business combination occurs, is as follows:

(a) the names of the combining companies;

(b) the number and the class of the securities that the company issued in respect of the combination;

(c) details of any other consideration that the company gave in respect of the combinations;

(d) the accounting treatment that the company adopted for the business combination, in other words, whether the acquisition or merger method of accounting was used; and

(e) the nature and the amount of any significant accounting adjustments that the combining companies made to achieve consistent accounting policies.

Acquisition accounting   If acquisition accounting is used, then the consolidated accounts should contain information about the results of any subsidiaries which the group has acquired during the year. The purpose of this requirement is to enable shareholders to appreciate the effect that the results of the subsidiaries have had on the consolidated results. The date from which the results have been brought into the consolidated accounts should also be given.

Merger accounting   Additional information is also required when merger accounting has been used that is:

(a) the fair value of the consideration that the issuing company gave in respect of the business combination;

(b) the amount of the current year's attributable profit before extraordinary items that relates to the part of the year before the business combination, and also the amount that relates to the part of the year after;

(c) an analysis of the attributable profit before extraordinary items of the current year up to the effect date of the combination;

(d) an analysis of the attributable profit before extraordinary items of the previous year between that of the issuing company and that of the subsidiary;

(e) an analysis of extraordinary items between those items relating to the period before the combination's effective date and those relating to the period after that date; and

(f) an analysis of extraordinary items indicating to which party to the combination the extraordinary items relate.

Goodwill

Nature   When a company purchases a business, it may find that the consideration paid for that business is different from the value of its separate net assets. That difference is called "goodwill" and while it is usually a positive figure, it is possible to have negative goodwill. Goodwill may also arise as a result of the accounting treatment of investments and assets when more than one business entity is combined in the preparation of consolidated or group accounts.

Definition   Statute does not define goodwill but a definition does appear in the accounting Standard on the subject, SSAP 22, "Accounting for Goodwill," which states that it is "the difference between the value of a business as a whole and the aggregate of the fair values of its separate net assets." Separate net assets includes intangible assets. In a company's balance sheet, purchased goodwill will appear as an intangible asset under the "Fixed asset" heading. It is, however, unlike other intangible assets in that its value is highly subjective and may fluctuate widely over short periods of time. When a business is purchased, for example, goodwill only exists at the moment when the business is bought and subsequently appears in a company's accounts as a "paper figure" necessary in order that the books balance. The figure representing goodwill will therefore be the amount over and above the worth of the business' assets which that particular purchaser was prepared to pay in the circumstances which existed at the time of the purchase. On the other hand, other types of intangible assets, such as patents and copyrights, have a value which can be gauged on the open market and are a saleable asset in their own right.

If goodwill was treated in the same manner as other assets, it would lead to a false impression being created in a company's balance sheet. Special rules have therefore been evolved to deal

Accounting   with the accounting treatment of goodwill. The Act itself makes
treatment   some limited provisions concerning the subject, but the majority of the rules governing goodwill are contained in SSAP 22. This Standard was approved in 1984 and governs all financial statements to which the true and fair rule applies for the accounting period beginning on or after January 1, 1985.

As has been seen above goodwill is shown under "Intangible assets" in a company's balance sheet, but only purchased goodwill may be included.[29] No revaluation of this asset is permitted either by statute,[30] or by SSAP 22; rather, goodwill must be eliminated from the company's accounts. If there is a permanent diminution in the value of any goodwill, it should be written down immediately, through the profit and loss account, to its estimated recoverable value.

Elimination   There are various methods by which goodwill may be dealt with in a company's accounts, but the preferred way is to eliminate it immediately it arises. As this might prove impracticable in certain situations and might lead to a company's financial statements not showing a true and fair view, the Act provides that goodwill must be written off over its useful economic life.[31] SSAP 22 provides various acceptable methods of elimination.

---

[29] Companies Act 1985, Sched. 4, para. 8, note 3 to the balance sheet.
[30] *Ibid.* Sched. 4, para. 31.
[31] *Ibid.* para. 21.

Where positive goodwill exists in financial statements for the accounting period beginning on or after January 1, 1985, (being the date on which the Standard became effective), it should normally be written off against reserves. Where such goodwill has not been amortised, a company, wishing to choose the amortisation method of elimination, should calculate the amount by which the goodwill would have been written down had that policy been followed from the date on which the goodwill was purchased up to the date the Standard became effective. The company should then write that amount off as a prior year adjustment to realised reserves. Any remaining balance should then be amortised over the useful economic life of the goodwill.

Transitional provisions

Transitional provisions exist for those companies and groups which have large balances of purchased goodwill. In these cases, the amortisation of the goodwill may begin on the date on which the Standard came into effect. Special rules also apply to those companies and groups which did not begin to write down goodwill until after the date of purchase. Here, the goodwill may continue to be amortised over the period of its useful economic life and no prior year adjustment need be made for the period during which the amortisation policy did not apply.

Goodwill purchased after the Standard came into effect should either be written off immediately or amortised over its useful economic life, although the Standard states that a policy of immediate write off is to be preferred. Where it is decided to eliminate goodwill over its useful economic life, the question then arises as to whether this policy will result in a reduction of

Realised reserves

realised reserves, thus affecting, *inter alia*, the amount of profits which a company will have available for distribution. The Standard reaches the conclusion that realised reserves will not be reduced immediately, unless the goodwill is considered to have suffered a permanent diminution in value. Purchased goodwill, however, must eventually result in a realised loss at the end of its useful economic life.

A company, therefore, may choose between writing goodwill off immediately against realised or unrealised reserves. In the latter case, the amount written off must be transferred systematically to realised reserves over the goodwill's useful economic life. The effect of this in practical terms is the same as if the company had applied a policy of amortisation. It is for the company to decide which unrealised reserve should be used for the immediate writing off of goodwill if this method is chosen.

Revaluation reserve

The Act, however, prohibits the use of the revaluation reserve for this purpose, as it does not include the writing off of goodwill as one of the methods allowed for the reduction of this reserve. Another reason for not allowing the revaluation reserve to be used in this way is that the amount will not be one which was previously charged to the profit and loss account or one which represents a realised profit.[32] There is doubt whether this would apply to goodwill arising on consolidation as the restriction is based upon the EC Fourth Directive which only applies to companies and not to groups.

Useful economic life

If it is decided to write goodwill off over a period time, it should be amortised systematically over its useful economic life,

---

[32] *Ibid.* para. 34.

the length of that life being determined by the particular company's directors.[33] As it is not possible to give an absolute period over which goodwill should be amortised in all circumstances, neither maximum nor minimum periods are set by statute or by SSAP 22, although the Standard does offer the guidance that the useful economic life of purchased goodwill should be "the period over which benefits may reasonably be expected to accrue from that goodwill."

When a company or group is determining the useful economic life of purchased goodwill, it should not take into account any actions or expenditure or other circumstances after the date of the acquisition. If these subsequent events create goodwill, it will be non-purchased goodwill, which cannot be included in a balance sheet.[34] The only goodwill which may therefore be taken into account when determining the period of useful economic life is that which existed and was recognised at the time of acquisition.

Among the factors which may affect the length of goodwill's useful economic life are:

(a) expected changes in products, markets or technology;
(b) the expected period of future service of certain employees; and
(c) expected future demand, competition or other economic factors that may affect current advantages.

A company should periodically review its policy towards goodwill. The Standard permits the shortening of its estimated useful economic life but this period may not be lengthened.

Negative goodwill   Negative goodwill will be created when the aggregate of the fair values of the separable net assets acquired exceeds the consideration given for the purchase. When it arises it should be credited direct to unrealised reserves. A separate reserve does not need to be created, either under the Act or SSAP 22, for negative goodwill. Should a company, however, wish to do so, then this reserve should be included under "Other reserves" in the balance sheet formats. Negative goodwill may be systematically transferred from unrealised to realised reserves, but if this is done it will have no effect on the profits available for distribution.

Disclosure   SSAP 22 requires that the accounting policy in respect of either positive or negative goodwill should be disclosed in a note to the accounts. The note should very briefly describe how the goodwill arose and in the case of purchased goodwill state whether it has been written off immediately or amortised. In the case of negative goodwill, the note should give a brief summary of it being credited to reserves and any accounting entries carried out in addition to that. If a company has made several acquisitions during the year, the amount of purchased goodwill should be shown separately for each acquisition, but this need only be done if the amount involved is material.

In cases where the amortisation method has been adopted, a company must show the amount of any purchased goodwill which has not been written off separately under the subheading "Intangible assets" in the balance sheet. In group accounts, this

[33] *Ibid*. para. 21.
[34] *Ibid*. para. 8, note 3 to the balance sheet.

figure might include not only purchased goodwill, but also goodwill arising on consolidation or purchased goodwill appearing in a subsidiary's balance sheet.

The Act also requires that the period chosen by the directors for writing off any goodwill appearing in the balance sheet, in other words, the length of its useful economic life, should be given in the notes to the accounts, along with the reasons for their choice.[35] The requirement that the directors' reasons be given for choosing a particular amortisation period does not apply to goodwill arising on consolidation.[36] As SSAP 22 does not require any disclosure of reasons for this choice, it will not apply to groups, although they are required by the Standard to show the length of the useful economic life of any goodwill.

Both the Act and the Standard permit, either expressly or by implication, companies to choose different amortisation periods for different elements of goodwill. Where this is done, the company or group will have to disclose each of the periods chosen. The Standard then requires that this information should be accompanied by the following particulars:

(a) the aggregated cost of goodwill both at the beginning of the financial year and as at the balance sheet date;

(b) the effect of any revision to that amount made during the financial year;

(c) the effect on that amount of any acquisitions or disposals made during the same period;

(d) any transfers effecting that amount during the financial year;

(e) the amount of any amortisation made in respect of the financial year;

(f) the amount of accumulated amortisation at the beginning and end of the financial year; and

(g) the amount of any other adjustments made in respect of the amortisation of goodwill during that year.

---

[35] *Ibid.* para. 21.
[36] *Ibid.* para. 66.

18 CHANGE OF COMPANY STATUS

Introduction

There are both advantages and disadvantages in a company having either public or private status. The advantages of the public company status are that a public company can offer its shares and debentures to the public, and if it so desires, seek a listing on the Stock Exchange. The disadvantages are that:

(a) a public company may not enter into quasi-loans or credit transactions for its directors or persons connected with them; this prohibition includes the provision of guarantees or security for such transactions and also engaging third parties to enter into the prohibited transactions on the company's behalf[1];

(b) whilst a public company may acquire its own shares, it may not purchase or redeem its own shares out of capital[2];

(c) a public company may only provide financial assistance for the purchase of its own shares if the giving of the assistance was not the main objective but an incidental part of some larger purpose, and the assistance was given in good faith in the interests of the company; a private company may also give financial assistance if in doing so it does not reduce its net assets and complies with certain other conditions.[3]

(d) the accounting records of a public company must be kept for six years under companies' legislation, whereas private companies are only obliged to retain their accounting records for three years, although other regulations may extend this period, for example, VAT requirements[4];

(e) a public company must lay its annual accounts before its members in general meeting and deliver copies of them to the Registrar of Companies within seven months of the end of their financial year; a private company has ten months from that date within which to comply[5];

(f) a public company may not register modified accounts with the Registrar of Companies or resolve not to have its annual accounts audited should it become dormant.[6]

The advantages and disadvantages of private company status are the mirror image of the advantages and disadvantages of being public: it may not offer its shares or debentures to the public but may take advantage of the options listed in the preceding paragraphs.

[1] See p. 141ff above.
[2] See p. 129ff above.
[3] See p. 125ff above.
[4] Companies Act 1985, s.222(4); see also pp. 8–9 above.
[5] *Ibid.* s.242(2).
[6] For modified accounts see p. 30ff above and for dormant companies see p. 122ff above.

Private company re-registering as public

Share capital

Authorised minimum 25 per cent. or more paid up

A private company which wishes to achieve public company status must meet the relevant share capital requirements. The requirements are that the nominal value of the company's share capital is not less than the authorised minimum[7] which is at present set at £50,000. Each of the company's allotted shares must be paid up at least to one-quarter of the nominal value of that share and the whole of any premium on it must be paid up.[8] Where any shares or premium on them have been fully or partly paid up by an undertaking regarding the performance of work or services, the undertaking must have been performed or otherwise discharged.[9]

If either the whole or part of any consideration in respect of any share or premium on it was that an undertaking other than one relating to the perfomance of work or services, would be honoured, then that undertaking must have been performed or otherwise discharged. Alternatively, it will be sufficient if there is a contract between the company and some person pursuant to which the undertaking is to be performed within five years from the date on which the special resolution relating to re-registration was passed.[10]

Procedure

Special resolution

Having satisfied the share capital requirements, a private company wishing to change its status must follow a certain procedure in order to re-register as a public limited company. First, it must pass a special resolution approving the alteration from private to public status.[11] The special resolution should change the company's memorandum of association so that it:

(a) states that the company is to be a public company;
(b) changes the company's name so that the words "public limited complany" or the letters "p.l.c." appear at the end of its name instead of "limited" or "ltd.";
(c) alters the company's share capital clause so that the value of the company's nominal share capital is not below the authorised minimum; and
(d) makes any other necessary alterations.[12]

The special resolution should also make such alterations to the company's articles of association as are necessary on the company becoming public.[13] An example of a necessary change to the company's articles might be the removal or changing of the restrictions on the transfer or transmission of the company's shares. Such an alteration would have to be made if it was envisaged that the company might seek a listing on the Stock Exchange at some future date.

Application to Registrar

Having passed the requisite resolution, a company must then apply to the Registrar of Companies for re-registration. The application must be in the prescribed form and cannot be made by a company which has previously re-registered as unlimited.[14]

[7] Companies Act 1985, ss.45(2), 118(1).
[8] *Ibid.* s.45(2).
[9] *Ibid.* s.45(3); see also s.45(5)–(7).
[10] *Ibid.* s.45(4).
[11] *Ibid.* s.43(1).
[12] *Ibid.* s.43(2).
[13] *Ibid.*
[14] *Ibid.* s.43(1).

The application must be signed by a director or the secretary of the company and be accompanied by the following documents:

(a) a printed copy of the memorandum and articles as altered by the special resolution;

(b) a copy of a written statement concerning the company's net assets made by the company's auditors;

(c) a copy of the relevant balance sheet, together with a copy of an unqualified report by the company's auditors in respect of that balance sheet;

(d) a copy of a revaluation report if shares have been allotted between the date at which the relevant balance sheet was prepared and the passing of the special resolution; and

(e) a statutory declaration in the prescribed form made by a director or secretary of the company.[15]

The auditors' statement, relevant balance sheet, valuation report and directors' declaration are examined in detail in the following paragraphs.

Auditors' statement

The auditors' written statement on the company's net assets must give the auditors' opinion that the relevant balance sheet shows that, at the balance sheet date, the amount of the company's net assets was not less than the aggregate of its called up share capital. The phrase "net assets" means the aggregate of the company's assets less the aggregate of its liabilities. A company's liabilities are to include any provisions for liabilities and charges.[16]

Relevant balance sheet

The balance sheet which must be included with a company's application for re-registration is one which has been prepared as at a date not more than seven months before the application is made.[17] If a balance sheet which forms part of a company's annual accounts (in other words, it is drawn up as at the company's accounting reference date) meets this criteria then it may be submitted with the company's application for re-registration. If not, then a company must prepare a balance sheet drawn up as at a date which is within the specified period namely, not more than seven months before the application is made. Whichever balance sheet is used, it must be accompanied by an unqualified audit report.[18]

Unqualified audit report

An audit report will be unqualified if it is without material qualification. A qualification will not be regarded as material, if the thing giving rise to it is not material in relation to the following matter. That matter is whether, according to the relevant balance sheet, the amount of the company's net assets was not less than the aggregate of its called up share capital and undistributable reserves. This question is to be determined as at the balance sheet date. In the event of the auditors reporting an immaterial qualification, their report must include a statement that the qualification is not material as it does not relate to the above matter.[19]

In addition to stating that the balance sheet is without

---

[15] *Ibid.* s.43(3).
[16] *Ibid.*
[17] *Ibid.* s.43(4).
[18] *Ibid.* s.43(3).
[19] *Ibid.* s.46(5).

material qualification, the auditors must express their opinion on the manner in which the balance sheet has been prepared and this will vary according to whether or not the balance sheet date is the company's accounting reference date. The audit report on a balance sheet which has been drawn up as at that date should state that, in the auditors' opinion, the balance sheet was properly prepared in accordance with with Companies Act 1985 and that it gives a true and fair view of the state of the company's affairs as at the balance sheet date.[20]

If the relevant balance sheet was not drawn up as at a company's accounting reference date, the auditors should give their opinion on whether the balance sheet presents a true and fair view of the state of affairs of the company as at the balance sheet date. The auditors must also report on whether they consider that the balance sheet complies with Schedule 4, in so far as it is applicable. It will be appropriate to include information which is additional to the requirements of the Schedule if such information is necessary to present a true and fair view. In the event of the Schedule's provisions not presenting a true and fair view, the true and fair override may be used, in which case, a note to the accounts must be given showing the particulars of the departure, the reasons for it and its effect.[21] It will be the auditors' task to ensure that any adaption of the Schedule requirements has been properly done, or, where the true and fair override has been used, that its use was justified. In addition to this, the auditors must ensure that the balance sheet has been signed on behalf of the board by two directors.[22]

Valuation report   It may be necessary to include with the documents to be sent to the Registrar of Companies a copy of a share valuation report. Such a report will be necessary if the company has allotted shares between the date of the relevant balance sheet and the passing of the requisite special resolution and those shares were allotted as fully or partly paid up as to their nominal value or any premium on them otherwise than in cash.[23] Where such an allotment has been made, the Registrar of Companies may only entertain the re-registration application if the allotment complies with certain conditions. Those conditions are:

(a) the consideration for the allotment has been valued by an independent person, who at the time that he made his report, was qualified to be appointed or continue to be an auditor of the company; the valuer may, however, elect for an independent person, who in the original valuer's opinion has the requisite knowledge and experience, to undertake the whole or any part of the valuation; and

(b) the report of the valuer must have been made during the six months immediately preceding the allotment of the shares.[24]

The valuer need not consider any part of the consideration for the allotment which has been satisfied by a company transferring

[20] *Ibid*. s.46(2).
[21] See p. 24ff above.
[22] Companies Act 1985, s.46(3).
[23] *Ibid*. s.44(1).
[24] *Ibid*. s.44(2).

an amount from either its reserve accounts or from its profit and loss account.[25] The valuation report must give particulars of the shares allotted and the consideration given in respect of them, along with other specific details, such as the method of valuation used. Where the valuer has delegated part of the valuation to another, details of the part delegated and of the delegatee must also be given.[26]

There will be no need for a valuation report where all or part of the consideration for the allotment is to be the transfer to the company of shares of another company or the cancellation of shares in that other company.[27] This provision will only apply, however, if it is open to the members of the other company to take part in the arrangement. Should the arrangement only concern a particular class of the other company's shares, then only holders of that class of share need be able to participate.[28]

Directors' declaration
The directors of a company which is seeking to re-register as public are required to make a statutory declaration. This declaration should state that:

(a) the requisite special resolution has been passed and that conditions regarding the allotment of shares between the relevant balance sheet date and the passing of the special resolution, and in respect of the company's share capital, have been met, in so far as they are applicable; and

(b) between the balance sheet date and the application for re-registration, there has been no change in the company's financial position that has resulted in the amount of its net assets becoming less than the aggregate of its called up share capital and undistributable reserves.[29]

The directors' declaration may be accepted by the Registrar as sufficient evidence that the requisite special resolution has been passed and the other conditions of re-registration satisfied.[30] Nevertheless, the special resolution will still have to be registered with the Registrar of Companies in compliance with normal company law procedure.

If the Registrar of Companies is satisfied that a private company has met all the requisite conditions, he must then issue the company with a certificate of incorporation which states that the company is a public company.[31] If before issuing the new certificate, however, it appears to the Registrar that there has been a court order which has the effect of reducing the nominal value of the company's share capital to below the authorised minimum, he may not issue a certificate.[32]

Once the certificate has been issued, the company becomes a public company by virtue of that certificate,[33] and it is conclusive evidence not only that the registration meets the legal

[25] *Ibid.* s.44(3).
[26] *Ibid.* s.108(4)–(7).
[27] *Ibid.* s.44(4).
[28] *Ibid.* s.44(5).
[29] *Ibid.* s.43(3).
[30] *Ibid.* s.47(2).
[31] *Ibid.* s.47(1).
[32] *Ibid.* s.47(3).
[33] *Ibid.* s.47(4).

requirements, but also that the company is public.[34] Further, upon its issue, any alterations to the memorandum and articles which are contained in the special resolution will become effective.[35]

Public company re-registering as private

It is possible that, either by choice or because the nominal value of its share capital has fallen below the authorised minimum, a public company may wish to re-register as private, in which the following procedure will have to be followed.

Procedure special resolution

A special resolution must be passed by the company,[36] which alters the company's memorandum so that it no longer states that the company is to be public. Consequential alterations to both the memorandum and articles of association should also be set out in the resolution,[37] such as, for example, changing the company's name so that it no longer ends with "public limited company" or "p.l.c.," but with "limited" or "ltd." instead and the placing of restrictions on the transfer or transmission of the company's shares.

Challenging re-registration

Company members not in favour of their company re-registering as private may challenge the application for re-registration in court. As this challenge may be made at any time within 28 days from the passing of the special resolution, re-registration may not take place within this period.[38]

Application to Registrar

An application for re-registration made on the prescribed form must then be lodged with the Registrar of Companies. The application must be signed by a director or the secretary of the company and be accompanied with a printed copy of the memorandum and articles of the company as altered by the resolution.[39]

If the Registrar of Companies is satisfied that all the requirements have been met, he will issue the company with a certificate of incorporation appropirate to a private company.[40] This will have the effect that the company, by virtue of the issue of the certificate, becomes a private company and the alterations to the memorandum and articles set out in the special resolution will come into operation.[41] As with other certificates of incorporation, the certificate which pronounces a once public company as private is conclusive evidence that the company is private and is entitled to be re-registered as such.[42]

Stock Exchange listing

Only public companies may apply to the Stock Exchange for a listing. The reason for this is that not only must their shares be

---

[34] *Ibid.* s.47(5).
[35] *Ibid.* s.47(4).
[36] *Ibid.* s.53(1).
[37] *Ibid.* s.53(2).
[38] *Ibid.* ss.53(1), 54.
[39] *Ibid.* s.53(1).
[40] *Ibid.* s.55(1).
[41] *Ibid.* s.55(2).
[42] *Ibid.* s.55(3).

freely transferable, but also the expected market value of securities for which the listing is sought must normally be at least £700,000 in case of shares, which is well above the authorised minimum nominal share capital required by company legislation for a public company. A company will be expected to have published or filed accounts covering the five years preceding the application, and those accounts, in the case of a company incorporated in the United Kingdom, must comply with the provisions of the Companies Act 1985.

The information which a company must supply to the Stock Exchange when applying for a listing is detailed and concerns not only the company's financial standing but also its business operations and management. As the obtaining of a Stock Exchange listing is a complex undertaking, companies wishing to apply for one will need to seek the advice of legal, banking and accounting experts. Such expertise should be sought well in advance of any application to the Stock Exchange. Before seeking a full listing on the Stock Exchange, companies should investigate a quotation on the Unlisted Securities Market, as a company wishing to trade its shares on this market will not have to provide such detailed particulars when seeking a quotation and the cost of preparing the necessary documents is substantially less.

APPENDIX I

Appendix I sets out the balance sheet and profit and loss account formats from which a company must choose.

Balance sheet formats

Format 1

A. Called up share capital not paid

B. Fixed assets
    I Intangible assets
        1. Development costs
        2. Concessions, patents, licences, trade marks and similar rights and assets
        3. Goodwill
        4. Payments on account

    II Tangible assets
        1. Land and buildings
        2. Plant and machinery
        3. Fixtures, fittings, tools and equipment
        4. Payments on account and assets in course of construction

    III Investments
        1. Shares in group companies
        2. Loans to group companies
        3. Shares in related companies
        4. Loans to related companies
        5. Other investments other than loans
        6. Other loans
        7. Own shares

C. Current assets
    I Stocks
        1. Raw material and consumables
        2. Work in progress
        3. Finished goods and goods for resale
        4. Payments on account

    II Debtors
        1. Trade debtors
        2. Amounts owed by group companies
        3. Amounts owed by related companies
        4. Other debtors
        5. Called up share capital not paid
        6. Prepayments and accrued income

    III Investments
        1. Shares in group companies
        2. Own shares
        3. Other investments

IV Cash at bank and in hand

D. Prepayments and accrued income

E. Creditors: amounts falling due within one year
    1. Debenture loans
    2. Bank loans and overdrafts
    3. Payments received on account
    4. Trade creditors
    5. Bills of exchange payable
    6. Amounts owed to group companies
    7. Amounts owed to related companies
    8. Other creditors including taxation and social
       security
    9. Accruals and deferred income

F. Net current assets (liabilities)

G. Total assets less current liabilities

H. Creditors: amounts falling due after more than one year
    1. Debenture loans
    2. Bank loans and overdrafts
    3. Payments received on account
    4. Trade creditors
    5. Bills of exchange payable
    6. Amounts owed to group companies
    7. Amounts owed to related companies
    8. Other creditors including taxation and social
       security
    9. Accruals and deferred income

I. Provisions for liabilities and charges
    1. Pensions and similar obligations
    2. Taxation, including deferred taxation
    3. Other provisions

J. Accruals and deferred income

K. Capital reserves
    I Called up share capital

    II Share premium account

    III Revaluation reserve

    IV Other reserves
        1. Capital redemption reserve
        2. Reserve for own shares
        3. Reserves provided for by the articles of
           association
        4. Other reserves

    V Profit and loss account

Format 2

Assets

A. Called up share capital not paid

B. Fixed assets
    I Intangible assets
        1. Development costs
        2. Concessions, patents, licences, trade marks and
            similar rights and assets
        3. Goodwill
        4. Payments on account

    II Tangible assets
        1. Land and buildings
        2. Plant and machinery
        3. Fixtures, fittings, tools and equipment
        4. Payments on account and assets in course of
            construction

    III Investments
        1. Shares in group companies
        2. Loans to group companies
        3. Shares in related companies
        4. Loans to related companies
        5. Other investments other than loans
        6. Other loans
        7. Own shares

C. Current assets
    I Stocks
        1. Raw materials and consumables
        2. Work in progress
        3. Finished goods and goods for resale
        4. Payments on account

    II Debtors
        1. Trade debtors
        2. Amounts owed by group companies
        3. Amounts owed by related companies
        4. Other debtors
        5. Called up share capital not paid
        6. Prepayments and accrued income

    III Investments
        1. Shares in group companies
        2. Own shares
        3. Other investments

    IV Cash at bank and in hand

D. Prepayments and accrued income

Liabilities

A. Capital and reserves
        I   Called up share capital

       II   Share premium account

     III   Revaluation reserve

     IV   Other reserves
         1. Capital redemption reserve
        2. Reserve for own shares
        3. Reserves provided for by the articles of
           association
        4. Other reserves

      V   Profit and loss account

B. Provisions for liabilities and charges
        1. Pensions and similar obligations
        2. Taxation including deferred taxation
        3. Other provisions

C. Creditors
        1. Debenture loans
        2. Bank loans and overdrafts
        3. Payments received on account
        4. Trade creditors
        5. Bills of exchange payable
        6. Amounts owed to group companies
        7. Amounts owed to related companies
        8. Other creditors including taxation and social
           security
        9. Accruals and deferred income

D. Accruals and deferred income

Profit and loss account formats

Format 1

1. Turnover
2. Cost of sales
3. Gross profit or loss
4. Distribution costs
5. Administrative expenses
6. Other operating income
7. Income from shares in group companies
8. Income from shares in related companies
9. Income from other fixed asset investments
10. Other interest receivable and similar income
11. Amounts written off investments
12. Interest payable and similar charges
13. Tax on profit or loss on ordinary activities

14. Profit or loss on ordinary activities after taxation
15. Extraordinary income
16. Extraordinary charges
17. Extraordinary profit or loss
18. Tax on extraordinary profit or loss
19. Other taxes not shown under the above items
20. Profit or loss for the financial year

Format 2

1. Turnover
2. Change in stocks of finished goods and in work in progress
3. Own work capitalised
4. Other operating income
5. (a) Raw materials and consumables
   (b) Other external charges
6. Staff costs
   (a) wages and salaries
   (b) social security costs
   (c) other pensions costs
7. (a) Depreciation and other amounts written off tangible and intangible fixed assets
   (b) Exceptional amounts written off current assets
8. Other operating charges
9. Income from shares in group companies
10. Income from shares in related companies
11. Income from other fixed asset investments
12. Other interest receivable and similar income
13. Amounts written off investments
14. Interest payable and similar charges
15. Tax on profit or loss on ordinary activities
16. Profit or loss on ordinary activities after taxation
17. Extraordinary income
18. Extraordinary charges
19. Extraordinary profit or loss
20. Tax on extraordinary profit or loss
21. Other taxes not shown under the above items
22. Profit or loss for the financial year

Format 3

A. Charges
1. Cost of sales
2. Distribution costs
3. Administrative expenses
4. Amounts written off investments
5. Interest payable and similar charges
6. Tax on profit or loss on ordinary activities
7. Profit or loss on ordinary activities after taxation
8. Extraordinary charges

B. Income
1. Turnover
2. Other operating income
3. Income from shares in group companies
4. Income from shares in related companies
5. Income from other fixed asset investments
6. Other interest receivable and similar income
7. Profit or loss on ordinary activities after taxation

9. Tax on extraordinary profit or loss
10. Other taxes not shown under the above items
11. Profit or loss for the financial year

8. Extraordinary income
9. Profit or loss for the financial year

Format 4

A. Charges
  1. Reduction in stocks of finished goods and in work in progress
  2. (a) Raw materials and consumables
     (b) Other external charges
  3. Staff costs
     (a) wages and salaries
     (b) social security costs
     (c) other pension costs
  4. (a) Depreciation and other amounts written off tangible and intangible fixed assets
     (b) Exceptional amounts written off current assets
  5. Other operating charges
  6. Amounts written off investments
  7. Interest payable and similar charges
  8. Tax on profit or loss on ordinary activities
  9. Profit or loss on ordinary activities after taxation
  10. Extraordinary charges
  11. Tax on extraordinary profit or loss
  12. Other taxes not shown under the above items
  13. Profit or loss for the financial year

B. Income
  1. Turnover
  2. Increase in stocks of finished goods and work in progress
  3. Own work capitalised
  4. Other operating income
  5. Income from shares in group companies
  6. Income from shares in related companies
  7. Income from other fixed asset investments
  8. Other interest receivable and similar income
  9. Profit or loss on ordinary activities
  10. Extraordinary income
  11. Profit or loss for the financial year

APPENDIX II

[The Joint Opinions on "True and fair" are reproduced with the kind permission of the Accounting Standards Committee, Leonard Hoffmann Q.C., Mary Arden and "Accountancy." References to the current legislation have been included.]

The Accounting Standards Committee— Joint Opinion

1. The Accounting Standards Committee ("ASC") from time to time issues Statements of Standard Accounting Practice ("SSAPs"). These are declared in the Explanatory Foreword to be "methods of accounting approved . . . for application to all financial accounts intended to give a true and fair view of financial position and profit or loss." They are not intended to be "a comprehensive code of rigid rules" but departures from them should be disclosed and explained. The Committee also noted in its Explanatory Foreword that "methods of financial accounting evolve and alter in response to changing business and economic needs. From time to time new accounting standards will be drawn at progressive levels, and established standards will be reviewed with the object of improvement in light of new needs and developments."

2. The ASC has recently undertaken a review of the standard setting process and decided that future standards will "deal only with those matters which are of major and fundamental importance and affect the generality of companies" but that, as in the past, the standards will apply "to all accounts which are intended to show a true and fair view of financial position and profit or loss." A SSAP is therefore a declaration by the ASC, on behalf of its constituent professional bodies, that save in exceptional circumstances, accounts which do not comply with the standard will not give a true and fair view.

3. But the preparation of accounts which give a true and fair view is not merely a matter of compliance with professional standards. In many important cases it is a requirement of law. Since 1947 all accounts prepared for the purpose of compliance with the Companies Acts have been required to "give a true and fair view": s.13(1) of the Companies Act 1947, re-enacted as s.149(1) of the Companies Act 1948. In 1978 the concept of a true and fair view was adopted by the EEC Council in its Fourth Directive "on the annual accounts of certain types of companies." The Directive combined the requirement of giving a true and fair view with extremely detailed provisions about the form and contents of the accounts but the obligation to give a true and fair view was declared overriding. Accounts must not comply with the detailed requirements if this would prevent them from giving a true and fair view. Parliament gave effect to the Directive by passing the Companies Act 1981. This substitutes a new s.149(2) in the 1948 Act [*Companies Act 1985*, s.228(2),] reproducing the old s.149(1) in substantially similar

words. The detailed requirements of the Directive appear as a
new Eighth Schedule to the 1948 Act [*Companies Act 1985*,
Sched. 4.] The old s.149(1) now renumbered s.149A(1)
[Companies Act 1985, s.258(1)] and the old Eighth Schedule
(now Sch. 8A) [Companies Act 1985, Sched. 9.] are retained for
the accounts of banking, insurance and shipping companies. So
far as the requirement to give a true and fair view is concerned, a
difference between 149(2) and 149A(1) [Companies Act,
ss.228(2) and 258(1)] is that the former has come into law via
Brussels, whereas the latter has no EEC pedigree.

4. "True and fair view" is thus a legal concept and the
question of whether company accounts comply with s.149(2) (or
s.149A(1) [Companies Act 1985, s.258(1)] can be authoritatively
decided only by a court. This gives rise to a number of questions
about the relationship between the legal requirement and the
SSAPs issued by the ASC, which also claim to be authoritative
statements on what is a true and fair view. What happens if there
is a conflict between the professional standards demanded by the
ASC and the decisions of the courts on the requirements of the
Companies Acts? Furthermore, the ASC issues new SSAPs "at
progressive levels" and reviews established ones. How is this
consistent with a statutory requirement of a true and fair view
which has been embodied in the law in the same language since
1947? Can the issue of a new SSAP make it unlawful to prepare
accounts in a form which would previously have been lawful?
How can the ASC have power to legislate in this way?

5. To answer these questions it is necessary first to examine
the nature of the "true and fair view" concept as used in the
Companies Act. It is an abstraction or philosophical concept
expressed in simple English. The law uses many similar
concepts, of which "reasonable care" is perhaps the most familiar
example. It is a common feature of such concept that there is
seldom any difficulty in understanding what they mean but
frequent controversy over their application to particular facts.
One reason for this phenomenon is that because such concept
represent a very high level of abstraction which has to be applied
to an infinite variety of concrete facts, there can never be a
sharply defined line between, for example, what is reasonable
care and what is not. There will always be a penumbral area in
which views may reasonably differ.

6. The courts have never attempted to define "true and fair"
in the sense of offering a paraphrase in other languages and in our
opinion have been wise not to do so. When a concept can be
expressed in ordinary English words, we do not think that it
illuminates that meaning to attempt to frame a definition. We
doubt, for example, whether the man on the Clapham omnibus
has really contributed very much to the understanding of
"reasonable care" or that accountants have found it helpful to ask
themselves how this imaginary passenger would have prepared a
set of accounts. It is much more useful to illustrate the concept in
action, for example, to explain why certain accounts do or do not
give a true and fair view.

7. It is however important to observe that the application of
the concept involves judgment in questions of degree. The
information contained in accounts must be accurate and
comprehensive (to mention two of the most obvious elements

which contribute to a true and fair view) to within acceptable limits. What is acceptable and how is this to be achieved? Reasonable businessmen and accountants may differ over the degree of accuracy and comprehensiveness which in particular cases the accounts should attain. Equally, there may sometimes be room for differences over the method to adopt in order to give a true and fair view, cases in which there may be more than one "true and fair view"of the same financial position. Again, because "true and fair view" involves questions of degree, we think that cost-effectiveness must play a part in deciding the amount of information which is sufficient to make accounts true and fair.

8. In the end, as we have said, the question of whether accounts give a true and fair view in compliance with the Companies Act must be decided by a judge. But the courts look for guidance on this question to the ordinary practices of professional accountants. This is not merely because accounts are expressed in a language which judges find difficult to understand. This may sometimes be true but it is a minor reason for the importance which the courts attach to evidence of accountancy practice. The important reason is inherent in the nature of the "true and fair" concept. Accounts will not be true and fair unless the information they contain is sufficient in quantity and quality to satisfy the reasonable expectations of the readers to whom they are addressed. On this question, accountants can express an informed professional opinion on what, in current circumstances, it is thought that accounts should reasonably contain. But they can do more than that. The readership of accounts will consist of businessmen, investors, bankers and so forth, as well as professional accountants. But the expectations of the readers will have been moulded by the practices of accountants because by and large they will expect to get what they ordinarily get and that in turn will depend upon normal practices of accountants.

9. For these reasons, the courts will treat compliance with accepted accounting principles as *prima facie* evidence that the accounts are true and fair. Equally, deviation from accepted principles will be prima facie evidence that they are not. We have not been able to find reported cases on the specific question of whether accounts are true and fair, although the question has been adverted to in the course of judgments on other matters; see for example *Willingale* v. *International Commercial Bank Ltd.* [1978] A.C. 834. There are however some cases on the analogous question arising in income tax cases of whether profit or loss has been calculated in accordance with "the correct principles of commercial accountancy" and there is a helpful statement of principle (approved in subsequent cases in the Court of Appeal) by Pennycuick V.-C. in *Odeon Associated Theatres Ltd.* v. *Jones (Inspector of Taxes)* [1971] 1 W.L.R. 442 at 454:

> "In order to ascertain what are the correct principles [the court] has recourse to the evidence of accountants. That evidence is conclusive on the practice of accountants in the sense of the principles on which accountants act in practice. That is a question of pure fact, but the court itself has to make a final decision as to whether that practice corresponds to the correct principles of commercial accountancy. No

doubt in the vast proportion of cases the court will agree with the accountants but it will not necessarily do so. Again, there may be a divergency of views between the accountants, or there may be alternative principles, none of which can be said to be incorrect, or of course there may be no accountancy evidence at all . . . At the end of the day the court must determine what is the correct principle of commercial accountancy to be applied."

10. This is also in our opinion the relationship between generally accepted accounting principles and the legal concept of "true and fair." The function of the ASC is to formulate what it considers should be generally accepted accounting principles. Thus the value of a SSAP to a court which has to decide whether accounts are true and fair is two-fold. First, it represents an important statement of professional opinion about the standards which readers may reasonably expect in accounts which are intended to be true and fair. The SSAP is intended to crystallise professional opinion and reduce penumbral areas in which divergent practices exist and can each have claim to being "true and fair." Secondly, because accountants are professionally obliged to comply with a SSAP, it creates in the readers an expectation that the accounts will be in conformity with the prescribed standards. This is in itself a reason why accounts which depart from the standard without adequate justification or explanation may be held not to be true and fair. The importance of expectations was emphasised by the Court of Appeal in what may be regarded as a converse case, *Re Press Caps* [1949] Ch. 434. An ordinary historic cost balance sheet was said to be "true and fair" notwithstanding that is gave no information about the current value of freehold properties because, it was said, no one familiar with accounting conventions would expect it to include such information.

11. A SSAP therefore has no direct legal effect. It is simply a rule of professional conduct for accountants. But in our opinion it is likely to have an indirect effect on the content which the courts will give to the "true and fair" concept. The effect of a SSAP may therefore be to make it likely that accounts which would previously have been considered true and fair will no longer satisfy the law. Perhaps the most dramatic example arises out of the recent statement by the ASC in connection with its review of SSAP 16 "Current Cost Accounting." The Statement puts forward the discussion the proposition that "where a company is materially affected by changing prices, pure HC accounts do not give a true and fair view." If this proposition were embodied in a new SSAP and accepted by the courts, the legal requirements of a true and fair view will have undergone a revolutionary change.

12. There is no inconsistency between such a change brought about by changing professional opinion and the rule that words in a statute must be construed in accordance with the meaning which they bore when the statute was passed. The *meaning* of true and fair remains what it was in 1947. It is the *content* given to the concept which has changed. This is something which constantly happens to such concepts. For example, the Bill of Rights 1688 prohibited "cruel and unusual punishments." There has been no change in the meaning of

"cruel" since 1688. The definition in Dr. Johnson's Dictionary of 1755" ("pleased with hurting others, inhuman, hard-hearted, without pity, barbarous") is much the same as in a modern dictionary. But changes in society mean that a judge in 1983 would unquestionably characterise punishments as "cruel" which his predecessor of 1688 would have thought to come within this description. The meaning of the concept remains the same; the facts to which it is applied have changed.

13. The possibility of changing accounting standards has been recognised both by the courts and the legislature. In *Associated Portland Cement Manufacturers Ltd.* v. *Price Commission* [1975] I.C.R. 27, esp. at 45–6, the court recognised changes since 1945 in the permissible method of calculating depreciation. Similarly para. 90 of the new Eighth Schedule to the Companies Act 1948 [Companies Act 1985, Sched. 4, para. 91] refers to "principles generally accepted . . . at the time when those accounts are prepared."

14. We therefore see no conflict between the functions of the ASC in formulating standards which it declares to be essential to true and fair accounts and the functions of the courts in deciding whether the accounts satisfy the law. The Courts are of course not bound by a SSAP. A court may say that accounts which ignore them are nevertheless true and fair. But the immediate effect of a SSAP is to strengthen the likelihood that a court will hold that compliance with the prescribed standard is necessary for the accounts to give a true and fair view. In the absence of a SSAP, a court is unlikely to reject accounts drawn up in accordance with principles which command some respectable professional support. The issue of a SSAP has the effect, for the two reasons which we have given in para 10 of creating a *prima facie* presumption that accounts which do not comply are not true and fair. This presumption is then strengthened or weakened by the extent to which the SSAP is actually accepted and applied. Universal acceptance means that it is highly unlikely that a court would accept accounts drawn up according to different principles. On the othe hand, if there remains a strong body of professional opinion which consistently opts out of applying the SSAP, giving reasons which the ASC may consider inadequate, the *prima facie* presumption against such accounts is weakened.

15. We therefore do not think that the ASC should be concerned by the possibility that a court may hold that compliance with one of its SSAPs is not necessarily for the purposes of the Companies Acts. This possibility is inherent in the fact that the courts are not bound by professional opinion. The function of the ASC is to express their professional judgment on the standards which in their opinion are required.

16. There are two further points to be considered. The first is the relationship between the "true and fair" requirement and the detailed provisions of the new Eighth Schedule [Companies Act 1985, Sched. 4]. The Act is quite explicit on this point: the true and fair view is overriding. Nevertheless it may be said that the detailed requirements offer some guidance as to the principles which Parliament considered would give a true and fair view. In particular, the Schedule plainly regards historic cost accounting as the norm and current cost accounting as an option alternative. In these circumstances, is a court likely to follow a SSAP which

declares that for certain companies, historic costs accounts *cannot* give a true and fair view? In our opinion, whatever reasons there may be for taking one view or the other, the provisions of the Eighth Schedule [Fourth Schedule] are no obstacle to accepting such a SSAP. As we have already pointed out, the provisions of the Schedule are static whereas the concept of a true and fair view is dynamic. If the latter is overriding, it is not impossible that the effect in time will be to render obsolete some of the provisions of the Schedule. But we think that this is what must have been intended when overriding force was given to a concept with a changing content.

17. Lastly, there is the effect of the adoption of "true and fair view" by the EEC. Because s.149(2) of the 1948 Act [Companies Act 1985, s.228(2)] now gives effect to a Directive, it must (unlike s.149A(1) [Companies Act 1985, s.258(1)]) be construed in accordance with any decision of the European Court on the meaning of Article 2.3 of the Directive. In practice we do not think that this is likely to affect the evolution of the concept in England. Just as the concept may have a different content at different times, so it may have a different content in different countries. Although the European Court may seek to achieve some uniformity by laying down minimum standards for the accounts of all EEC countries, it seems to use that they are unlikely to disapprove of higher standards being required by the professional bodies of individual states and in consequence, higher legal criteria for what is a true and fair view being adopted in the national courts of some member states.

18. So for example Article 33 of the Directive gives member states the right to "permit or require" companies to use current cost accounting instead of historic cost principles. In the UK, as we have said, current cost accounts are permitted by the Eighth Schedule [Fourth Schedule] but the only circumstances in which they may be required is if a court should decide, on the basis of prevailing principles, that they were necessary to give a true and fair view. In Germany, on the other hand, the equivalent of the Eighth Schedule [Fourth Schedule] does not even permit current cost accounts. In Germany therefore, the only way they could be permitted would be if the German court applied "true and fair view" as an overriding requirement. For the reasons given in para 16, we do not regard it as illogical or impossible that even a German court may take this view. But having regard to the Directive, we think it is very unlikely that the European Court would decide as a matter of community law that there are circumstances in which historic cost accounts do not give a true and fair view. Developments of this kind are more likely to be left to national courts to make in the light of local professional opinion.

Lincoln's Inn   Leonard Hoffman
13 September 1983   M. H. Arden

The Accounting Standards Committee—Supplementary Joint Opinion

1. This opinion is intended to be supplementary to our Joint Opinion dated 13 September 1983. We do not propose to repeat the contents of that Opinion more than is necessary in order to make this one intelligible. The two Opinions should therefore be read together.

2. The ASC proposed to issue a Statement of Intent concerning the future of SSAP 16 "Current Cost Accounting." In summary, the proposal is that all public limited companies ("PLCs") other than insurance companies, property companies and investment-based companies ("value-based companies") should show the effects of changing prices when these effects are material, but this should be indicated in a note and not in separate current cost accounts. The present position is that SSAP 16 applies only to large and quoted companies (as therein defined) and does not apply to value-based companies, whatever their size. The ASC is not satified that a method has yet been developed for producing useful information about the effects of changing prices on the business of private companies and value-based companies at a cost that can be justified. It is therefore commissioning further work on the application of current cost accounting to these companies. However, the ASC draws attention to the principal factors which have led them to their conclusion that significant benefits result from the disclosure of current cost information by PLCs, including the large number and wide range of users of their accounts and in many cases the sophistication of those users. These factors generally do not apply to private companies. The benefits of providing information about the effects of changing prices on the businesses of private companies are therefore likely to be significantly less than in the case of PLCs.

3. The Statement of Intent therefore recognises that while in principle and subject to cost-effectiveness, all accounts should, in order to give a true and a fair view, show the effects of changing prices when such effects and material, there are practical difficulties about devising cost-effective methods for implementing this principle in the case of certain companies.

4. This practical approach has been criticised on the ground that if a footnote about the effects of changing prices is regarded as necessary for accounts to give a true and fair view, this requirement should apply to all sets of accounts. Questions of cost and expediency are said to be irrelevant to whether or not the accounts give a true and fair view and it is argued that there can be no justification for the ASC distinguishing between different kinds of companies.

5. We think that this criticism is misconceived. In the first place, questions of cost-effectiveness are in our opinion relevant to whether accounts give a true and fair view or not. "True and fair view" is not an absolute and unique concept. If that was what the legislature had meant, it would no doubt have said "the true and fair view." More than one view may be true and fair and whether a particular set of accounts satisfies this test or not involves questions of degree and a consideration of many factors

relating both to the affairs of the particular business and the
reasonable expectations of the people likely to use the accounts.
In paragraph 7 of our Joint Opinion we said:

> "Again, because "true and fair view" involves questions of
> degree, we think that cost-effectiveness must play a part in
> deciding the amount of information which is sufficient to
> make accounts true and fair."

Some elaboration of this statement may be useful. The
information contained in accounts may vary in its
comprehensiveness, the usefulness and degree of precision.
These are all factors which bear upon the question of whether the
accounts are "true and fair." The accounts must satisfy criteria of
acceptability in regard to each of these and other matters. But the
question of whether it is necessary for particular kinds of
information to be included must take into account the cost and
difficulty of providing such information. There is in our opinion
nothing illogical in saying: "This information would be useful to
(say) investors in assessing the condition of the business. If it
could be provided relatively easily, we think that fairness to
investors demands that it should be included. *Prima facie*
therefore, accounts which do not include such information would
not be true and fair. On the other hand, if the information could
be provided only with great expense and difficulty, we do not
think that it would be reasonable to insist upon it. Therefore we
would accept accounts without such information as still being
true and fair."[1]

6. In our earlier Opinion we mentioned for another purpose
the analogy of the legal concept of reasonable care. On this point
too, we think that reasonable care provides a useful comparison.
The question of whether a person has taken reasonable care to
guard against some danger depends upon weighing a number of
factors, including likelihood that the risk may materialise, the
seriousness of the loss or injury which may be caused if the risk
does materialise, the importance of the activity giving risk, and
the cost of taking various kinds of precautions. As Lord
Wilberforce put it, more succinctly than we have done:

> "What is reasonable depends on the nature and degree of the
> danger. It also depends upon the difficulty and expense of
> guarding against it."[2]

This process of weighing risks against the difficulty and expense
of guarding against them would apply equally to the question of
whether an accountant had taken reasonable care in the
preparation of a set of accounts. And although the question of
whether reasonable care has been taken in the preparation of
accounts is not the same as whether they are true and fair, we

---

[1] In saying this we have in mind expense and difficulty applicable to any
company of that kind. We are not saying that it would be right to take into
account the difficulty which a particular company might have in providing
certain information, *e.g.* because its records had been badly maintained. There
is again an analogy here with "reasonable care" (see paragraph 6) in which
difficulties or handicaps peculiar to an individual are usually disregarded on the
ground that a person suffering from such a difficulty or handicap should not
have undertaken the activity that gave rise to the risk.

[2] *Herrington* v. *British Railways Board* [1972] A.C. 877, 920.

think that the questions of "reasonableness" and "fairness" have enough in common to make the analogy a valid one.

7. At this point the critic may say: "Well, I can see that questions of cost-effectiveness may enter into the decision on whether accounts are true and fair and that information about the effects of price changes may have to be given in the accounts of some companies but not others. But the SSAP should still be capable of expression in general terms. How can one justify an arbitrary dividing line which requires such information in the accounts of one company which happens to be a PLC and does not require it in the accounts of a private company of the same size and carrying on a substantially similar business?"

8. This criticism in our opinion misses the true function of SSAPs, which is to reduce the level of abstraction at which rules of good accounting practice are expressed. The more abstract the rule, the more pure and universally applicable it is, but the less useful it is to the practitioner seeking to apply it to the facts of a particular case. If universality were all that one wanted, the proposition that accounts should be true and fair would be sufficient. The point of a SSAP is to concretise that proposition, while recognising that every case must depend upon its own facts and that any rules expressed at a lower level of abstraction must to a greater or lesser extent be "rules of thumb." This point is made with great clarity in the Explanatory Foreword. We therefore see nothing illogical in a SSAP which gives guidance to the profession by taking a (necessarily) arbitrary but practical dividing line and saying that for PLCs which are not value-based companies it will ordinarily be assumed that the public benefit from the provision of information about the effects of changing prices will be sufficient to justify the cost of providing such information, whereas this will not be assumed, or will not yet be assumed, in the case of private or value-based companies.

9. We said in our earlier opinion that "true and fair" was a dynamic concept and that its detailed content could change by degrees over time. We also said that one of the functions of the ASC was to initiate and promote such changes. A SSAP in accordance with the draft Statement of Intent seems to us to give effect to that function.

Lincoln's Inn   Leonard Hoffman
20 March 1984   M. H. Arden

APPENDIX III

[The following Technical Releases are reproduced with the kind permission of the Consultative Committee of Accountancy Bodies]

Technical Release 481, The Determination of Realised Profits and Disclosure of Distributable Profits in the Context of the Companies Act 1948 to 1981, and Technical Release 482, The Determination of Distributable Profits in the Context of the Companies Act 1948 and 1981, were issued in September 1982 by the Consultative Committee of Accountancy Bodies (CCAB), whose members are as follows: The Institute of Chartered Accountants in England and Wales; The Institute of Chartered Accountants of Scotland; The Institute of Chartered Accountants in Ireland; The [Chartered] Association of Certified Accountants; The Institute of Cost and Management Accountants; and The Chartered Institute of Public Finance and Accountancy.

Technical Release 481—The Determination of Realised Profits and Disclosure in the context of the Companies Acts 1948 and 1981

Explanatory note

The Consultative Committee of Accountancy Bodies wishes to draw readers' attention to the fact that the attached (*sic*) guidance statement does not deal with the special problems arising in connection with the determination of realised profits in the context of foreign currency translation. It is intended that these problems should be dealt with in the future by the issue of an accounting standard on foreign currency translation.

The following statement of guidance on the determination of realised profits and disclosure of distributable profits in the context of the Companies Acts 1948 to 1981 is issued by the Councils of the member bodies of the Consultative Committee of Accountancy Bodies. The guidance given in this statement may need to be amended as the law is interpreted in particular cases, or as existing Accounting standards are revised and new Standards are issued.

The statement and its appendix have been considered and approved by Counsel. They are, however, not definitive. Interpretation of the law rests ultimately with the courts.

[As the title of TR 481 suggests, the release originally referred to the Companies Acts 1948 and 1981. These references have been replaced by the relevant provisions of the Companies Act 1985, and all references are now to that Act.]

Realised profits: The statutory framework

1. The term 'realised profits' was introduced into UK company law statutes as a result of the implementation of the 2nd and 4th EEC directives on company law in the [Companies Act 1985 (Part VIII)]

(1) [Part VIII] imposes statutory restrictions on the distribution of profits and assets by companies. These restrictions include a prohibition on the distribution of unrealised profits★.

(2) Paragraph 12(a) of [Schedule 4] requires that 'Only profits realised at the balance sheet date shall be included in the profit and loss account.' Paragraph [34(3)] contains a similar requirement applicable to transfers from the revaluation reserve to the profit and loss account. These requirements are extended to consolidated accounts by paragraphs 61 to 66 of [Schedule 4]. They do not apply to accounts prepared under [Schedule 9].

★There is an exception to this rule where distributions are made in kind (see Section [276]).

2. [Schedule 4] states that 'reference . . . to realised profits . . . are references to such profits . . . as fall to be treated as realised profits . . . in accordance with principles generally accepted with respect to the determination for accounting purposes of realised profits at the time when those accounts are prepared' [Schedule 4 para. 91]. The term 'principles generally accepted' for the determination of realised profits is not defined in the Act.

3. This statement gives guidance as to the interpretation of 'principles generally accepted' for the determination of realised profits in the context of these statutory requirements. Both the statutory requirements and the following guidance must throughout be viewed in the context of Section [228] which states that the requirement for company accounts to give a true and fair view overrides all other provisions of the [Companies Act 1985] as to the matters to be included in a company's accounts. Section [230] imposes a corresponding requirement for group accounts.

'Principles generally accepted' for realised profits

4. 'Principles generally accepted' for the determination of realised profits should be considered in conjunction with, inter alia, the legal principles laid down in [Schedule 4], statements of standard accounting practice ('SSAPs'), and in particular the fundamental accounting concepts referred to in SSAP 2 'Disclosure of accounting policies.' As stated in the Explanatory Foreword to Accounting Standards, SSAPs describe methods of accounting for all accounts intended to give a true and fair view. They must therefore, where applicable, be considered to be highly persuasive in the interpretation of 'principles generally accepted' for the determination of realised profits.

5. Accounting thought and practice develop over time. This is recognised in the statutory requirement that realised profits

should be determined 'in accordance with principles generally accepted . . . at the time when those accounts are prepared.' Because of this, the guidance set out in this statement is itself liable to amendment from time to time.

6. In determining whether a profit is realised, particular regard should be had to the statutory accounting principles at paragraphs 12 and 13 of [Schedule 4] and to the parallel fundamental accounting concepts of 'prudence' and 'accruals' as set out in SSAP 2.

7. Paragraph 12 of [Schedule 4] requires that 'The amount of any item shall be determined on a prudent basis' and, in particular, as already noted, that 'only profits realised at the balance sheet date shall be included in the profit and loss account.' SSAP 2 amplifies the prudence concept as follows:

> 'revenues and profits are not anticipated, but are recognised by inclusion in the profit and loss account only when realised in the form either of cash or of other assets the ultimate cash realisation of which can be assessed with reasonable certainty.'

In the light of the new statutory requirements, it should be borne in mind that the phrases 'ultimate cash realisation' and 'assessed with reasonable certainty' are intended to clarify the extent to which a profit can be said to be 'realised' under the prudence concept in circumstances other than where the profit had already been realised in the form of cash. 'Reasonable certainty' is the limiting factor.

8. This approach is consistent with paragraph 13 of [Schedule 4] which requires that:

> 'All income and charges relating to the financial year to which the accounts relate shall be taken into account, without regard to the date of receipt of payment.'

The statutory requirement corresponds with the accruals concept as explained at paragraph 14(b) of SSAP 2. This states that:

> 'revenue and costs are accrued (that is, recognised as they are earned or incurred, not as money is received or paid) matched with one another so far as their relationship can be established or justifiable assumed, and dealt with in the profit and loss account of the period to which they relate.'

9. In determining realised profits, it is also necessary to comply with paragraph 12(b) of [Schedule 4], which states that:

> 'all liabilities and losses which have arisen or are likely to arise in respect of the financial year to which the accounts relate or a previous financial year shall be taken into account, including those which become apparent between the balance sheet date and the date on which it is signed on behalf of the board of directors . . .'.

This statutory requirement corresponds with the prudence concept as explained at paragraph 14(d) of SSAP 2. This states that:

> 'provision is made for all known liabilities (expenses and losses) whether the amount of these is known with certainty or is a best estimate in the light of the information available.'

Realised profits: Summary of guidance

10. A profit which is required by statements of standard accounting practice to be recognised in the profit and loss account should normally be treated as a realised profit, unless the SSAP specifically indicates that it should be treated as unrealised. *See Appendix.*

11. A profit may be recognised in the profit and loss account in accordance with an accounting policy which is not the subject of a SSAP, or, exceptionally, which is contrary to a SSAP. Such a profit will normally be a realised profit if the accounting policy adopted is consistent with paragraphs 12 and 13 of [Schedule 4] and with the accruals and prudence concepts as set out in SSAP 2.

12. Where, in special circumstances, a true and fair view could not be given, even if additional information were provided, without including in the profit and loss account an unrealised profit, the effect of Section [228(3)] is to require inclusion of that unrealised profit notwithstanding paragraph 12(a) of [Schedule 4]. Moreover, paragraph 15 of [Schedule 4] allows the directors to include an unrealised profit in the new profit and loss account where there are special reasons for doing so. Where unrealised profits are thus recognised in the profit and loss account, particulars of this departure from the statutory accounting principle, the reasons for it and its effect are required to be given in a note to the accounts.

Distributable profits

13. The definition of realised profits contained in [Schedule 4] is extended by Section [742(6)] to apply to any [provision] of the Companies [Act 1985]. It therefore applies to the provisions of Part [VIII] dealing with distributions. In that context this guidance should be read in conjunction with the statutory rules as to what constitute distributable profits and losses in particular circumstances for the purposes of that part of that Act.

14. It is essential that all companies should keep sufficient records to enable them to distinguish between those reserves which are distributable and those which are not. While most realised profits will be passed through the profit and loss account, there may be some realised profits which will originally have been brought into the accounts as unrealised profits by way of direct credit to reserves. Similarly, while most unrealised profits will be credited direct to reserves, there may be some unrealised profits passed through the profit and loss account (see paragraph 12 above). Subsequently, when such profits are realised either in whole or in part, a reclassification needs to be made between unrealised and realised profits.

15. There is no legal requirement for a company to distinguish in its balance sheet between distributable and non-distributable reserves as such. However, where material non-distributable profits are included in the profit and loss account or in other reserves which might reasonably be assumed to be distributable, it may be necessary for this to be disclosed and

quantified in a note to the accounts in order for them to give a true and fair view.

16. Distributions are made by companies and not by groups. It follows that the profits of a group are only distributable to members of the group's holding company to the extent of the holding company's distributable profits. The concept of distributable profit is not, therefore, strictly applicable to groups. However, it is reasonable to assume that the distributable retained profits of subsidiaries can be distributed to the holding company. Where this is not the case, the requirements of paragraph 36 of SSAP 14 'Group accounts' should be complied with. This states:

> 'If there are significant restrictions on the ability of the holding company to distribute the retained profits of the group (other than those shown as non-distributable) because of statutory, contractual or exchange control restrictions the extent of the restrictions should be indicated.'

Appendix to TR 481

Accounting standards and realised profits: Examples

1. As statements of standard accounting practice are revised and as new standards are issued, it is expected that they will deal with any matters relevant to the determination of realised profits.

2. This has already been done in the case of SSAP 1 'Accounting for Associated Companies' revised in April 1982. This provides an example of the way in which the true and fair view requirements should be satisfied by giving additional information rather than by including unrealised profits in profit and loss accounts (see paragraph 12 above). As far as an investing company is concerned, the profits of its associated companies are not realised until they are passed on as dividends; the true and fair view, however, requires that they should be reflected in the investing company's financial statements. There is no problem where group accounts are prepared because specific provision is made for this situation in paragraph 65(1) of [Schedule 4]. Where, however, the investing company does not prepare group accounts, the revised SSAP 1 states that it should show the information required as to its share of the associated company's profit by preparing a separate profit and loss account or by adding the information to its own profit and loss account in supplementary form in such a way that its share of the profits of the associated company is not treated as realised.

3. An example of the principle that profit recognised in accordance with an Accounting Standard should normally be treated as realised (see paragraph 10 above) is provided by SSAP 9 'Stocks and work in progress.' This requires that long-term contract work in progress should be stated in periodic financial statements at cost plus any attributable profit, less any foreseeable losses and progress payments received and receivable. There was initially some concern as to whether profit thus

recognised on long-term contract work in progress would be construed as realised profit within the provisions of the Companies [Act 1985]. However, the relevant principles of recognising profits in SSAP 9 are based on the concept of 'reasonable certainty' as to the eventual outcome and are not in conflict with the statutory accounting principles. Such profits should be treated as realised profits. The Department of Trade does not dissent from this view.

Technical Release 482, The Determination of Distributable Profits in the Context of the Companies Acts 1948 to 1981

Guidance statement issued in September 1982 on behalf of the Councils of the constituent members of the Consultative Committee of Accountancy Bodies, on the determination of distributable profits. This statement gives guidance on the interpretation of [Part VIII of the Companies Act 1985] and on the determination of the maximum amount of profit which can be legally distributed under that Act.

It should be emphasised that it does not seek to deal with the many commercial factors which need to be taken into account before a company decides on the amount of a distribution to be recommended to its shareholders. It should also be borne in mind that its guidance relates solely to the determination of profits legally available for distribution and that it does not give guidance on the recognition of profits in the accounts.

This statement should be read in conjunction with the guidance statement issued by the Councils of the constituent members of the CCAB on 'The determination of realised profits and disclosure of distributable profits in the context of the Companies Act 1948 to 1981,' issued in September 1982.

This statement has been considered and approved by Counsel. However, it is not definitive. Interpretation of the law rests ultimately with the courts.

[As the title of TR 482 suggests, the release originally referred to the Companies Act 1948 to 1981. These references have been replaced by the relevant provisions of the Companies Act 1985, and all references are now to that Act.]

Introduction

1. The [Companies Act 1985] restricts distributions of both public and private companies. Previously the determination of legally distributable reserves and profits was governed only by a company's articles of association, Sections 56 to 58 of the 1948 Act, and a significant body of case law. After the commencement of the provisions of the [Companies Act 1980 now consolidated in the Companies Act 1985] a company must restrict its distributions to those permitted by the [Companies Act 1985] subject to any further restrictions imposed under its memorandum or articles of association.

2. In general, companies are only able to make distributions out of realised profits less realised losses, but further restrictions are imposed on public companies (see paragraph 6 below). The [Companies Act 1985] also includes special provisions for certain investment companies and insurance companies (ss.[265 to 268]): these are not discussed in this guidance statement.

Provision of the Companies Act [1985]

Distribution

3. A 'distribution' is defined [s.263(2)] as 'every description of distribution of a company's assets to members of the company, whether in cash or otherwise, except distributions . . . by way of—

    (*a*) an issue of shares as fully or partly paid bonus shares;

    (*b*) [the] redemption or purchase of any of the company's own shares out of capital (including a new issue of shares) or out of unrealised profits;

    (*c*) [the] reduction of share capital; and

    (*d*) a distribution of assets to members of the company on its winding-up.

Profits available for distribution

4. A company may only make a distribution out of profits available for that purpose [s.263(1)]. A company's profits available for distribution are stated to be its accumulated, realised profits (so far as not previously distributed or capitalised) less its accumulated, realised losses (so far as not previously written off in a reduction or reorganisation of its share capital) [s.263(3)]. Realised losses may not be offset against unrealised profits. Public companies are subject to a further restriction (see paragraph 6 below).

5. A company may only distribute an unrealised profit when the distribution is in kind and the unrealised profit arises from the writing up of the asset being distributed [s.276].

Public companies

6. A further restriction is placed on distributions by public companies [s.264(1)]. A public company may only make a distribution if, after giving effect to such distribution, the amount of its net assets (as defined in [s.264(2)]) is not less than the aggregate of its called up share capital and undistributable reserves. This means that a public company must deduct any net unrealised losses from net realised profits before making a distribution, whereas a private company need not make such a deduction (see also paragraphs 29 to 31 below).

7. Under section [264(3)] the following are undistributable reserves:

    (*a*) share premium account (see also [s.130];

    (*b*) capital redemption reserve (see also [s.170];

    (*c*) the excess of accumulated, unrealised profits, over the accumulated, unrealised losses so far as not previously written off in a reduction or reorganisation of its share capital;

(*d*) any other reserve which the company is prohibited from distributing by any enactment, or by its memorandum of articles of association (or equivalent).

Section [264] only applies to public companies. However, because of the effect of [sections 130, 170 and 263], none of the above mentioned reserves is distributable by private companies. (The restrictions which are placed upon public companies which have distributed or utilised unrealised profits prior to the commencement of the Act are discussed at paragraph 30 below).

Relevant accounts

8. Whether or not a distribution may be made within the terms of the [Companies Act 1985] is determined by reference to 'relevant items' as stated in the 'relevant accounts.' A 'relevant item' is defined by s.[270(2)] as profits, losses, assets, liabilities, provisions, share capital and reserves. Thus, valuations or contingencies included in notes to the financial statements, but not incorporated in the accounts themselves, have no effect on the amount of distributable profit. There is no requirement the distributions can only be made out of distributable profits described as such in the accounts.

9. The 'relevant accounts' (annual, interim or initial) are defined in Section [270(3)(4)] and, except for the initial or interim accounts of private companies, must be properly prepared in accordance with [Sections 271 to 273].

10. Annual accounts must be accompanied by an audit report complying with Section [236] and must have been laid before the company in general meeting in accordance with [Section 241 (s.270(3)]. Interim and initial accounts of public companies (there is no such requirement for private companies) must have been delivered to the Registrar of Companies [ss.272(4) and 273(6)]. Initial accounts of public companies must be accompanied by a report by the auditor stating whether in his opinion the accounts have been properly prepared [s.273(6)]. The interim accounts need not be accompanied by an audit report.

11. There are requirements in Section [271(3)(4)] and Section [273(4)(5)] where an auditor has issued a qualified report on either annual or initial accounts as appropriate, that before a distribution may be made in reliance on those accounts the auditor must issue an additional statement. In this statement he must express an opinion whether the subject of his qualification is material for the purposes of determining whether the proposed distribution complies with the requirements of the Act.

Adjustment to relevant accounts

12. Adjustments to distributable profits calculated from the relevant accounts are required where one or more distributions have already been made 'in pursuance of determinations made by reference to' those accounts [s.274(1)]. Adjustments are also required where a company has, since those accounts were

prepared, provided financial assistance for the purchase of its own shares which depletes its net assets or made certain payments in respect of or in connection with the purchase of its own shares [s.274(2)(3)].

Basis for calculating profits available for distribution

13. The starting point in determining profits available for distribution, the 'accumulated, realised profits . . . less accumulated, realised losses,' will be the profit or loss recognised in the relevant accounts. That is the accumulated balance on the profit and loss account. This figure may require adjustment to take into account any items which are required to be excluded in the determination of distributable profits (*e.g.* see paragraph 21 below). The amount so arrived at will require further adjustment for any items taken to reserve accounts which may properly be included in the determination of distributable profits. For example, an unrealised profit on an asset revaluation will originally be credited direct to a revaluation reserve. On a subsequent disposal of the asset part or all of the profit is clearly realised notwithstanding the fact that it may not have been passed through the profit and loss account.

14. If an item has not been recognised in the relevant accounts, it cannot be taken into account in determining the profits or net assets available for distribution.

Aspects requiring special consideration

Realised losses

15. Section [275(1)] states that certain provisions are to be treated as a realised loss. These are provisions of any kind mentioned in paragraphs [88 and 89] of [Schedule 4], namely:

' . . . any amount written off by way of providing for depreciation or diminution in value of assets' and ' . . . any amount retained as reasonably necessary for the purpose of providing for any liability or loss which is likely to be incurred, or certain to be incurred but uncertain as to amount or as to the date on which it will arise.'

16. Section [275(1)] makes one specific exception to the rule that any provision of any kind mentioned in these paragraphs is to be treated as realised loss, namely a provision arising on a revaluation of a fixed asset when all the fixed assets, or all fixed assets other than goodwill, have been revalued (see paragraph 19 below).

17. In view of the requirement of s.[275(1)], any loss recognised in the profit and loss account will normally be a realised loss. (An exception to this rule at [275(2)] is discussed at paragraph 21 below).

Revaluation of assets

18. A surplus over original cost recognised on revaluation of any asset is unrealised. There is no statutory requirement specifying whether the balance, if any, of the surplus that represents the writing back of past depreciation or of provisions for diminution in value should be regarded as realised or unrealised. Moreover, there is at present no unanimity of opinion as to whether such a surplus, to the extent that it represents the writing back of a realised loss, particularly where the realised loss arises from past depreciation, constitutes a realised profit. In view of the division of opinion on this matter, and in the absence of any statutory rule or clearly decisive precedent in case law, it is considered inappropriate to offer guidance on the question in this statement. Where reliance is placed on such a profit being realised in order to make a distribution, it may be appropriate for the directors of the company to seek legal advice. To the extent that the surplus represents the writing back of unrealised loss, it should be treated as an unrealised profit.

19. A deficit on the revaluation of an asset (unless offsetting a previous unrealised surplus on the same asset) gives rise to a provision and is required to be treated as a realised loss. A realised loss thus created cannot be reduced by being offset wholly or partially against revaluation surpluses on other assets, whether or nót of the same class. However, there is an exception to the general rule where a provision for diminution in value of a fixed asset arises on a revaluation of all the fixed assets (other than goodwill) [s.275(1)]. Although not explicitly stated, the Act implies that such a provision may be treated as unrealised, and therefore that it does not reduce the profits available for distribution.

20. For the purpose of s.[275(1)] a 'revaluation' of all the fixed assets may comprise actual revaluations of some of the fixed assets combined with consideration by the directors of the value of the remaining fixed assets. However, if an actual revaluation of all the fixed assets has not occurred, the director must be satisfied that the aggregate value of all fixed assets 'considered' but not actually revalued is not less than the aggregate amount at which they are for the time being stated in the company's accounts (s.[275(4)(5)]. If the accounts include 'revalued' fixed assets which have been 'considered' but which have not been subject to an actual revaluation, certain additional information is required to be disclosed for the 'revaluation' to be valid. (s.[275(6)].

Revalued fixed assets and depreciation

21. Provisions for depreciation of revalued fixed assets require special treatment to the extent that these provisions exceed the amounts which would have been provided if an unrealised profit had not been made on revaluation (s.[275(2)]). For the purpose of calculating the amount of profit which is legally available for distribution, s.[275(2)] requires an amount equivalent to this excess depreciation to 'be treated . . . as a realised profit,' thereby reducing the provision for this purpose to that relating to the original cost of the asset. As a result, while the depreciation of a surplus on a fixed asset revaluation will affect

the published profits, it will not normally affect the amount of a company's distributable profits, provided of course that this revaluation surplus has not been capitalised ('capitalisation' in this context is defined at s.[280(2)].

Disposal of revalued assets

22. On the disposal of a revalued asset any surplus over cost immediately becomes realised. Any loss which has been treated as unrealised (see paragraph 20 above) should on disposal of the · asset be redesignated as a realised loss.

Development costs

23. Development costs carried forward in accordance with SSAP 13 'Accounting for research and development' will not normally affect distributable profits. Although Section [269(1)] requires that development costs shown as an asset should be treated as a realised loss, this requirement does not apply (s.[269(2)] if the directors justify the costs carried forward not being treated as a realised loss. This they will normally be able to do if the costs are carried forward in accordance with SSAP 13. Such justification must be included in the note on capitalised development costs required by paragraph 20(2) of the [Schedule 4].

Holding company

24. It should be noted that although the whole of the distributable profits of a subsidiary are (subject to the interests of minority shareholders and tax on distributions) available to the holding company, the latter cannot distribute these profits to its own shareholders until such time as they are recognised in the accounts of the holding company.

25. It is not normal practice to take credit for dividends from investments unless the amounts are declared prior to the investing company's year-end. However, dividends receivable from subsidiaries and associates in respect of accounting periods ending on or before that of the holding company are normally accrued in the holding company's accounts even if declared after the holding company's year-end. Such dividends should be treated as realised by the holding company whether they are paid or passed through a current account, provided that, in the latter case, an appropriate reassessment of the realisable value of the current account balance is made.

26. Exchange control or other restrictions may affect the ability of overseas subsidiaries to remit dividends to the UK. In accordance with the prudence concept such dividends receivable should be treated as realised only when their eventual receipt can be assessed with reasonable certainty.

27. Whilst there is no legal requirement for a holding company to take into account its share of the net losses (if any) of its subsidiaries in determining its distributable profits, the holding company may need to make a provision against a permanent diminution in the value of its investment in any such subsidiary (paragraph 19(2) [Schedule 4]).

Current cost accounts

28. It will normally make no difference to a company's legally distributable profit whether its relevant account are drawn up under the historical or the current cost convention. Where net assets under the current cost convention exceed net assets under the historical cost convention, the difference consists of net unrealised profits which form part of the current cost reserve. The remainder of the current cost reserve consists of an amount equal to the cumulative current cost adjustments charged in the profit and loss account each year. According to SSAP 16 this amount is regarded as realised (in the case of the depreciation adjustment the [Companies Act 1985] specifically requires it to be so treated). This part of the current cost reserve, being realised, is legally distributable even though there would be a reduction in the operating capability of the business as a result of making such a distribution, which might, therefore, be commercially inadvisable.

Transitional provisions

Determination of distributable profits at the commencement date

29. Where the directors of a company are, after making all reasonable enquiries, unable to determine whether a particular profit or loss made before the commencement date of the 1980 [Companies] Act is realised or unrealised, they may treat such profit as realised and such a loss as unrealised (s.[263(5)]). Such a position will occur when there are no records of the original cost of an asset or the original amount of a liability.

30. Where a public company has distributed or utilised (otherwise than by capitalisation) unrealised profits prior to the commencement date of the 1980 [Companies] Act and such profits have not substantially been realised, an amount equal to the unrealised profits so distributed or utilised falls to be included as part of the undistributable reserves (s.[264(3)] and s.[280(3)]). This prevents a public company which has so distributed or utilised unrealised profits in the past from making any further distribution until the shortfall has been made good.

31. If, prior to the commencement of the 1980 [Companies] Act, a company has realised losses (insofar as they have not been previously written off in either a reduction or a reorganisation of capital), such losses must be made good before making any distribution (s.[263(3)]).

32. [. . .]

INDEX